Advancing Your Tech Career:
A Handbook

Stephen A. Di Biase, PhD

Published by

Premier Insights, LLC
10 E. Ontario Street
Chicago, IL, 60611

www.premierinsightsllc.com
premierinsightsllc@gmail.com

ISBN-13: 978-1508817000
ISBN-10: 1508817006

DEDICATION

To my beloved Denise (Tix) who is my best friend, supporter, confidant, and greatest gift always being there for me.

To all my fine colleagues who helped me so much over the years, allowing me to compile this memoir which I hope is useful to the next generation of technologists.

CONTENTS

STEPHEN A. DI BIASE

ACKNOWLEDGMENTS

"We who have been given much must give much back to those who follow."
~ Author Unknown ~

There are many definitions of an innovator. For me it's a person who's embraced change, making something out of nothing in the face of huge obstacles using little more than their imagination. Our imaginations are most fertile before we clutter our minds with knowledge arguably, around the age of five, when we've learned enough to ask a question but have not learned enough to have an answer.

A simple and actionable definition of innovation is this: *A human response to, and exploitation of, a change that creates wealth in the present.* A cornerstone of the innovative mind is curiosity, because it drives inquiry and seeks understanding that leads to an innovative act, in turn leading to something better. The catalyst driving innovation is the opportunity for a better life. Often this better life results from the innovator transforming into the entrepreneur.

Those who immigrate to any foreign land, making a life for themselves against all odds, are truly entrepreneurs. I say anyone willing to make the journey, and the sacrifices, are welcome to my home because they're what we want future Americans to embody. Intrinsically, only innovators and entrepreneurs will risk leaving their homes for a better life. They should be welcomed always.

My grandfather emigrated from Italy to the United States in 1920, right after World War I, without resources or language skills, and with my grandmother in tow. They had seven children, all of whom became successful professionals. My grandpa was the "Chairman of the Board" for the "Family Enterprise," but my grandma was the "CEO" who focused on getting results that improved the life of the family. Together my grandparents, and my parents who followed, made it clear that being an entrepreneur is all about getting results, something I learned early from these generous teachers.

Beyond family, I've had the privilege of spending my youth with some of the most innovative and entrepreneurial people imaginable. I learned much from watching them become successful business people with essentially no formal education. The thought of obtaining a business degree, let alone an MBA, simply wasn't a possibility. These entrepreneurs learned by watching and by doing what those who came before them did to be successful, like apprenticing with a master. They taught me much.

My high school chemistry teacher owned a chain of successful dry cleaning facilities and taught me about the interface of technology and business. As a teen I worked for an Italian baker who invested 50 years of his life building an enterprise. He taught me much by his example of loving his customers. Reaching the workforce after graduate school, and while the topics of innovation and entrepreneurship were still embryonic, my exposure to those who simply innovated out of need and passion was significant. It is to these Masters I owe much.

Once in the real world, I watched other Masters innovate and build businesses where judgment-based decision-making was excellent. There weren't troves of data, and what was available was always too little or too late to be useful. I learned that a little knowledge combined with purpose, imagination, curiosity, passion, determination, and judgment will allow someone to be both an innovator and entrepreneur, creating wealth for the many they touch.

The lesson learned was simple: There is no recipe for innovation and entrepreneurship. It's hard but pleasurable work, and very situational. I also learned that successful entrepreneurs and innovators are attentive and observant of opportunities, taking advantage of those opportunities to make their own luck.

Finally, my blessing was these many generous and effective mentors helping me avoid many of the common, and sometimes fatal, errors that befall the inexperienced. These selfless professionals put up with my immaturity and ignorance because they saw more in me than I could see in myself. They deserve the greatest credit for anything I have accomplished. Without this select group of humanitarians I would have failed for sure.

For anyone who has benefited like me, it's our responsibility to give back to those who follow, which is the main driver for writing this book. I Share some of my learning in order to enlighten and catalyze the thinking of the next generation of successful innovators and entrepreneurs.

I've explicitly left all of my many mentors anonymous because it would be unfair to single out the few among the many who were there for me. Being the kind of mentors I envy, they would prefer to be anonymous because what counts most is doing good for its own sake, without any expectation of return.

PREFACE

You just graduated from college, where you worked very hard to acquire a technical degree, be it information technology, biology, physics, engineering, or something else. You may also now be entering the workforce with significant debt. A recent estimate made by the government suggests that the average debt for graduating students today is nearly $30,000. This is a huge burden given a slowly growing economy and wage stagnation. Your first priority is finding a decent paying job that can lead to a financially successful career.

None of the courses you took prepared you for a career in industrial R&D. Such a course simply does not exist. Wouldn't an easy-to-read handbook to help you launch and advance your tech career be nice? Well, this is it.

Unfortunately, most new technical professionals enter the workforce with no idea how the system works and having to learn it all on the job. Everyone has to learn on the job to some degree, but this process is greatly enhanced by combining an educated point of view on how industrial R&D is done with on-the-job experience.

My premise for writing this book is that making a simple and actionable framework for entering the workplace readily available will be valuable to new technologists. Further, I wanted to create a text that helped new employees be more innovative because that is what all employers expect these days. Many may not even know how to define innovation let alone do it. My intent is to help new technical professionals develop an educated point of view on what their careers might be, and how to be innovators, as early as possible.

The innovation process is plagued with uncertainty, risk, surprise, and failure. For US-based companies, more than 90% of all innovation initiatives are either abandoned or fail, costing Fortune 1,000 firms alone nearly $80 billion per year.[1]

Fortunately, the innovation process doesn't have to be a chance occurrence or a random event that is contingent on serendipity or luck. There is a better way, but it requires technical professionals to think differently about innovation.

---

[1] This information is based on the findings of Kuczmarski and Associates, a Chicago-based consultancy, and a footnote in *Wellspring of Knowledge*, Chapter 7.

It begins by recognizing that innovation is not an art form or random event, but rather a critical business process; a process with specific steps that can be managed and controlled to yield desired and predictable results.

If you Google the term innovation, you'll obtain at least 120 million hits in seconds, suggesting there's a lot of information available on the topic. Some of the greatest minds in the field, such as Peter Drucker,[2] Clayton Christianson,[3] James Utterback,[4] Steven Johnson[5] and many others, have written about innovation from many points of view. However, these are also often beyond the grasp of a new technical professional.

Innovation can be treated as a skill that anyone, from students to senior executives, across any field, can learn. I'm not advocating a universal recipe for becoming an innovator. That would be a fool's errand. I'm asserting that certain basic elements of innovation can be learned, taught, and mastered, *making innovation a discipline.* Innovation is natural to human beings, and is something they can learn at an early age and master to a significant degree and never forget how to do. In fact, learning how to become innovative should be as easy as learning how to ride a bicycle, and is a skill that can be developed at a very early age. How does one synthesize what has been published about innovation, allowing an individual to acquire an educated point of view useful in developing innovative behaviors?

Accepting the definition of innovation as being a human response to, and exploitation of, a change that creates wealth in the present, then it seems reasonable that a process can be delineated that enables the technical professional to become more innovative. This happens by first recognizing change, defining its meaning to the individual's circumstances, assessing what responses to make and why, combined with a starting point of how to exploit the change force, creating wealth in the present, and then preserving the wealth created.

A precondition for such a process to work is that innovation must have common features that are independent of the context in which they occur. These common features suggest that innovation is fractal, looking the same from whatever vantage point you view it.

The approach for developing this educated point of view is combining the thinking of thought leaders in the field of innovation with the experiences of actual practitioners to create a holistic framework. This

---

[2] Edersheim., Elizabeth Haas. *The Definitive Drucker*, McGraw-Hill, 2007.

[3] Christensen, Clayton. *The innovator's dilemma: When new technologies cause great firms to fail*, Harvard Business Review Press, 2013.

[4] Utterback, James M. *Mastering the Dynamics of Innovation*, Harvard Business Press, 1996.

[5] Johnson, Steven. *Where Good Ideas Come From: The Natural History of Innovation*, Riverhead, 2004.

framework begins with a strategic view that defines what change forces should be responded to, why they're valuable to the endeavor, and which specific choices will be made as to where to invest time and money, all supported by specific plans yielding measurable and desirable results.

This text is divided into 8 chapters beginning with the context for R&D and finishing with the critical partnerships an R&D employee must learn to cultivate. The first chapter begins with a case study of my own career where I joined a firm as an individual contributor and rose to the position of vice president of R&D in about 15 years, managing 700 professionals with a $120 million annual budget. This role eventually led to me managing a start-up business within a multi-billion dollar firm. By sharing my experience, I hope to provide a 360-degree view of how a technologist could begin in a lab and wind up running a business.

Obviously, my career path is but an example, and not the rule, for a modern technologist. However, what I learned along the way is valuable, such as the role of adversity in developing character and capability, and the importance of selfless leadership and encouraging others to do more than they believe they are capable of doing. While not a detailed road map, I hope my experiences can provide a framework from which the next generation of technologists can succeed more quickly than I did. Most importantly, I entered the workforce with average skills at best, and many of you are much more gifted than I was in the beginning.

Chapter 2 begins with a brief history of R&D, followed by an in depth consideration of organizational designs. Organizational design impacts innovation because it influences how people experience their roles. If the designs are insightful, they can promote innovation rather than inhibit it. The wrong design and norms of behavior can prevent even the most innovative technologists from being successful.

Chapter 3, titled the Innovation Imperative, covers the historical context for innovation, the foundations of innovation, and how one becomes more innovative. All innovation comes from the application of human knowledge in a given context defined by a change force leading to an adaptation of something that already exists to create something that was previously undoable. Context is the set of circumstances, or facts, surrounding a particular event or situation. What is the context in which innovation can occur smoothly and easily within an R&D function? This simple question defies a simple answer, but one can establish a framework favoring innovation by recognizing those contexts that inhibit it.

Chapter 4 considers how the enterprise determines the right things to do by knowing what its objectives are, as well as what they are not and why, allowing resources to be deployed in an effective manner. The tactical elements of innovation consider the handful of basic approaches enabling people to interact with their environments in more innovative ways.

Chapter 5 considers the critical nature of leadership and how new R&D employees need to understand what makes a leader effective while being cognizant of what causes leaders to fail. This chapter begins with a definition of what a leader does. *A leader is an individual who has a continuous stream of insights that are so compelling that followers will subordinate their self-interest to the leader's objectives.* How the leader acquires these insights begins with considering the essentials of leadership, along with appropriate norms of behaviors, educating new R&D employees about what they need to know and do first. The chapter closes with the concept of Inquiry Driven Leadership, which is leading with questions that prompt insightful answers.

Building on the first four chapters, chapter 6 begins to consider how a new R&D employee begins developing their career from the first day of work. This chapter contains concepts developed by Peter F. Drucker, the 20th century's greatest management advisor, about managing oneself, defining how the individual will perform using their strengths, while demoting their weaknesses. Following this is a description of a Career Progression Process more commonly known as a "Technical Ladder." This chapter closes with how to align the employee's performance with the firm's objectives in the context of discreet metrics.

Chapter 7 moves from the overall R&D function, and the employee's experience within it, to the critical processes leading to actionable plans. Many of these basic processes are well described in the literature, so my treatment is more of a summary of their key features. The processes covered include roadmapping, business ethics, intellectual property management, creating the investment portfolio, open innovation, Stage Gates, project management, and big data.

Chapter 8 rounds out the book by looking at the interfaces between the R&D and those other functions of a company required to satisfy the firm's customers. The other functions critical to R&D being successful include marketing and sales, human resources, manufacturing, finance, and corporate administration. How an R&D employee collaborates with these partner functions is important in helping R&D meeting its objectives.

Most people learn from their own experiences, but then there is a smaller population who can learn from the experiences of others, by witnessing or by reading about, events. These people are wise and constitute the audience to which I'm reaching out. During my 40-year career in industry and academics I've often learned the hard way, by trial and error. My contribution is to synthesize an educated point of view from the great minds in the field, such that anyone can advance their tech career by just reading this book.

Chapter 1: A Personal Case Study

How did a less-than-average student from a lower-middle class family end up spending more than half of his career as a senior executive in the chemical industry? Answering this question should spur others like me to aspire to things they only imagine at present. The intent behind sharing my story is to share experiences that taught me well and that might appear in your own lives and careers. Specifically, learning from adversity and challenge, having mentors and failures, helping others succeed, sharing success with others and, most importantly, discovering my own strengths and leveraging them (rather than trying to fix weaknesses) provided me with many teachable moments.

Learning from Adversity and Challenge

That which does not kill us, makes us stronger.
~ Friedrich Nietzsche ~

Life began in the spring of 1952. I was born to August (Gus) and Mary Di Biase in Rochester, New York, living in a lower-middle class neighborhood. My sister followed two years later, and mom died in 1956 when I was 4 years old. This was by all accounts a disaster. Dad was a firefighter working "trick work," meaning he didn't have a stable schedule. Raising two toddlers was a huge challenge, not to mention this was long before there was any such thing as daycare. Being a single dad in the 1950s was an impossible task. We ended up living with our paternal grandmother in the same house dad grew up in, located in "Little Italy," where life was tough. Even though we bounced around among relatives and never had a stable home, my dad was an incredible father.

Time passed and dad continued as a single parent while I did my best navigating catholic grammar school with some difficulty. The Sisters f St. Joseph ran a Special Ops school into which I didn't fit very well. I came to learn years later my biggest issue was being partially deaf. I couldn't hear a woman's soft voice, which the sisters interpreted as insubordination. All this made grammar school miserable. Dad wanted me to do better than he did, which meant going to college and becoming a professional, such as a doctor, lawyer, or dentist. For this dream to come true, I needed to get into a college prep high school. Given my grades, that seemed unlikely. I took the entrance exam for such a school, the Aquinas Institute, and was on the waiting list with hundreds of other kids like me. It didn't look good.

Dad was, and still is, an "operator," which meant he would not be deterred. He approached the principal of my grammar school and began lobbying her for help in talking with the admissions officer at Aquinas. I recall her response to this day. She said "Mr. Di Biase, Stephen is incapable of doing college work. You should begin educating him in the trades." Dad was always polite, so he thanked the sister and we left. Outside he said to me, "She's full of sh*t. You can do anything you want." Before I knew it I was in college prep high school, struggling along but not flunking out with a C+ average.

Being in an all-boys Catholic college prep high school managed by the Basilian Fathers was like boot camp. To make things more challenging, I became seriously ill with what turned out to be a chronic condition that would persecute me for the rest of my life.

It took the doctors 3 months to diagnosis me with Crohn's disease, by which time my weight was down to 90 pounds and I had missed 3 months of school. Dad was terrified of losing a child after losing his wife, while I faced the prospect of flunking out of high school. Things looked very grim.

I was never a star student in any of the schools I attended. I barely got into this college prep high school, and now missing 3 months with a serious illness made it seem like I'd have to start over my sophomore year, if I wasn't asked to leave outright. I managed to recover enough to rejoin my class 3 months before comprehensive final exams covering the whole year's content and administered by the State of New York. My teachers had no way to help me. I had to pass these tests on my own or flunk out.

On the surface this looked daunting, but sometimes you learn a lot about yourself when adversity strikes. I did the best I could to catch up. The final exams were 3-5 hour affairs in the heat of June, and air conditioning was rare. I needed to pass English, chemistry, world history, and math to advance. The passing grade was 65 (out of 100), but even the best students would not do much better than 70. I took the tests with everyone else. Afterwards, as we all compared our answers, I was horrified. Very few of my classmates had answered the way I had. I prepared for the worse. When the results came back, I had achieved a B+ on every test. My teachers we're amazed, as was I. Dad just beamed from ear to ear.

What came from this adversity was a discovery that I could teach myself better than being taught by someone else. In addition, the freedom to manage information according to the way I think was critically important, especially since I still couldn't hear in high school. My hearing loss wasn't treatable until 2004. I did very well whenever the context allowed me to work independently, which was exactly what graduate school was like, and where I excelled. When I didn't fit the norm of education, and many other structured parts of American life, I experienced significant adversity. The old saying is true – *what doesn't kill you makes you stronger* – and the adversity *did* make me stronger. High school led to college and eventually to graduate school. Along the way I struggled to do better than a C+. In graduate school I managed to reach a little better than B+ because I had to teach myself – being an independent learner was the expectation.

I discovered I wanted to be a technologist, specifically a chemist, at a very early age. I was mixing stuff in my grandparent's garage when I was 7 and miraculously managed to *not* poison myself in the process. I was and am driven by an insatiable curiosity about how things work, reinforced with a vivid imagination about what might happen. What I lacked in book smarts I made up for in street smarts expressed as a desire to discover new things.

We didn't have much money, so I worked to help pay for high school and college. Gratefully, graduate school came with a stipend and grant or I could have never gone. My first job was in an Italian bakery making pizza. My big break came in 1972, during my sophomore year in college, working for Eastman Kodak in one of their quality assurance labs.

It was the night shift but the pay was good and the experience even better for an aspiring chemist. I was in heaven. This meant school during the day, work at night, very little sleep, and almost no time to study, but I did well enough to get accepted by Pennsylvania State University for graduate school where I was a teaching assistant and did research in an environment that was largely unstructured. I had to figure it out on my own, which was perfect for me.

I loved doing research and trying to discover things no one had ever found before. I worked long hours on multiple projects, some of which failed, but I made progress quickly. My advisor was a new professor aiming for tenure, which helped me get results faster. Marriage and our first son came along half-way through graduate school. The stipend, which seemed so generous at first, was not enough for a family of three, so I needed to graduate and make better money.

During my second year in the program (a doctorate took an average of five years to complete), I had the opportunity to interview for a job with Lubrizol Corporation. Lubrizol was a small but very successful specialty chemical company in Cleveland, Ohio. I met the head of human resources off of interstate 80 where he interviewed me over lunch. I thought this was unusual, but I was the only student interested in the company, so he agreed to meet me on his way to Philadelphia. One thing led to another and within three months I had a job offer less than three years into my doctorate program. I figured if they were willing to pay me I must be ready to graduate. My advisor didn't see it that way at all, so we negotiated a completion date just after the three-year mark.

I later came to appreciate how adversity in my life opened up opportunities for me to learn and excel because these events revealed the strengths I'd come to use over my lifetime. I thrive on ambiguity, working in an unstructured environment where I need to figure things out. The struggles with poor grades and worse hearing made me adapt where others could excel without really trying. Adversity for them was harder to overcome since they had gotten used to things being easy.

The hardest part of growing up was being rejected by everyone for being different because my mom had died. This, along with the teachings of Christianity taught to me by the Sisters of St. Joseph, made me realize I never wanted to treat others the way I had been treated. I would never reject anyone for being different. This "skill" was very critical in launching a career that shouldn't have happened, given my raw talent.

Learning from Mentors and Failure

Mentors, by far, are the most important aspects of businesses.
~ Daymond Johnson ~

Many of life's failures are people who did not realize how close they were to success when they gave up.
~ Thomas Edison ~

I left graduate school in late May and arrived at work on June 5, 1978. It was an exciting time, being a well-paid research scientist, with an industry-leading firm in a growing economy.

I was one of the first of nearly fifty new R&D employees hired between 1978 and 1981, followed by one of the worst recessions since the Great Depression, only to be outdone by the Great Recession of 2008. Lubrizol hadn't laid people off in three decades and now they were facing the need to reduce costs quickly. We didn't appreciate this was the beginning of a more than two-decade contraction of the core lubricant additive business. That's a sobering backdrop in which to begin a career.

Lubrizol was a very innovative company over its entire history, driven by avoiding too much bureaucracy. No one predicted the slow growth period we faced. Lubrizol's aversion to too much structure was evident in the R&D division in that there were only four layers from an entry level scientist to the VP–R&D, there wasn't any evidence of a technical ladder or even a performance planning process. It was clearly a company driven by its technical leadership. The first four CEOs came from R&D, and every CEO had a technical degree in either chemistry or engineering. This was unusual in that a fifty-year-old chemical firm would have migrated to a leader educated in marketing or sales by then. It spoke to the importance of innovation for sustaining the business.

However, joining Lubrizol from graduate school, which was very data-driven and formal, was challenging. Lubrizol understood that innovation requires a degree of chaos in order to be effective, which was counterintuitive to what I learned in graduate school where every conclusion had to be supported with data. As a result, my first year of employment was challenging, but made easier by my first supervisor and mentor. Fred was about 10 years older than me, had a doctorate in chemistry, and was skilled in the culture of the company. Most importantly, Fred was patient with my frustrations about the way research was conducted at Lubrizol. The most important lesson I learned was that knowing why something worked was not necessarily as important as using it. This became even clearer as I learned about managing intellectual property, especially filing patents. A strong patent depended on commercial utility. Lubrizol was superb at developing its intellectual property estate and defending it successfully in court.

Interestingly, I'm not sure that anything I did my first year was useful. As a new chemist, I was assigned a problem that was deemed to be unsolvable. The intent behind the assignment was to see if someone new to the company could identify a solution. I solved this problem by doing what others thought made no sense – inducing the chemical reaction in the absence of a solvent. This eventually led to a new fuel additive detergent that had eluded Lubrizol for many years.

While the final product was a marginal commercial success, it demonstrated to my managers that I could innovate, and it taught me to embrace utility over understanding. Critically important to any success in an industrial R&D environment is recognizing that your understanding must be bounded by utility. Said another way, understand your products only to the extent required for them to be used and valuable. Greater understanding than this wastes money.

Helping Others Succeed

It is literally true that you can succeed best and quickest by helping others to succeed.
~ Napoleon Hill ~

I learned in graduate school that it was important to know how to teach others to research. I learned this as a teaching assistant, as well as assigning work to undergraduate technicians in my research group. Both of these experiences required patience and a willingness to explain things repeatedly so the students would learn. I brought this mindset to my career and found that many of my colleagues appreciated the time I spent helping them be successful.

Unexpectedly, at a company social event, the vice president of R&D at the time approached me and gave me some feedback that others were speaking highly of my willingness to help do the work. He went on to explain that this is very important to him and how it demonstrated I had leadership skills. Little did I know at the time that I was being considered for my first management position as a group leader, which happened almost three years to the day from when I joined the firm.

Putting the Company First

Employee loyalty is the adhesive that bonds the firm to its customers.
~Stephen A. Di Biase ~

Inconveniently, my health took a turn for the worse just as I was being offered my first supervisory role. I accepted the role while recovering from surgery. This happened again when I was promoted to become the VP of R&D about ten years later. The lesson learned was that my performance spoke louder than my personal health struggles. I spent the next six years successfully leading my research group to commercialize new products, solve manufacturing problems, and provide service to our customers.

Unbeknownst to me, my performance was being carefully watched by not only the VP of R&D, but also the chief operating officer of the company. Apparently I was being considered for additional senior roles within the company, the next one of which arrived in 1987. This assignment was interesting in that it involved me becoming part of the business unit to give me commercial experience. At the time there was competition between R&D and the business units for talent. The business units offered higher salaries to the best in R&D to lure them away.

I was requested to take a position in the business unit without a salary increase – a lateral move – to demonstrate to other R&D employees that not everyone secured a higher salary by moving out of R&D. I readily accepted the job without any negotiations because it was the right thing to do for the company, which created significant goodwill between me, the VP of R&D and the chief operating officer.

I had the same experience two years later when R&D wanted me to return, something that had never happened before, to take on a newly formed department, again as a lateral move. This time the business unit responded with a very substantial double-digit increase in salary and the decision was left up to me. I knew that the correct decision for the company was to take the R&D offer and turn down the money, which I did. Shortly after making this decision the chief operating officer personally thanked me for making his job easier and reducing the competition occurring between various divisions within the company. About 18 months later I was offered the VP–R&D role, at which time my salary more than made up for the two lateral moves!

Sharing Success

A rising tide lifts all boats.

I joined the C-suite, a term of the most senior executives of the company. It was 1993 and just shy of my 41st birthday, making me one of the youngest officers in the firm. I progressed from managing 50 people with a budget of $8 million to leading a global division of 700 employees with a budget of over $100 million. Needless to say, this was a breath-taking assignment. Concurrent with my promotion there was a company-wide restructuring, which meant I had to restructure the R&D division as I became its leader. This consumed my first year as an executive, during which I removed almost all of the past R&D leadership to align with the new mantra for how the company would operate. Lubrizol had come of age and now needed to evolve from a top-down, high-control organization to one that empowered employees to make the best decision for the customer, shareholder, and company. This was a radical departure and required an inclusive leadership style – one that is selfless – at every level to succeed. I provided leadership that lifted up employees based on their achievements and not my own. My success depended now on providing the resources required for others to be successful, whether that be money, knowledge, guidance, or other forms of support.

As VP–R&D I distributed an award, termed a "cash award," recognizing individual employees and teams for exceptional performance. The cash awards often totaled a month's pay, representing about an 8% pay increase on top of whatever merit increase was offered that year, and had a material impact.

My last assignment with Lubrizol was to commercialize a new diesel fuel system that dramatically reduced emissions from trucks and buses. This fuel was an innovation I championed for mixing up to 20% water into a diesel fuel. By burning fuel in the presence of water, the peak combustion temperature is lower, which reduces soot and nitrous oxide emissions. The product was a technical success but failed commercially because the value proposition was poor. The key lesson learned? All innovations must create wealth for enough stakeholders to be successful. Ideally, all stakeholders benefit, and in reality there needs to be at least one significant stakeholder to drive adoption. A meaningful value proposition only existed for a niche market in underground mining, where emissions control was expensive.

Chapter 1 Summary

Here are several pertinent lessons from my personal case study:

- **Adversity and Challenge:** Embrace adversity as a chance to grow rapidly, albeit painfully. Accept challenges that others have failed to meet since they offer opportunities to differentiate yourself from the pack. Do this without complaint or fear. If this adversity and challenge leads to persecution, accept it. Rise above the temptation to strike back. Instead, demonstrate you're better than that.

- **Mentors and Failure:** Find a mentor who sees themselves in you and helps you avoid the mistakes they made while helping you learn at an accelerated pace. Mentors often find you, but you consider bosses to be default mentors and strive to learn from them by asking great questions. Most importantly, listen to and accept their advice.

- **Help Others Succeed:** Always consider your colleagues, peers, and subordinates as your students. Teach them whenever you can. Be a mentor and advisor without expectation of return, for they'll speak highly on your behalf to those above you. This multiples your achievements many times over.

- **Putt the Company First:** This seems obvious, but too often self-interest dominates our decisions, which can have a short-term benefit and a long-term cost. I put the company first twice instead of seeking money, which turned out to be the correct choice. Often this sacrifice comes in the form of longer hours, more travel, and less family time, all of which is being to management. But it also shows a commitment to the firm. Smart employees make these sacrifices for the company.

- **Sharing Success:** Here's a paradox: The more power one acquires, the less one can use it. This requires senior leaders to use influence to get employees to do what makes the firm successful. This is even more critical today in the age of knowledge workers who demand and deserve to be empowered to make decision on behalf of the firm. While thanking employees verbally and in writing is important, giving them extra money is more impactful.

- **Leveraging your strengths:** Perhaps the greatest lesson to share is this: Greater success comes by identifying the things you're really good at and using them consistently versus trying to improve on weaknesses. As Peter Drucker points out, improving a weakness rarely leads to anything better than mediocre performance. My strengths are being able to teach myself, the ability to relate things that seems unrelated, and to work well with everyone, using the strengths of the team to do more than all the individuals could do alone.

Chapter 1 Critical Questions

1. What drives your personal objectives?
2. How are these drivers critical to your happiness? Why?
3. What do you think of when you here the term *narcissistic?*
4. How did you overcome your greatest challenge and what did you learn from it?
5. Who were your best mentors and what did you learn from them?
6. What did you learn from your biggest failure?
7. Describe how you helped someone succeed and how it made you feel?
8. What sacrifices have you made for your firm and why?
9. Can you describe three instances where you shared your success with others?
10. What happened to you as a result of sharing your success?

Chapter 2: The Context

A Brief History of R&D

Industrial R&D began when Thomas Edison's Menlo Park laboratory began operations in the 1870s. This humble beginning led to the formation of General Electric, a conglomerate with $150 billion in revenues. Edison believed in specialization of labor, creating the concept of scientists and technicians working to meet market needs. He famously waited ten years before introducing his first light bulb so the electric infrastructure would be in place to support lighting a city like New York. Edison provided a framework for doing R&D in a centralized way and showed the importance of timing your innovation to meet an immediate need.

Prior to Edison's approach to R&D, research was either informal – a person solved a problem at hand and moved on, rarely documenting anything. This is how pre-industrial societies worked. Successful innovations were handed down from one generation to the next generation through an apprenticeship approach.

Complementing this "do or die" approach to innovation was the entitled class of rich people, often land owners, who would satisfy their own curiosity themselves or by sponsoring others who solved problems that were captured in more formal ways upon which civilization began evolving quickly. Many of the pre-industrial giants of science became so through this approach. Men like Sir Isaac Newton, Galileo, and Leonardo da Vinci, along with many others, laid the foundation enabling the Industrial Revolution to take off in the late part of the 19th century.

Following Edison were Henry Ford (Ford Motor Company), Andrew Carnegie (US Steel), John D. Rockefeller (Standard Oil), and Alexander Graham Bell (AT&T), among many other titans of the industrial age. The industrialization of R&D made investments easier to leverage because innovation requires the collaboration of many disciplines that wouldn't normally interact with each other at all, let alone in the same physical space.

Early R&D organizations preserved the autonomy of the inventor by adopting the military approach of top-down, high command-and-control structures. Edison is the classic example of being highly directive in his laboratory. This structure had many qualities, such as being highly effective in a crisis where time was critically important and too much debate was unacceptable. Two such cases were the world wars in the first half of the 20th century. Highly structured R&D led to the development of systems and weapons that helped win those wars, such as the race between the United States and Germany to develop the first atomic bomb.

As a consequence of the second world war and the beginning of the cold war, significant R&D happened in the military-industrial complex, made up of companies working on projects for national governments. As markets developed for consumer products, of all kinds industrial R&D emerged to meet those needs, again using the military model of organization. Modern management of R&D began with Peter F. Drucker coining the word *management* in the late 1930s.

The last 70 years have seen R&D morph in a variety of ways to get faster at introducing innovations at lower costs to more customers. This desire for speed and greater impact from innovation forced the command-and-control philosophy to give way to more empowered organizational designs where employees were encouraged to collaborate, moving away from the *great inventor syndrome* where a few inventors took responsibility for all of a firm's innovations. This migration towards empowerment made the primary source of innovation become managing people and budgets. Innovation was being delegated to project teams where empowered employees, closer to the customer, were more effective. Individual power has never been greater with the knowledge accessible through the Internet.

DuPont Case Study[6] –R&D in Multidivisional Firms

DuPont pioneered the adoption of the multidivisional structure in the early 1920s. The firm decentralized its research activities to the divisional level, representing specific business units. Although DuPont never entirely eliminated its corporate-level Development and Chemical Departments— the sources of the technologies that supported its initial diversification in the prior decade—in 1921 the firm began to allocate virtually all research budget and decision making authority to division-level R&D groups. What little corporate R&D function remained was essentially required to solicit budgetary funds from the business divisions.

---

[6] Hounshell D, Smith JK. 1988. Science and Corporate Strategy: Du Pont R&D, 1902–1980. Cambridge University Press: New York.

The history of DuPont's organization of R&D illustrates some of the key determinants of R&D organization structure in large multidivisional firms. DuPont's decentralization of research was driven by complaints from DuPont's business unit managers that the Department of Chemicals, known today as Central or Corporate R&D, was unresponsive to manufacturing and sales needs. Allowing the divisions to have their own chemical departments, these managers argued, would result in less conflict and would foster better relationships between research and plant personnel. DuPont's corporate-level Executive Committee agreed.

By the late 1920s, however, DuPont's central Chemical Department staged a comeback under the sponsorship of Chemical Department Director Charles Stine. Stine argued that the Department was too tied up with work to do anything new. The Executive Committee was convinced, and dramatically increased corporate funding for the Chemical Department, so that by the end of that decade the Chemical Department was once again on top.

Research activity continued at significant levels within the divisions as well. This balanced hybrid structure for research appears to have prevailed at DuPont for the rest of the century, although debates about the appropriate organization of research were common amongst tech-intensive firms. By the early 1990s, nearly all large firms in the US had adopted some variation of the hybrid structure, having both centralized and decentralized structures.[78] However, a 1994 survey by the Industrial Research Institute indicates there are wider variations in R&D organizational structures than in overall corporate structures.

Organizational Design Options

Despite all our gains in technology, product innovation and world markets, most people are not thriving in the organizations they work for.
~ Stephen Covey ~

Establishing an innovative culture requires an understanding of organizational designs and how they impact employee performance. The role of all organizational structures is to facilitate information flows that lead to the creation of actionable knowledge. Modern organizational design concepts evolved from the changing needs of the enterprise as they

---

[7] Fligstein N. 1990. The Transformation of Corporate Control. Harvard University Press: Cambridge, MA.
[8] Teece DJ. 2000. Economic and sociological perspectives on diversification and organizational structure. In Economics Meets Sociology in Strategic Management: Advances in Strategic Management, Vol. 17 Baum JAC, Dobbin F (eds). JAI Press: Greenwich, CT; 79–86.

migrated from an owner model to modern private and public companies.

The industrial revolution was thunderous. You could hear the factories and trains; you could see cities transforming; you could smell the changes. This revolution led to organizational designs based on the *machine bureaucracy*, where formal lines of control are supported by a hierarchical structure and standardized procedures leading to massive increases in productivity. Key to this design architecture was the specialization of work into the smallest possible tasks that could be done repetitively. The critical success factors allowing this design were first that employees be uneducated, secondly that they be driven exclusively by economic need, and finally that the market be stable and unchanging over long periods of time.

These conditions do not exist today in that employees are motivated least by economic need, and market change is constant and profound. These external changes drive employee perceptions of the workplace, their role within it, and their expectations of how they'll perform their work and how they'll create value for the enterprise. The enterprise's response to these change forces must be embodied in their organizational designs.

These changes are profound but largely silent. We can't look out our windows and see the catalysts for the opportunities that will change the way we organize our companies and employees do their work. However, it's becoming clear that this silent revolution is built around human assets. It's all about knowledge, information, collaborative connections, and partnering that impact how companies are designed and work performed.

The results of this silent revolution are far from quiet. The role of management at every level is amplified, as is the influence of the customer. The employee's ability to learn and work collaboratively within an ever-increasing complex design is far more important than ever before. In this revolution, leaders are seeing the heightened risks of bad organizational design decisions, no decisions at all, or poor execution of the right decisions. Companies are navigating in a new world that is interconnected on every level. Distance isn't important when services can arrive instantly online. Time has a new meaning when we measure progress in milliseconds rather than minutes, hours, and days. In short, organizational design is fast becoming a critical and sustainable source of competitive advantage, and must be done with both intelligence and purpose.

Human organizations began during the time when humans were hunter-gatherers in family units comprised of a few individuals and led by the strongest member who provided food and defense. As humans transitioned into an agriculturally based society, the availability of food and nutrition allowed for specialization of activities where different members of the group performed a variety of tasks for the entire community. With agriculture, the first signs of hierarchy emerged based on power, resulting from access to resources, leading to the emergence of a perceived deity.

Ancient civilizations from Greece to Rome are useful examples of these kinds of design. The fall of the Roman Empire in the fifth century left a huge void in western civilization's societal structures. This void was filled by the Catholic Church, whose hierarchical design has remained largely unchanged for 1,500 years. It's fair to conclude that as societies became more stratified, organizational designs arose to manage human activities from governments to military to religion.

Early commercial entities were often organized along lines of "owners" and "workers," with little attention to the work being performed or the value created. With the Industrial Revolution, designs began evolving around enterprise productivity. Some of the earliest descriptions of these designs were written by Frenchman Henry Fayol, the head of one of Europe's largest but also disorganized enterprises, a coal mining company. Others in the US, such as J. P. Morgan, John D. Rockefeller, and Andrew Carnegie, began exploring designs for doing work and managing employees.

These structures were called *machine bureaucracies* where employees were treated like machines doing well-defined tasks and were considered largely interchangeable parts. This approach to design and management has also been referred to as the *scientific method of management*. These designs have evolved but remained largely unchanged until the advent of the Internet.

Historically, organizational design has been considered a means to an end versus an end in itself. The best minds in organizational design theory today have concluded that organizational designs are increasingly becoming a source of sustainable competitive advantage.

The reasoning follows that with increasingly complex business environments, the key measure of an enterprise's competitiveness is their employees' abilities to meet strategic objectives. Core to employee effectiveness are working relationships and processes within the company as well as unique alliances with major customers and suppliers, all targeted at dealing with an ever-changing business environment.

Drivers of Organizational Design

The key drivers of organizational design today are as follows:

- Power is moving (irreversibility) from suppliers to customers.
- Offerings are favoring total solutions and partnerships.
- The Internet has provided an explosion of information.
- Business relationships have become multi-dimensional.
- The pace of change has increased exponentially.

As power shifts towards customers, the organization must reflect a new level of intimacy that was previously considered optional. This requires employees to successfully engage customers on a recurring basis within designs making this contact effective. With increased customer intimacy, and more demanding markets, offerings are moving towards total solutions versus component sales. Not only are total solutions more sophisticated, the organizations supplying them must also become more sophisticated. However, increased sophistication can deter employees from adapting to more demanding designs requiring far more analysis and planning.

The lifeblood of any design is how it facilitates information to flow where it's needed, enabling employees to respond to customer demands in a timely fashion. The challenge isn't the *availability* of information but its *interpretation* and *use* leading to actionable knowledge for doing work that creates value. Designs failing to manage information flows effectively or that confuse employees with too much information can cause the organization to lose competitiveness. Traditional business associations between entities are evolving rapidly into multi-dimensional relationships among suppliers, competitors, and interested third parties such as non-governmental organizations (NGOs) and academic institutions. This evolution increases the impact of an organization's decision-making capabilities. Designs must facilitate insightful decisiveness. Finally, the rapid pace of change increases demands for designs that help employees quickly adapt. This is significant because it is human nature to resist change.

Why Organizational Design is Important

Effective design is not only important, it is critical to the future of any enterprise. Recognizing that competitive advantage is the goal, the following are additional outcomes that the designer must consider to have an educated point of view and reap the advantages sought:

1. *Organizational designs provide a framework from which to develop organizational capabilities.* Leading companies who have successfully employed design to their advantage have recognized that designs are a collection of formal and informal relationships that give their company a particular feel and functionality. These relationships embody values, beliefs, and behavioral norms that make up an organization's culture. It is an enterprise's culture that, when combined with strategy, structure, work, and people, yields an environment within which the organization can develop increased competitiveness.

2. *Design offers a powerful tool for shaping performance.* Designs maximizing the flows and utilization of information yield more effective decision-

making and a higher-performing enterprise. Using information expressed in employee activities from performing simple tasks to developing sophisticated analysis inform strategic options. However, poor designs inhibiting information utility negatively impact organizational and individual performance, as well as learning capabilities. In today's highly changing business environment, even temporary disadvantages can result in major negative consequences.

3. *Certain concepts apply to every level of design offering scalability.* Design at any level involves a series of decisions about groupings and linkages aimed at enhancing the organization's ability to process information and coordinate cross-functional work. The route to value creation is the enterprise's ability to gather, channel, and process information into actionable knowledge. Done well, similar design elements can be applied broadly, allowing the organization to be consistent.

4. *Design processes are driven by a series of actions and decisions applicable at any level of an organization.* Presuming design can happen quickly, in a vacuum, or without careful analysis is a grave error. Design must flow from alignment with strategy, consideration of both formal and informal elements of the enterprise, weighting the impact the design will have on the rest of the organization. The process must include the articulation of concrete goals and the widest range of possibilities, along with the construction and assessment of feasible groupings and linkages.

5. *There are no perfect designs; only trade-offs between pros and cons.* No matter what design is selected, there are inherent trade-offs that must be explicitly defined and considered. As business environments become more complex and sources of competitive advantage more difficult to obtain, companies find it necessary to focus simultaneously on several strategic objectives at once, making matrix designs ever more popular. However, they are also the most difficult to implement and manage, and so must be more carefully analyzed for trade-offs. A question to ask as one embarks on a new design is this: If we were going to invent this company from scratch, what would it look like? From here the designers should challenge every assumption about the current design relative to the company's strategic objectives.

6. *The best designs call upon the knowledge, experience, and expertise of people throughout the organization.* A tempting approach that usually fails is to narrow those involved with the redesign to a few executives and a short timeframe. This approach is sometimes referred to as a *cocktail napkin approach* to design where a few executives draw some boxes on a

cocktail napkin over drinks and then begin rolling out the new design. A classic failure was the 1984 redesign attempted by General Motors (GM.) It lasted eight years and is considered among the worst design projects in corporate America. What is required is a thoughtful process involving as many people as reasonable (e.g., 3-4 levels down in the organization) who have educated points of view about how work gets done and information flows to assist in the process. This now yields both the best outcomes and the greatest buy-in.

7. *The best designs can be derailed by ill-planned, poorly-executed implementation.* Great designs fail with poor implementation. Design teams and management must not underestimate the degree of change employees experience in a major redesign. This level of change almost always requires a transition state migration from the present design to the new one while carefully managing communication with employees about new roles and impact on career paths, changes in performance metrics and rewards, and so on. Implementation must carefully consider change management challenges to avoid many difficulties.

8. *Continual redesign is becoming a fact of life, and successful organizations learn to use flexible architectures.* Accepting the proposition that constant change is the hallmark of the competitive environment, strategies need to evolve to keep pace. Changes in strategy invariably dictate changes in the design of structures, processes, skills, and working relationships necessary for pursuing the strategy and creating competitive advantage. Today "organizational Legos" are being contemplated where organizations construct modular units that can be rearranged without seriously disrupting the overall design while upgrading its capability.

9. *Flexible architectures and designs that leverage competitive strengths will themselves become ultimate competitive weapons.* Successful competitive architectures feature not only flexible internal designs but also porous external boundaries. These architectures will embrace a broad range of organizational arrangements capable of leveraging each company's core competencies while expanding its access to new technologies and markets. The emerging reality that success in the future will come from collaboration specifically impacts design elements in that they must facilitate working with parties external to the organization as if they are internal to it.

The Star Model: A Proven Innovation Enabler

All successful designs must stem from the enterprise's strategic objectives. The more complex the business, the more formal the design process should be to ensure a successful outcome.

The *STAR model* is a design framework developed by renowned organizational design expert Jay R. Galbraith. Its five elements include Strategy, Structure, Processes, Rewards, and People. By using the STAR methodology, designers begin with well-defined success factors.

The first and most critical element is *strategy*. An enterprises' strategy sets the direction the firm will pursue over a defined period of time, often 3-5 years. Much was written about strategy in the 1980s, and the best treatise of the topic was by Michael Porter at Harvard. The basis of Porter's teaching is that a successful strategy must be informed by five choices:

- What are our aspirations?
- Where will we play?
- How will we win?
- What capabilities must be in place to succeed?
- What management systems are required?

Figure 1. The Star Model[9]

Each of these questions must be carefully answered before a design can be contemplated. It's easy to understand why a design can only be as effective as the strategy from which it is derived.

---

[9] http://www.jaygalbraith.com/images/pdfs/StarModel.pdf

Only after the strategic objectives are clear should a designer then address what *structures* are possible. Structure simply determines the location of decision-making power. This is a critical feature of any design since decision-making authority determines how resources will be used to achieve specific objectives.

Decision-making itself is a complex subject involving very carefully defined rules, often termed *decision rights*, where certain individuals within an organization have the right to make final decisions. Well-defined decision rights combined with a design aligned with strategy provide the basis of a successful organization.

Following strategy and structure are *processes*. Processes are the methods by which decisions are communicated and implemented. *Vertical processes*, or those that move top to bottom in an organization, allocate resources such as money and people. Outputs form vertical processes are items like the budget and annual plan. *Horizontal processes* are those by which the direction from vertical processes are implemented to do the work, such as new product development, performance evaluation, and so on.

The final elements of the STAR model are *rewards* and *people*, both of which are intimately linked in driving the behavior of the people doing the work of the organization. Rewards must be carefully aligned with strategy, structure, and processes to be effective. If the rewards system drives behaviors incongruent with strategy, then people will behave by their own self-interest, which could be at odds with the best interests of the company.

In today's fast-changing business climate, processes, rewards, and people are becoming more critical than structure in facilitating innovation. Strategy is always dominant, but where flexibility and speed are critical success factors, the combination of business processes, compatible reward systems, and adaptable employees becomes a source of competitive advantage. The STAR model provides five leverage points for the designer and company leadership to respond to a changing business environment.

Strategy

Environmental conditions, organizational resources, and history cannot be changed in the short-term and must be taken as constants, providing the setting within which the organization operates. Each must first develop and articulate a vision of how it intends to compete and what kind of organization it wants to be given the realities of the environment. From vision flows strategy, a set of business decisions about how to allocate resources against the demands, constraints, and opportunities in the environment. Strategy can be defined as explicit choices about markets, offerings, technologies, and distinctive competencies.

However, no matter how well thought out or creative a strategy is, it will fail if it's not aligned with the structural and cultural capabilities of the organization required to execute it. But a clear and compelling strategy can also create silos that become misaligned and counter-productive. The designer must include the proper linkages within the organizational structure so silo-ization is avoided or minimized.

Structure

When organizational design is discussed, it's often in the context of boxes on paper referred to as the organization chart. While this approach is insufficient on its own in today's business climate, it does provide a helpful view of possibilities. There are five basic structural designs types: *Functional, Product line, Processes, Market- driven* and *Geographical.* Within each basic design there are four additional features: *Specialization, Shape, Distribution of Power* and *Departmentalization.* Combining the basic structural designs with the appropriate features gives an organization shape and mobility.

Specialization refers to the types and number of job specialties.

Shape refers to the number of people constituting the departments or spans of control at each level of the structure. Spans of control are increasing as modern information technology systems are making accurate information readily accessible to empower knowledge workers. This results in "flatter" designs enabling decision-making to occur lower in the organization. This can increase speed and responsiveness, which are sources of competitiveness.

Distribution of Power refers to centralization or decentralization of decision-making and vertical information flows. The choice to centralize or decentralize takes into consideration many elements of how to execute the strategy. Decentralization often provides greater responsiveness whereas centralization offers greater control.

Departmentalization is the formation of departments at each level of the structure.

Processes

Processes and systems are vital for coordinating activities and enabling people to link their efforts into productive work. Think of an organization like a human body. The body cannot function if its efforts aren't all linked or coordinated. A person cannot move a limb unless a message is conceived in the brain, communicated to the limb, and the muscles activated to move the limb according to the directive from the brain. If this coordination is absent, then the body will malfunction or is paralyzed. The same is true of processes and systems within an organizational design.

Processes are best described as sequences of collaborative efforts by groups and individuals, at various organizational levels and frequently across structural boundaries,

21

performed in the pursuit of a common objective. The related term *systems* refers to mechanisms that use human or physical technology to enable people and groups to perform the work required by a particular process.

Rewards

The purpose of rewards or incentives is to align the goals of people with the goals of the organization. Rewards provide motivation to drive a specific kind of behavior that is deemed effective and compatible with the organization's culture or norms. They must be equitable but also personalized to be effective. Often, rewards are synonymous with money, but today effective recognition programs reach well beyond financial tools. Money historically has been proven to *satisfy* employees but not *motivate* them in any significant way. In fact, excessive monetary recognition, in lieu of other forms of recognition, can become de-motivate employees. Forms of non-monetary recognition include the following:

- Telecommuting.
- Verbal or written recognition.
- Work assignments.
- Paid time off.
- Attendance at conferences.

Regardless of the methodology, effective reward programs must have several features as follows:

- They must be linked clearly to performance measured by specific standards and objectives. If a team's objective is customer satisfaction, then that should be measured directly.
- They must be aligned with the nature of the performance at each level of the organization. Executives should be recognized based on overall company performance whereas an individual contributor might be recognized only for their own outputs.
- The must put performance directly within the control of the individual or work group, and should be directly linked to recognition. If the employee or work group has no control over an objective, they can't be held accountable for the outcome.
- The timeframe of measurement should be aligned with the timeframe of recognition. If an objective should be accomplished in three months, that's when the recognition for the accomplishments should be available.
- Finally recognition programs must be equitable without everyone getting the same recognition.

People

Employees are every organization's most valuable resources, and how successful those employees are is impacted by the design in which they work as well as how they are directed by company leadership and policies.

Human resource policies must build the organization's capabilities to execute strategy in a manner that fits the culture and expected norms of behavior. The workers of the 21st century are far more sophisticated, educated, and demanding than those of the previous generations. This is especially true of workers just entering the work force, who tend to be not only more educated but independent and uncommitted to the historical norm of lifetime employment. This mindset, combined with much greater access to information and productivity tools, creates an entirely new dimension for the relationships among the employee, design, manager, and associated processes and systems. Employees today expect greater autonomy and decision-making authority enabled by designs that leverage their education and capabilities.

A critical dimension of the modern organizational design is to enable leaders to fit the strategy of the company with the design required to deliver that strategy while enabling employees to leverage their specific strengths and knowledge individually and as part of collaborative teams.

An additional element of the 21st century worker is that they choose to work for companies which fit their image of desirability. For example, some younger workers are selecting companies based on their eco-footprint or commitment to sustainability and not on location, role, or compensation.

Linking Strategy to Design

Historically designs were largely hierarchical reflecting the limitation inherent to information flows and automation. The hierarchy was required so decisions could be made with the limited knowledge available, which was most often aggregated at the top of the organization. With the advent of information technology, the Internet and social networks information has become widely available and designs have flatted allowing decision-making by employees closest to the work. As previously described the twenty first century worker has evolved from this new information rich environment to demand greater autonomy and individual recognition. These realities have increased the latitude available to Designers relative to levels of a given design and hybrid designs better suited to complex business conditions.

Dimensions of Structure

It's premature to declare the hierarchy dead because it's still very useful for transmitting information, making decisions impacting large numbers of people, resolving conflict, and negotiating with external parties. The following are four key articles of structure independent of hierarchy:

STEPHEN A. DI BIASE

- Specialization.
- Shape.
- Distribution of Power.
- Departmentalization.

Specialization

Specialization refers to the types and numbers of specialties to be used in performing work. In the past, when employees were expected to contribute by accomplishing specific and routine tasks, the greater the specialization the more effective the organization because subtasks could be performed more efficiently. This trend has shifted to less specialization for low to moderate skilled workers, allowing greater ease in coordination among varied but related activities along with more job rotation. This has resulted from more educated workers and greater access to information. However, for highly skilled activities, greater specialization has developed so deep knowledge can be created in an ever-increasing competitive environment. These diametrically opposed trends challenge the designer to be focused and creative in structuring a diverse workforce. This has led to the development of hybrid designs capable of greater flexibility. The key is to find the correct balance between the two concepts. Less specialization simplifies management but reduces the organization's capability to respond quickly. Overspecialization makes information processing more complicated and increases the opportunity for conflict.

Shape

Shape determines the number of people forming departments at each hierarchical level. Span of control is the number of people under a given manager. The more people, the greater the span of control. As spans of control increase, the number of levels *within* a given department decreases, yielding a "flatter" design. Generally the effective maximum number of direct reports for any given manager is 5-8, although up to 17 direct reports is reported in the literature. It's important to recognize that span of control is very situational. The more a leader can empower employees through information transfer, knowledge management, and processes, the greater the span of control.

The trend today is to significantly increase spans of control to maximize responsiveness of the design and reduce the time and cost to serve. Experience of the worker, work content, roles of individual employees, and metrics can also influence span of control. If the employees are experienced and the work is readily measurable, the spans of control can increase without loss of effectiveness. Regardless of the design, the ability of the leader to delegate and communicate effectively will impact the span of control and overall effectiveness of the workgroup. Effective leaders tend to invest less in administering the work group, resulting in higher productivity.

When looking at the shape of an organization, it's wise to recognize that spans are easier to change than levels within the hierarchy. Levels, more than spans of control, are directly aligned with power such that changes in spans of control cause less anxiety.

Distribution of Power

Power drives decision-making. Power within the organizational structure has two dimensions: Vertically (in levels) and horizontally (across levels). The vertical power structure is formal and defined by titles and control over resources. Horizontal power is more informal, projected via influence on decisions and actions. Both are very real and critical to how a design works. In effective organizations, power flows from where value is being created. In a mature business, power generally flows from the customer-facing entities to the ones serving those entities.

In a start-up power may flow from the product development function if the offering is the key source of value, but it will eventually shift back to the customer. Given the changes in the balance of power favoring the customer, power must always be used to serve the customer, and designs must recognize this. New designs cause major changes to influence and distribution of power. All organizations are political entities made up of individuals, groups, and coalitions competing for power. As the design approaches implementation it's critical that the designer and leadership prepare for a major spike in political activity. Both individually and collectively, people are likely to engage in politics if they sense a major shift in power is about to occur. This activity can take the form of support, resistance, or just positioning if the outcome is perceived as neutral.

Managing political events requires the designers to clearly communicate impacts of the impending changes and answer WIFM (what's in it for me) questions. When employee concerns are addressed, even if it means a loss of power, implementation is smoother.

Departmentalization

Departmentalization refers to the choice of departments to integrate the specialized work and form a hierarchy of departments. The most common designs are based on the following:

- A function or specialty.
- A product line.
- A customer/market segment.

- A geographic area.
- A workflow process.
- Hybrids.

Functional or specialty design

There is a clear link between department selection and business life cycle where simplicity is desired early in the life cycle with increasing sophistication, driven by need, as the business grows and matures. The most common option is the functional or activity-based design. A functional design has many advantages. It allows people with like roles to share ideas, knowledge, and contacts, yielding a more productive workforce. It stimulates greater levels of specialization and helps the company present a single face to the customer. It also helps leverage capital investments more efficiently. Examples of functional designs that take advantage of these attributes are R&D and manufacturing. A company opts for a functional design if it's driven by the need to standardize practices, reduce complexity, operate at a lower cost, and become faster. Functional structures are desired under the following organizational conditions:

- Small-sized with a single product line.
- Operates in an undifferentiated market.
- Has scale or expertise within the function.
- Has long product development cycles.
- Utilizes common standards.
- Is early or late in its lifecycle.
- Is cost driven.

A functional design has two fundamental weaknesses. The first appears as reduced efficiency when the business becomes more complex, whether from offering many products/services or having varied customers and channels to serve. The second is reduced communication when intra-functional sharing becomes difficult. There are relatively few businesses today with uniform offerings. As the business becomes more diverse, the design should follow the lines of value creation. For instance, if the primary source of value is a diverse product line, the functional design would evolve to a product line structure or hybrid between the function and product.

A sign that the functional design is losing its effectiveness is when the leadership team's decision-making capacity is overloaded. Product-based start-up companies often evolve as their product range and customer base expands. Another weakness is that departments within the design become isolated, focusing too much on their own specialties. This weakness is harder to detect until significant issues occur through customer dissatisfaction, increasing costs to serve, and/or slower responsiveness.

Apple is a classic example of a product-driven company moving from a functional design to a product design. When Apple radically simplified its product line, it reverted back to a functional design. It's important for the leadership team to willingly adjust design choices based on business needs.

With the advent of increased information flows, globalization of many markets, and the ever-present need to increase productivity, the functional design option has given way to hybrids and other options.

Product Structures

Functional structure is often followed by a product design once a product line reaches a critical mass of sales, manufacturing volume, and profitability to support its own functional design. Hewlett-Packard and 3M are classic examples of companies that set up multiple business units around product lines with a functional design overlay.

Product line structures generally have the advantages and disadvantages of the functional structures within them. However, several weaknesses need to be managed. It's common that the self-contained business unit structures will compete for control of resources for their unit at the expense of other units. This often promotes duplication of equipment, people, and competencies, thereby reducing margins. In addition, for smaller product lines, the business can lose economies of scale. Very clear work processes and decision rules, along with shared corporate functions, can help manage these disadvantages. At 3M it's common for a product line business unit to share a manufacturing plant with many other business units. The same is true for sophisticated R&D resources. Ultimately, product line structures evolve into hybrids to promote growth. Product line structures are desired when value creation is...

- Product focused and performance driven.
- Based on multiple products for separate customers.
- Defined by short product development and life cycles.
- A minimum efficient scale for the functions or outsourcing is required.
- Early in the business life cycle.

An example of a hybrid is used by Boeing, which has adopted a design where product line and functions are integrated around the parts of the airplane. The "narrow body" and "wide body" product designs are augmented with a central fabrication unit for economies of scale. Each body unit has functional groups around engineering, quality control, and so on.

The most significant challenge of the product line design is where a customer buys from more than one product division. This could be handled by a central sales unit to manage customer requests within the company. However, as customers begin demanding specific offerings and services such as total solutions, individualized websites, and service models, the product line option loses its effectiveness. The product line option is often selected by manufacturing companies where a focus on lateral processes and more sophisticated internal designs are created.

Customer or Market Segment Structures

A popular and increasingly relevant design option is based on customers, markets, or industries. There are several drivers supporting this transition. First and primary is a shift in power to the customer or buyer. This change has occurred as globalization and production efficiencies have created more supply than demand. In addition, the Internet has made auctions a possibility for highly standardized offerings where blind bidding drives additional buyer power. A second driver is a decline in the manufacturing scale required to be profitable. This has been further augmented by high volume, single-sourcing arrangements where a dedicated unit can be deployed for a single customer or market. For instance, high-volume retail businesses like 7-Eleven have sole-sourced some of its food needs to Ajinomoto. Third is the tendency to out-source activities not considered core to the business. If a function's scale is not critical to the business, it is often cost-effectively out-sourced to an entity where it is core. Fourth is a shift in competitive advantage to those who have superior knowledge of the market or customer served. The information explosion, combined with rapid data mining techniques, has made knowledge generation much less expensive and time consuming. An example is the music business, where intimate knowledge of trends attracts recording artists and hence market share. Fifth is the shift in value to service offerings and total solutions versus product-based sources of value. Companies in telecommunication, hospitality, and finance often elect market-segmented structures. Customer or market segment structures are desired when...

- Customers or market segments are critical to value creation.
- Products or services are unique to a segment or customer.
- The purchaser has power in the relationship.
- Customers have knowledge advantages.
- There are rapid product development cycles and customer service.
- Minimum scale is required to compete.

Market-based structures share weaknesses common in product line designs. They can suffer from duplication and silo-based processes and systems, leading to difficulty in sharing products/services. These weaknesses can be mitigated with shared service arrangements for common activities like finance and human resources, or the use of hybrids. Proctor and Gamble (P&G) has developed a front-back design where customer-facing units like sales are organized by customer (the "front") and support functions like manufacturing or R&D are functionally aligned (the "back"). P&G use this hybrid, along with highly sophisticated customer teams and joint business planning processes, to serve large customers like Walmart.

Geographic area structures

Geographic structures are effective when the supplier must be physically close to the customer. Often, proximity is driven by a low volume-to-transport cost ratio where the product is too low-value to transport very far and remain profitable. Historic examples are commodity-based offerings like timber, cement, and coal, but with increased competition, businesses like retail increasingly select geographical designs. Pizza Hut and McDonalds are two examples. However, the wide availability of information has made it feasible for geographically organized businesses, such as consultants, to adopt alternative designs. Of all design options, geography requires the most analysis before adoption. For instance, oil refining, insurance, pharmaceuticals, and elevators have been able to move from geographical designs to other options due to increased availability of information, knowledge, and globalization. A geography-based structure is desired when...

- The offering has a low volume-to-transport cost ratio.
- Service is delivered onsite.
- Proximity to the customer is required for product delivery or support.
- Perception of the organization is local.
- Geographical segmentation is necessary.

Weaknesses of geographic designs can be duplication, high working capital requirements, and poor leverage across capabilities. Despite these drawbacks, the selection of geographic structures are sometime mandatory where the offering has a low volume-to-transportation ratio.

Workflow process structures

A relatively new design option is that based on a work process. An example is organizing around the order fulfillment process where individual activities become elements of the structure. To be effective, each part of the process has employees totally responsible for the entire process they work within. Each process element or process team is integrated so that final outcomes are smooth and effective. Process-driven designs grew out of the total quality movement, the need to reduce cycle time, and a desire to re-engineer the workplace enabled by increases in information flows. The process design option is gaining new sources of competitive advantage from emerging information technology systems, a fresh look at how work is done, and an increased capability to measure outcomes. Process-driven designs have become tarnished with the rush to re-engineering in the 1990s, but should be revisited. Some advantages are the potential to reduce cycle time, time to market, cost to serve, lower inventories and associated reduced working capital, faster receipt of cash, reduced duplication, higher profitability, and greater productivity. Their relative novelty means they must assessed carefully prior to wide adoption. A weakness in this option is that the hand-off between different process types like product development and order fulfillment can be inefficient. A work flow process structures is desired when...

- An alternative to a functional design is required.
- There is the potential for new or radically changed process.
- Reducing working capital is required.
- Reductions in process cycle times is a competitive advantage.

Lastly, hybrid structures are desired when the other options are inappropriate or ineffective. Hybrids must be carefully selected based on business strategy where a dominant option is then strengthened with complementary designs.

As the pace of business increases and options for serving customers and markets evolve the need for highly flexible organizational designs will increase. The concept of continuously variable designs is becoming a reality and source of competitive advantage for companies capable of adopting rapid change.

R&D Design Options[10]

A great deal of attention has been given to exploring the relationship between a firm's organization of its research efforts and the generation and application of such knowledge leading to innovations that increase shareholder value. Over the last fifteen years or so, however, academic research has focused on the inter-firm organization of R&D activities, specifically the role of alliances and networks through processes like Open Innovation, almost to the exclusion of intra-firm organization.

There are two general choices for structuring R&D: Decentralized and within the business unit, or centralized as a corporate enterprise-wide function. Many hybrids may be designed as well. Centralized functions enable the firm to generate deeper knowledge bases, whereas decentralization can result in greater breadth of knowledge. Both are required and often the extent of which depend on the size of the firm and resources available. Larger firms will often have both structures where the centralized design is a corporate function paid for by the business units on a "taxing model" (each business unit has to contribute money based on its revenues). Smaller firms can often only afford a decentralized effort focused on the business at hand and not on knowledge generation for its own sake or some future use.

---

[10] Argyres, Nicholas,. Silverman, Brian,. Strat. Mgmt. J., 25: 929–958 (2004).

It's often argued that decoupling research from the immediate demands of the business will generate innovations that have a larger impact on future technological developments within and outside the firm, as well as a wider impact across technological domains. Further, centralized R&D will generate innovations that draw on previous innovations developed in a wider range of organizations and technological domains.

Conversely, decentralized R&D, since it ties research efforts directly to specific product-markets, produces innovation that has less overall impact, and that influences a narrower range of technological domains but has greater impact on the existing business in the short term, although possibly at the expense of that business in the future.

Firms that have the resources to do both tend to increase shareholder value more effectively than smaller firms where there are only enough resources to support the current business. The exact critical mass required for a firm to afford both options is difficult to estimate. However, the vast availability of data, information, and knowledge combined with the concept of open innovation facilitates smaller firms doing both more effectively.

I don't argue that one R&D structure is superior for all firms. Rather, variation of the designs may be more aligned with the diversity of the firm's businesses and its overall size. Larger firms not only have the resources for both a centralized and decentralized R&D structures, but as their businesses become less alike the need for specialization takes priority and hence dedicated, centralized structures become more effective.

The organization of research within these large firms typically takes on one of three structures as shown in Figures 2, 3, and 4. In the centralized structure, there is a single executive in charge of the firm's research activities who reports directly to a corporate-level executive such as the CEO or President. In the decentralized structure, research is conducted exclusively within divisions or business units, and R&D directors report to division general managers. In the hybrid structure, research is conducted both within a centralized function whose leader reports to corporate management, and within the firm's divisions or business units. An R&D director at the divisional level reports to his/her division general manager, who in turn reports to corporate management. Separate from the authority relations in R&D, the hybrid example highlights the fact that the source of research funding within large firms can be the business units, corporate headquarters, or some combination of the two. In either case, R&D budgets are typically allocated through an annual process in which the senior management of the corporation (or business unit) determines the size of the budget that the R&D function will receive, often based on an assessment of the projects proposed by R&D personnel. This is why portfolio management is so important – it drives the investment decisions.

Figure 2. Centralized R&D Example

Figure 3. Decentralized R&D Example

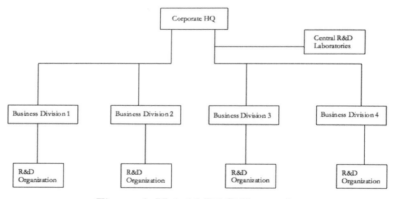

Figure 4. Hybrid R&D Example

R&D Structures Impacting Innovation

Historically, corporate and academic Research teams preferred to function as silos unto themselves. This was what Thomas Edison began, and what emerged as the standard model of centralized research. However, in a time of ever-increasing amounts of data, globalization, heightened competition, the emergence of knowledge workers, and customers demanding total solutions, individual firms cannot respond as they may have in the past – doing everything on their own. External relationships are becoming critical to the success of most firms today.

The new technologist in an R&D organization must quickly assess the importance of external technical activities to their overall effectiveness and the basic strategies their new company employs. The structure of R&D (centralized vs. decentralized) reflects the balance of internal vs. external efforts. Figure 5 shows how innovation efforts are impacted by structure.

Centralization of R&D investments will tend to limit support for near-term customer-intimate strategies in favor of those driven by market trends. Alternatively, decentralization provides incentives for divisional managers to invest in R&D focused on short-term customer wants as seen in process improvement innovations reducing cost and incremental product improvement innovations leading to new and improved products targeted at retaining market or customer share.

However, R&D investments often have uncertain payoffs, encouraging divisional managers, who are accountable for short-term performance, to skimp on long term R&D. By contrast, corporate managers, who can take a longer-term view, may be charged with finding new to the firm growth opportunities leading to centralization of R&D. The new Technologist needs to understand how these biases can effective their role and performance.

From a different perspective, firms that make substantial R&D investments are those that seek growth through innovations, which can create new lines of business. Such firms will tend to centralize R&D because managers of existing lines of business are not likely to invest in exploring opportunities that will not directly benefit their own division.

This is illustrated by the history of R&D at DuPont. After experimenting with decentralization in the 1920s, DuPont centralized R&D because existing business units could not be relied upon to invest in promising new lines of research.[11] This centralization also coincided with an increase in the scale of R&D and breakthroughs such as Nylon and acrylic fibers, which were produced by central R&D labs.

---

[11] Hounshell, D. A., & Smith, J. (1988). Science and Corporate Strategy: Du Pont R&D, 1902-1980. New York: Cambridge University Press.

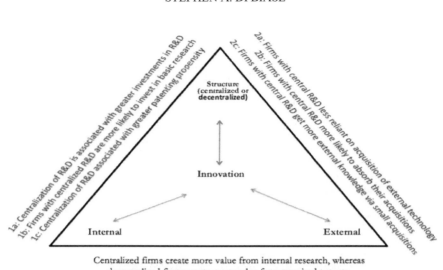

Centralized firms create more value from internal research, whereas
decentralized firms create more value from acquired patents.

Figure 5. Innovation vs R&D Structure

Table 1. Centralized versus Decentralized R&D Organizations

Centralized	Innovation Bias	Decentralized	Innovation Bias
Greater investment in R&D as percent of sales.	Longer term and larger impact portfolio. Hard to measure and value.	Lower investments in R&D as percent of sales.	Greater customer intimacy and more likely to invest in incremental innovation projects.
Portfolio favors basic research.	Knowledge oriented.	Portfolio favors applied research.	Development and application oriented.
Greater patenting, tendency towards breadth.	Large patent portfolio Targets excluding competition.	Fewer and narrower patent estate – defend existing business.	Smaller patent estate focused on freedom to operate.
Less reliant on acquiring external technologies while absorbing acquired R&D functions.	Risk of losing value of acquired technologies.	More reliant on acquiring external technologies without integrating the R&D functions.	Bias for exploiting acquired technologies as acquired while merging it with their own.
More dependent on internal knowledge generation.	Insulated from external sources of knowledge.	More receptive to acquired knowledge.	Open to learning from third parties.
Greater value on internal capabilities and knowledge.	Self-reliant but prone to Not-Invented-Here syndrome.	Greater value on acquired knowledge and patents.	Less susceptible to Not-Invented-Here syndrome.

General Observations:

The greater the centralization of R&D the greater investments in R&D. The centralization of R&D at DuPont also resulted in significantly higher investments in basic research, which is consistent with a number of theories. Basic research has higher potential economies of scale,[12] which would favor centralization of efforts. Further, individual business units are less likely to invest in basic R&D, projects which would provide benefits to other units in the firm.[13] Basic R&D also tends to have longer time horizons, unappealing to divisional managers with shorter-term objectives. Conversely, divisional managers may have superior access to local knowledge, such as information about customer needs or about production problems.[14] This implies that R&D managed by divisional managers is likely to be more tightly focused on improving existing products and lowering costs. Generally, decentralized R&D results in lower-impact research outcomes, as well as research that is narrower in technical and organizational scope.

Firms with centralized R&D are more likely to invest in basic research. The difference in the types of research projects undertaken also has implications for patenting behavior. Decentralized R&D projects are focused on improving existing products, so their results may be intrinsically less patentable. Similarly, decentralized R&D is focused on improving existing production processes, which also implies fewer patents per R&D dollar because process innovations are more likely to be protected through secrecy or tacit knowledge rather than patents.[15] Conversely, centralized R&D projects that are broader in scope and more scientific in orientation typically result in more patentable outcomes.[16]

---

[12] Kay, N. 1998. The R&D function: corporate strategy and structure. In G. Dosi, C. Freeman, R. Nelson, G. Silverberg, & C. Soete (Eds.), Technical Change and Economic Theory. London.

[13] Hitt, M., Hoskisson, R. 1990. Mergers and acquisitions and managerial commitment to innovation in M-form firms. Strategic Management Journal, 11: 29-47. Nobel, R., & Birkinshaw, J. 1998. Innovation in multinational corporations: control and communication patterns in international R&D operations. Strategic Management Journal, 19(5): 479-496. Feinberg, S. E., & Gupta, A. K. 2004. Knowledge spillovers and the assignment of R&D responsibilities to foreign subsidiaries. Strategic Management Journal, 25(89): 823-845.

[14] Henderson, R., & Clark, K. 1990. Architectural innovation: the reconfiguration of existing product technologies and the failure of established firms. Administrative Science Quarterly.

[15] Cohen, W. M., Nelson, R. R., & Walsh, J. P. 2000. Protecting their intellectual assets: Appropriate conditions and why US manufacturing firms patent (or not). NEER working paper. National Bureau of Economic Research Cambridge, Mass., USA.

[16] Arora, A., Fosfuri, A., & Gambardella, A. 2001. Specialized technology suppliers, international spillovers and investment: evidence from the chemical industry. Journal of Development Economics, 65(1): 31-54.

Further, central R&D labs may have greater incentives to patent as a way of signaling their productivity and justifying their budgets. By contrast, decentralized R&D is more likely to be measured by how it contributes to the performance of the unit rather than by measures such as patenting and publication. For all these reasons, greater decentralization should be associated with fewer patents, due to lower R&D intensity.

Greater centralization of R&D should be associated with greater patenting propensity, R&D structure, and the acquisition of external knowledge. There is an extensive literature on how and why firms acquire external knowledge through acquisitions.[17] A central question in this literature is whether external knowledge is a substitute or complement for internal knowledge, and the factors that condition this relationship.[18] The external orientation of firms relates to their organizational structure and to internal R&D. The more decentralized the function the more market and customer-facing the strategies and portfolios will become. The issue is not whether internal development (e.g., centralized R&D) or acquisitions (e.g., decentralized R&D) are the most appropriate means for investing resources, but how each of the two approaches provides distinct contributions.

Decentralization is associated with a modular organizational structure,[19] with decentralized firms finding it easier to deal with larger acquisitions. This is because the target may be more likely to be left alone, with a degree of autonomy, and managed as other business units are managed. Whether and when the acquired firm is integrated or recombined would depend on the potential synergies with more existing units.[20] By contrast, centralized firms will often have to rapidly integrate the acquisition or allow it to function autonomously. The first would be costly, while the second implies increased decentralization, which is counter to a centralized R&D strategy.

---

[17] Kogut, B., & Zander, U. 1992. Knowledge of the firm, combinative capabilities, and the replication of technology. Organization Science, 383-397. Institute of Management Sciences. Fleming, L. 2001. Recombinant Uncertainty in Technological Search. Management Science, 47(1): 117-132. Hitt, M., Hoskisson, R. 1990. Mergers and acquisitions and managerial commitment to innovation in M-form firms. Strategic Management Journal, 11: 29-47.

[18] Helfat, C. E., & Eisenhardt, K.M. 2004. Inter-temporal Economies of Scope, Organizational Modularity, and the Dynamics of Diversification. Strategic Management Journal, 1232(January 2002): 1217-1232.

[19] Karim, S. 2006. Modularity in organizational structure: the reconfiguration of internally developed and acquired business units. Strategic Management Journal, 27(9): 799-823.

[20] Karim, S., & Mitchell, W. 2000. Path-dependent and path-breaking change: reconfiguring business resources following acquisitions in the U.S. medical sector, 1978-1995. Strategic Management Journal, 21(10-11): 1061-1081.

Decentralization enables firms to be more outward-oriented in their acquisition of external knowledge. Conversely, acquisitions by centralized R&D firms often result in the acquisition being integrated, which can result in losing some of the acquired knowledge, know-how, and non-patent intellectual property.

More subtle organizational issues may also be at work. It is possible that large centralized labs, with a strong research orientation, suffer more from a not-invented-here syndrome (NIH) as compared to smaller, more customer-oriented labs.[21] This NIH might be a different mechanism driving a favoring of internal development versus external sourcing.[22] By contrast, decentralized firms are less likely to have an NIH bias and adopt the acquired technology more readily. In sum, decentralized firms should on average face lower costs of managing a technology-intensive acquisition, and therefore be more likely to grow through the acquisition of external knowledge.

Centralized firms will be less reliant on acquisition of external technology. However, the literature has a seemingly contradictory finding that centralized firms are more likely to build on external technology.[23] This may be a result of the external technology being far from homogenous, so it is important to consider not just how much, but also what kind of external technology is accessed by different firms.

If centralized and decentralized firms systematically differ in the type of R&D they engage in, these firms should have different absorptive capacities.[24] Thus, a firm with strong basic research focus should acquire different types of complementary knowledge.[25] For example, firms with a basic research focus should be more likely to acquire uncertain technology that needs to be built upon and whose future value is hard to assess. By contrast, firms without a strong research base will lack the ability to acquire unproven or immature technology and thus should be more likely to acquire technology that is proven in the market.

---

[21] Katz, R., & Allen, T. J. 1982. Investigating the Not Invented Here (NIH) syndrome: A look at the performance, tenure, and communication patterns of 50 R&D project groups. RBD Management, 12(1): 7-19. Chesbrough, H. 2006. Open Innovation: A New Paradigm for Understanding Industrial Innovation.

[22] Laursen, K., & Salter, A. 2006. Open for innovation: the role of openness in explaining innovation performance among U.K. manufacturing firms. Strategic Management Journal, 27(2): 131-150.

[23] Argyres, N. S., & Silverman, B. S. 2004. R&D, organization structure, and the development of corporate technological knowledge. Strategic Management Journal, 25(89): 929-958.

[24] Cohen, W. M., & Levinthal, D. A. 1990. Absorptive capacity: a new perspective on learning and innovation. Administrative Science Quarterly, 35(1): 128-152. JSTOR.

[25] Cassiman, B., & Veugelers, R. 2006. In Search of Complementarity in Innovation Strategy: Internal R&D and External Knowledge Acquisition. Management Science, 52(1): 68-82.

If centralized firms acquire different types of targets, they will also differ in how they deal with them. Specifically, they may tend to leverage the acquired knowledge in the short term rather than investing on its future potential. Studies show that when small technology-based firms were integrated into the firm that acquired them, their technology was more likely to be built upon, but the small firms were less likely to innovate in the future.[26]

The foregoing arguments lead us to testable implications. First, they suggest that firms with decentralized R&D are more likely to engage in bigger acquisitions, meaning larger pools of patents that represent refined and developed technology. Conversely, centralized firms would favor acquiring technologies that would complement their internal R&D, perhaps filling important holes in existing capabilities, but not substituting in internal research. This is more likely to be in the form of small acquisitions.

Second, if one views integration as a way of building upon the existing knowledge brought by the acquisition, then we would expect that centralized firms are more likely to integrate the acquisition by absorbing the target. By contrast, decentralized firms should be more likely to preserve the autonomy of the acquired firm. Insofar as larger targets are more difficult to integrate and absorb, these two empirical predictions are mutually consistent. This leads to the following two conclusions:

1. Conditional on acquisition, centralized firms are more likely to integrate (absorb) their acquisitions. Conversely, decentralized firms will be less likely to absorb targets.
2. Centralized firms gain a greater proportion of their externally acquired knowledge through small acquisitions than decentralized firms.

Organization of R&D and Outcomes

A study of the relationship between organization and performance outcomes suggest that neither theory nor historical experience suggest any specific form of organization is superior to the other, since myriad trade-offs are involved. For example, decentralized research might neglect spill-overs and under-invest in longer-term research, resulting in unrealized opportunities for value creation. But just as well, central R&D labs might be less knowledgeable about, and less responsive to, the needs of customers,[27]

---

[26] Puranam, P., & Srikanth, K. 2007. What they know vs. what they do: How acquirers leverage technology acquisitions. Strategic Management Journal, 825(April): 805-825.

[27] Furman, J. L. 2003. Location and organizing strategy: Exploring the influence of location on the organization of pharmaceutical research. Advances in Strategic Management, 20: 49-88. JAI PRESS INC. Jensen, M. C., & Meckling, W. H. 1992. Specific and General Knowledge and Organizational Structure. In L. Werin & H. Wijkander (Eds.), Contract Economics. 251-274.

or they may be more susceptible to wasteful expenditures on scientifically interesting pet projects with limited value for the firm.[28]

Knowledge sourcing frameworks do not give clear predictions either. Even if firms with decentralized R&D rely on acquisitions to grow, there is no consensus as to whether this will help or hurt. Similarly, although a large proportion of the academic work on R&D conceptualizes incremental research as being less valuable, there is ample evidence that minor, incremental improvements are also a significant source of profits and productivity.[29] Firms may choose their organizational form, external orientation, and R&D focus based on an idiosyncratic and complex combination of history and environment. Thus, comparing the performance of one set of choices with another cannot be prescriptive.

First, if indeed centralization of R&D goes hand in hand with a firm's underlying strategy of growth and value creation through internally generated innovations, we would expect that internally generated knowledge is the key source of value for these firms. Second, whereas decentralization reflects a strategy of creating value through acquiring and assimilating external knowledge, firms with decentralized R&D should derive proportionally more value from externally acquired technology. Therefore it seems reasonable that centralized firms create more value from internal research and intellectual property, whereas decentralized firms create more value from intellectual property.

Conclusions: R&D Structures Impacting Innovation

Centralized firms invest more in research, which is more basic and more rooted in science. They also patent more per dollar. Centralization is also related to orientation towards external knowledge. Both centralized and decentralized firms access external technology via acquisitions, however, centralized firms do so less frequently, and tend to acquire firms with fewer patents. Further, acquired firms are often integrated and absorbed by centralized firms, whereas firms acquired by decentralized firms tend to remain distinct within the parent firm.

The choices firms make along the three dimensions are mutually supportive and coherent, and reflect an underlying firm strategy for growth through innovation. Firms that choose to seek innovations primarily by developing new knowledge internally cannot rely simply on incremental

---

Oxford: Blackwell Publishing. Von Hippel, E. 1998. Economics of product development by users: The impact of" sticky" local information. Management Science, 44(5): 629-644. JSTOR
[28] Seru, A. 2010. Firm boundaries matter: Evidence from conglomerates and R&D activity. AFA 2008 New Orleans Meetings Paper.
[29] Rosenberg, N. (1979). Technological interdependence in the American economy. Technol- ogy and Culture, 20(1),   25-50. Hollander, S. The Sources of Increased Efficiency: The Study of du Pont Rayon Plants (Cambridge, Mass., 1965).

research that merely improves on existing goods and services. Instead, such firms must invest in more basic, long-term research. Typically, such research is easiest to manage in central labs, because existing business units are unlikely to support it adequately. It is not that these firms do not seek external knowledge. They do, but mostly to complement internal knowledge.

By contrast, other firms may be unwilling or unable to make the same large investments in internal research to fuel innovation and growth. Their internal R&D is likely to be focused on improving existing products and processes, which is best managed by the business units that produce them. Such firms are more likely to look outside for new technologies.

The point is not that one or the other type of strategy is better. Rather, firms likely choose one or the other based on their initial founding conditions and capabilities, their environment, and how those evolve. What may matter more than the particular strategy is how well it fits the firm's capabilities, and how well the firm executes on it. The upshot is that both types of strategies can create value, albeit in different ways.

Consistent with this, centralized firms derive value from internal R&D, while decentralized firms derive value from externally acquired patents. The firm's organization plays an important role in developing internally coherent but markedly different strategies to grow either via internal development or external acquisition of knowledge.

It appears that the organizational structure is the bedrock on which strategy is founded. The new technologists must understand their role in the context of their firm's R&D structure, given how it influences choices between internal development and accessing external knowledge. If the technologist is in a centralized R&D function, their scientific knowledge will be more valued than if they're in a decentralized group where knowledge of the customer and solving near-term problems is more important. Conversely, knowledge-intensive highly centralized R&D functions will value the technologist's scientific capabilities leading to broad patents and transforming knowledge generation.

The Future of R&D

The only thing certain about predicting the future is that it will be wrong. However, looking at the future with a lens carefully polished by 40 years of experience may be useful to consider. Starting a career as a technologist today in R&D, I'd want to know who works at the interface with marketing where the value propositions are developed for customers, regardless of the structure selected. Marketing represents the first and most important set of "power brokers" to understand. Next are those R&D employees accountable for spending money through the projects they lead, ultimately creating offerings for customer as products, services, or both.

These are the project leaders normally residing within the R&D organization. Beyond decision-making authority, knowledge will rule the future R&D organizations, so employees with highly valuable domain knowledge are the next set of "power brokers" to deal with. Lastly comes the management team that administers the procurement of funds for the budget and is accountable for the spending measured by agreed-upon metrics.

Comparing this picture of the future with the reality of the past suggests that the real power in R&D will migrate to those with the knowledge to meet customer demands and not the management team who administers the resources. Customers will continue to demand total solutions for their problems, solutions often not available from one organization. This total solution approach will force R&D functions to embrace open innovation, partnering relationships with other firms and universities, and a more open approach to meeting customer demands. Firms with a deep not-invented-here mentality will lag behind more nimble and open-minded firms.

The conclusion one might draw from this picture of the future of R&D is that each employee needs to proactively manage their own careers with the help of HR, their superiors and peers, and most especially well-educated mentors. In many ways, the future of R&D is going "Back to the Future" in that the individual scientist or engineer is becoming the dominate player as it was in the time of Edison, Carnegie, Bell, and Ford. Evidence for this is everywhere in the digital space when you study Facebook, Google, Amazon, Microsoft, and Oracle. These companies were all built by highly entrepreneurial scientists and engineers even though their founders may not have been educated as such.

Most R&D organizations today are designed as matrices combining functional groups by discipline such as engineering, science, application development, performance testing and technical service and so on where the people in these groups are deployed against projects. This organizational design is more challenging to manage because individual employee performance is buried within a project team where the project leader may not be the employee's manager. Employees entering the R&D workplace need to be comfortable with the reality that their performance, and career aspirations, can be impacted by almost everyone they interact with in the organization.

Further complicating the role of new R&D employees is that their project teams and leaders may reside in a different country, raising challenges in norms of behavior, language, and societal norms. For example, imagine you're a US-based employee working on a global project and your project leader is Japanese, located in Tokyo. Your communication burden goes up exponentially with the language differences, you need to deal with significant time zone differences, and the cultural norms of behavior are radically different. None of these are insurmountable, but they require a very different mindset than what was normal just 20 years ago.

Ultimately, the role of an organizational design is to facilitate the flow of information to where it needs to be converted into knowledge leading to informed decision-making. Using this role of the organization, combined with the fact that digital tools make information flows rapid and nearly zero-cost, designs of the future can become more flexible. For example, the traditional designs as described above can become virtual designs where employees work remotely, being part of external entities and measured by several supervisors. The virtual design allows smaller firms to access the resources to perform like firms with much greater resources. Conceptually this might be thought of as a *virtual design* that is *continuously variable*, adopting whatever construct is required to achieve the desired outcomes.

The greatest impediment to this approach is the historical reality that information flows through *people*, and therefore the more people one manages the more power they have over this information. Today, these hierarchical designs often find the manager as the choke-point for information flows, depreciating the performance of the R&D function, whereas in the past these managers played a critical role in knowing where information needed to flow and why. The digitization of organizational designs makes this role not only moot but likely harmful. The true power of the R&D organization may belong to knowledge workers, empowered with digital tools, and deployed against a compelling portfolio of projects.

Summary: Organizational Designs

Effective design is critical to the future of any enterprise seeking to install an innovative culture as a source of competitive advantage. Recognizing that competitive advantage is the goal, there are a series of additional outcomes that the designer must consider to have an educated point of view and reap the advantages sought.

Historically, designs were largely hierarchical, reflecting the limitation inherent to information flows and automation. The hierarchy was required considering the limited knowledge available, which was most often aggregated at the top of the organization. With the advent of information technology, the Internet, and social networks, information is widely available and designs have flattened, allowing decision-making closest to the work by knowledgeable, and therefore empowered, employees.

As previously described, the 21st century worker has evolved from this new information rich environment to demand more freedom and individual recognition, often in the form of greater autonomy. These realities have increased the designers' latitude relative to levels of a given design, and hybrid designs better suited to complex business conditions. While designs around function, product, markets, customers, geographies, and processes will remain, hybrid designs are becoming more common.

The STAR model provides a framework from which to approach modern organizational design. It relies on fitting the company's structure to its strategy and then populating the structure with employees who are governed and recognized in ways facilitating the achievement of the strategic objectives. While the STAR model has found utility for the last 30 years, the rapidly changing business climate, driven by the availability of information, globalization of economies, shifts in demographics, and the migration of power to customers, has created the need for deeper and broader collaboration among employees and companies. These radical and irreversible changes have increased demands for finding ways to use organizational design to yield lasting competitive advantage.

Centralized firms invest more in research, which is more basic and more rooted in science. They also patent more per dollar. Centralization is also related to orientation towards external knowledge. Both centralized and decentralized firms access external technology via acquisitions, but centralized firms do so less frequently, and tend to acquire firms with fewer patents. Further, acquired firms are often integrated and absorbed by centralized firms, whereas firms acquired by decentralized firms tend to remain distinct within the parent firm.

It appears that the organizational structure is the bedrock on which strategy is founded. The new technologist must understand their role in the context of their firm's R&D structure, given how it influences choices between internal development and accessing external knowledge. If the technologist is in a centralized R&D function, their scientific knowledge will be more valued than if they're in a decentralized group where knowledge of the customer and solving near term problems is more important.

Conversely, knowledge-intensive highly centralization R&D functions will value the technologist's scientific capabilities leading to broad patents and transforming knowledge generation.

Chapter 2 Summary

The technologist today entering the R&D function of a modern enterprise faces an organization that is vulnerable to drastic change. In some ways, the R&D structure of the future may reflect the elements that were prevalent before Edison designed the first centralized R&D function, except that the individual contributors are now empowered with vast amounts of low-cost information made available by the Internet. This information, combined with willingness and the ability to collaborate, allows the individual technologist to be much more innovative for the firm than at any time in history.

A case study outlining the progression of the DuPont central research organization is instructive in teaching technologists of the future what they could've expected to experience when they took their first job. However, reflecting on that standard as what the future holds could be misleading. Given that organizational designs are created to manage information flows leading to informed decision-making, historically this has been the role of R&D managers to facilitate. If this role is being displaced with digital tools, these historical structures may be replaced as obsolete.

Conceptually, the future of the R&D organization could take on elements of being continuously variable, allowing flexibility and responsiveness unheard of in the past. This flexibility may be required to meet the demands of the future driven by customers wanting total solutions not readily available from one organization. These total solutions may require significant access to external resources, especially knowledge, assembled in innovative ways. The future may belong to those technologists capable of playing the role of "self-managed knowledge workers" who own the processes of how value is created.

Chapter 2 Critical Questions

R&D

About the Employee

1. How is success measured for a new employee?
2. What are the "Norms of Behavior" in the R&D Division?
3. How is performance measured?
4. How many people evaluate my performance?
5. What role do R&D employees play in launching new products?
6. How important is it for me to publish my work?

About the Function
1. How is intellectual property managed?
2. How many patents does R&D generate each year?
3. Does your firm have a "Technical Ladder" and if so can you explain how it works?
4. Where have R&D professionals ended up in the firm?
5. How do R&D professionals interface with the business groups especially marketing and sales?
6. What metrics are used to measure R&D?
7. How much money does the firm spend on R&D as a percent of revenues?
8. How has the R&D budget increased or decreased over the past 10 years?

9. How is R&D structured – centralized or decentralized – and how does this impact the innovation strategy?

Organizational Design

1. What does the term "organizational structure" mean?
2. What are the building blocks of an organizational structure? What are the most important influences on the design of the organizational structure?
3. What dimensions are typically used for profiling and comparing organizational structures?
4. What are the key questions and challenges for organizational designers?
5. What are the most important goals and objectives when establishing the organizational structure?
6. How should we best structure and organize to be able to deliver strategy?
7. What capabilities do we need to improve upon or to add in order to deliver strategy?
8. How do we build a high performance/high commitment workforce good enough to deliver strategy?
9. How do we create an operating environment suitable to deliver strategy?
10. How do we sharpen our competitive edge and best leverage our capabilities to deliver differentiated value?
11. How do we assure synergy of operation and action?

Chapter 3: The Innovation Imperative

Historical Context for Innovation

Context is the set of circumstances or facts surrounding a particular event or situation. What is the context in which innovation can occur smoothly and easily? This simple question defies a simple answer, but one can establish a framework favorable to innovation by recognizing those contexts that inhibit innovation.

All innovation comes from the application of human knowledge in a given context defined by a change force that leads to an adaptation of something that already exists to create something that was previously undoable. If human knowledge is the root of all innovation, then two critical questions must be considered as one looks at being innovative in the present: How is human knowledge created? How will new human knowledge differ in the way it is generated in the future? Understanding the past helps frame possibilities for the future because most transitions occur by building on what has already happened or what has already been mastered. An additional nuance is that human knowledge is not the sole endeavor of one individual. It is a collective effort of humans interacting around a common goal described by the changes being experienced. This helps explain how many innovations occur simultaneously in multiple locations at the same time. What makes up human knowledge? How has that changed in the last 100 years?

In order to understand the context of human knowledge today, it is useful to reflect upon a general definition of knowledge. Human knowledge is the assembly of experiences, described as *data*, into a form that communicates something about those experiences. This *information*, once understood, yields knowledge that can be utilized by anyone.

Historically, knowledge was the providence of the few who had the resources to observe the world around them versus just staying alive. In the *Dark Ages*, his was typically confined to the power class of people who owned the most valuable resource of the time, which was land.

During the *Enlightenment*, there was a transition in education away from the apprenticeship model, where people learned by working under those who knew more than them, towards the classroom model where knowledge could be acquired by listening to what others knew. A powerful catalyst of this transition was the advent of Gutenberg's printing press, which made the sharing of understood experiences much easier, making knowledge available to anyone who could read. As formal education evolved and reading became widespread, Innovation flourished, paving the way for the *industrial revolution*. The American colonies' ability to communicate quickly via the first pony express, established by Benjamin Franklin, enabled the upstart rebels to defeat the world's only superpower of the time, Great Britain. This is an example of how knowledge often trumps physical might.

It took humans hundreds of thousands of years to move from being hunter-gathers to a society based on agriculture. The agricultural revolution lasted 10,000-15,000 years, eventually replaced by the industrial revolution beginning around 1700 (give or take 100 years). The industrial revolution has since given way to the *information revolution* in the last 30 to 50 years.

A key observation is that each transition has occurred roughly ten times faster than the previous, highlighting the powerful nature of knowledge when it is widely disseminated. If the industrial revolution took 400 years, then one might expect the information revolution to be complete in 40 years. In fact, it may already be over without it being recognized as such. If the information revolution is complete, what follows it? Most likely the *knowledge revolution*, which consists of humanity's ability to use knowledge widely and in novel ways, enabled by low-cost computing power.

One catalyst of the information revolution was the advent of the Internet as a public "utility" around 1995. It developed at least in part from the Cold War need to protect the Western world's military command and control systems from being disabled by nuclear attack. This is one of countless innovations enabled by humanity's desire to wage war. Prior to becoming a public utility, the Internet was something protected and developed by the military-industrial complex, largely managed by the United States after World War II when the rest of the world was rebuilding.

Because the US suffered essentially no physical destruction during World War II, it had a huge advantage in leading both the information and knowledge revolutions. Whether the latter proves to be the case over time is an open question, but most major Internet companies are US-based.

Three major changes since WWII have had the greatest impact on the innovative capacity of people: The movement of productive capacity from physical labor to knowledge, the establishment of major metropolitan areas where people can collaborate more intimately, and the ability to communicate broadly, deeply and ever more quickly with each other.

Knowledge workers can freely share data across time and geographic boundaries, radically increasing people's ability to respond to, and exploit, change-creating wealth. A new critical success factor is the ability to convert raw data into information that describes changes in ways that can be understood, which in turn creates the knowledge required for innovation to flourish. Many innovations occur without a fundamental understanding of how they work, but understanding how they create wealth is critical to entrepreneurship. The deeper this understanding, the greater will be the wealth created by the entrepreneur.

In addition to establishing a strategic framework and context for innovation, companies must recognize the need to address the human element on a personal level, especially how people manage themselves and how the company manages the emerging class of knowledge workers. This class of worker, while present in the past, is emerging as a primary source of labor. These workers will be more educated, more skillful, and more demanding of a work climate aligned with their intellectual capabilities more than with physical skills. This presents new challenges to management in motivating, developing, and retaining these knowledge workers.

Given the pace of change in the economy, along with the advent of the Internet and large databases, competitiveness will change much more rapidly than in the past. The inability to manage knowledge workers effectively will lead to the deterioration of competitive advantage. Once lost, knowledge workers will be hard to replace given the time and money required to develop their skill sets.

Knowledge workers, likewise, will be required to continuously increase their skills in order to remain valuable. This will require a much greater level of self-management and self- development than previously experienced. Given that only people can innovate, a new partnership between knowledge workers and management must evolve in order for innovation to flourish; one based on collaboration, which is the root of innovative activity.

New ventures of the 21st century will require skills, resources, and vision unlike anything seen before, but the opportunity to create high-value enterprises has also never been greater. The Internet can significantly reduce the cost of delivering offerings, in some cases to near zero. This lower delivery cost, combined with access to large communities of customers whose needs are understood, will lead to the rapid creation of very profitable enterprises. Examples of such enterprises already in the marketplace include Amazon, Google, Facebook, and a host of others that have all taken advantage of low delivery cost and wide access to large customer bases with intimate knowledge of the customers' needs.

It appears that the 21st century will be a 100-year period of incredible innovation and tremendous increases in the overall wealth and living standards of the world's population. This is occurring now in Asia at an incredible rate. The most significant challenges humankind faces are to innovate effectively enough to deal with the climate change that threatens the stability of the entire planet and its ability to sustain life. As the Chinese proverb says, *may you live in interesting times.* Indeed, the next hundred years of innovation should be very interesting.

Innovator Agency: Common Characteristics among Innovators and Entrepreneurs

The innovator's agency defines a collection of individual choices and behaviors facing the entrepreneur leading to solutions generating wealth expressed not only in companies but also in entire industries, often in the image of the entrepreneurs themselves. Interestingly, these change forces are common over time, suggesting the plausibility that the characteristics of successful innovators and entrepreneurs are also timeless. If so, then both the change forces leading to major innovations and those capable of taking advantage of these changes can be studied and mimicked, leading to a discipline, albeit one that is difficult to master.

This agency, within a context of events, appears to be timeless, and while visible to many, only a few succeed in creating value and wealth from the experience. To test the premise that change drives innovation, and that the characteristics of innovators to take advantage of these changes in becoming wealth-creating entrepreneurs, have common elements, and can be learned, I investigated six entrepreneurs and their successful enterprises over three centuries by consulting the work of Nancy Koehn, where she provides an analysis of the six entrepreneurs.[30]

The study addresses, from a historical perspective, six illustrative entrepreneurs in six different industries, all working to create new markets for their wares. The book opens in late 18th-century Britain, when Josiah Wedgwood tried to increase widespread consumer interest in fine china. It then jumps 100 years forward to the US-based efforts of Henry Heinz and Marshall Field in developing markets in food processing and mass-retailing. The book then analyzes three twentieth-century businesspeople and the new sectors in which they worked: Estée Lauder in prestige cosmetics, Howard Schultz of Starbucks in specialty coffee, and Michael Dell in personal computers. It uses these illustrative examples to draw lessons from these entrepreneurs on how they reacted to change in their time to create wealth.

The six entrepreneurs had many things in common. Perhaps the most important was an understanding of what rapid social and economic change meant for consumer needs and wants. They used their knowledge of both the supply and demand sides of the economy to create high-quality goods,

---

[30] Koehn, Nancy, F. *Brand New*, Harvard Business School Publishing, 2001.

meaningful brands, and other connections with customers, building companies that satisfied and anticipated changing customer preferences.

Four of these people made tangible products: Wedgwood made earthenware, Heinz made pickles, Lauder made cosmetics, and Dell made personal computers. The other two entrepreneurs created "encounters" that proved appealing to consumers: Field created the department store environment and Schultz created the café experience. In addition, Wedgwood's showrooms, Dell's customized order process, and Lauder's in-store demonstrations added an important element of experiential shopping to the sale of the things they made.

These six individuals thoroughly understood that economic expansion and social transformation affected what consumers want, have, and can afford, as well as what companies choose to make. Each pursued new business opportunities relentlessly, undeterred by initially limited resources.

Exploiting available opportunities depended on comprehending emerging consumer needs, developing a product that met those needs, communicating back and forth with customers, and actually delivering the product or service effectively. It also depended crucially on building a company that could perform all of these disparate functions well.

In 1759, for example, Josiah Wedgwood founded his own pottery workshop with the idea of developing a large market for dinner plates and other fine china. He had ambition, experience, and imagination, but virtually no cash and few connections. Like Wedgwood, the other five entrepreneurs developed particular tools to take advantage of the possibilities they confronted. These tools included rigorous quality control measures, focused employee training policies, innovative selling and distribution methods, and strong brands. All of these initiatives were coordinated toward one goal: Making a market from novel goods and services.

The accomplishments of all six entrepreneurs, especially early on, resulted from improvising or making it up as they went along. In starting their own businesses, they had few employees, meager revenues, and only rudimentary management systems. Two of the six made the first products in their kitchens. A third worked from his college dorm. A fourth worked from a room in the back of his café. All six shared an obsession with creating a quality offering, a determination to bring it to a large number of customers, and the ability to appreciate how social and economic shifts impacted consumer wants. In a sense, each was lucky in confronting new business opportunities growing out of major societal changes. But in every case, as an oft-stated business axiom puts it, the harder each one worked, the luckier he or she became. In addition to their personal traits, each encountered historical forces that they were able to recognize, interpret, understand, and respond to in creating products to sell into growing markets. These historical forces included the following:

- Accelerating economic change, presenting unusual opportunities for each of the entrepreneurs.
- Greater productivity, increasing the proportion of hours of working capital employed occurred across the entire market, creating consumers with greater purchasing power.
- Population growth was significant and became centralized in urban centers, creating concentrations of customers that could be reached effectively and efficiently.
- Supporting greater productivity, population growth, and urbanization were radical improvements in transportation and communication that allowed the entrepreneurs to reach more customers at lower cost in less time, much as the Internet has done in recent times.
- Michael Dell recognized that the personal computer would revolutionize everyone's life and understood that customizing the computer to user needs would be paramount.
- These changes created new expectations in consumers, satisfying social and psychic needs beyond the more fundamental requirements of everyday life. These new expectations are reinforced by the great availability of data that can be assembled into information and understood to create knowledge, making consumers more educated and more demanding.

Many were called, few were chosen, and most failed.

These six entrepreneurs built their enterprises as follows:
1. Having deep knowledge and experience of their product/service.
2. Learning quickly from their mistakes and making rapid corrections.
3. Creating meaningful brands that distinguish their offerings and respond to changing customer priorities, reflecting the value they were providing in a consistent way, creating loyalty.
4. Initiating a process of reciprocal learning with customers that resulted from ongoing two-way communication, using their brands to build bridges between themselves and their customers. This constant two-way communication created insights about what their customers and markets demanded in the present, and what they expected in the future. Often this communication occurred face-to-face.
5. Creating a range of organizational capabilities that delivered on brand promises.
6. Demonstrating unyielding passion and ambition for their vision of the enterprise.

7. By accessing, in some cases, financial resources from wealthy investors.
8. Demanding excellence in everything they did and, more importantly, everything that their employees did on behalf of their brand.
9. Displaying enormous energy on a personal level to do whatever was necessary to be successful.

All six entrepreneurs exhibited the same traits, despite the very different times in which they lived, suggesting that they are timeless and therefore applicable in the present to be a basis for creating a discipline of innovative entrepreneurship. Clearly, each of these six entrepreneurs faced daunting challenges from competitors, economic downturns, and unexpected challenges, such as the following:

1. Wedgwood, while able to conceive the products the customer wanted, needed skilled craftsman to make them, and these people were not available and needed to be developed by him for his business.
2. Henry Heinz went bankrupt twice during the 1860s and 1870s, but recovered to create an enterprise driven by a large, educated, competent sales force.
3. Marshall Field faced enormous competition in his home city of Chicago and survived his primary businesses burning down twice in five years.
4. Estée Lauder and Howard Schultz both encountered enormous organizational challenges in delivering their products and services to large numbers of consumers. Building effective organizations was the critical core competency allowing them to beat their competitors.
5. Michael Dell faced similar organizational challenges in customizing a mass-market product and providing service to a large number of customers in a way that created brand loyalty.

The historical context and the traits of these entrepreneurs provide a framework from which today's innovators and entrepreneurs can build their enterprises. They need to do what others have done successfully before them: Reflecting on the changes occurring around them, characterizing the opportunities these changes present, conceiving options customers are willing to pay for, and paving the way for adoption of these solutions.

Foundations of Innovation

Real integrity is doing the right thing,
knowing that nobody's going to know whether you did it or not.
~ Oprah Winfrey ~

Hope is not a Strategy
~ Author Unknown ~

The paradox called innovation has precepts that are easy to understand but difficult to implement. Innovation is not exclusively the domain of the technical community; it requires the participation of the entire enterprise to be successful. The components of successful, sustainable innovation are surprisingly common sense. The enterprise must *want* to innovate as a key part of their strategy. This commitment must begin with top management and be continuous and long-term in nature. Desire without commitment wastes organizational time and energy, squandering shareholder value. Because it is *people* that innovate, the collective talent of the organization's human capital is the raw material of innovation.

More important than the raw skills of people is their innate curiosity and desire to understand changes occurring around them, which the enterprise must then convert into advantages. These advantages benefit the enterprise's customers, markets, communities, shareholders and employees. Unless the advantages from innovation have broadening impact over time, they are unlikely to be significant or sustainable.

The systems and procedures by which an enterprise conducts business must also facilitate innovation. Information about change described in ideas is at the root of innovation, assembled into knowledge that transforms observations into meaningful innovations that can create wealth. *Knowledge management* has become a key core competency for industry innovation powerhouses like Proctor and Gamble (P&G), and are increasingly a condition of existence for most enterprises. In addition, successful innovation requires the enterprise to avoid "self-inflicted injuries" such as the following:

- Arrogance, especially by the leadership team.
- Unrealistic expectations. Innovation is not easy, quick, or large (at first).
- Simplicity. Being "clever" invites expensive failures.
- Unwillingness to recognize that innovation must first be in the present. The future will take care of itself.
- Inability to calculate and manage risk. Successful innovators are not *risk takers* so much as *risk managers*, deferring risk whenever possible.

For the entrepreneur, all innovations start small. In the beginning, innovations that become big are indistinguishable from those that stay small. Unless an organization is capable of successful, systematic organizational and business innovation, it cannot create sustainable shareholder value over time. Reinventing the business to lead events in the world and marketplace requires a sense of constant urgency and willingness to embrace change, thereby creating the future. Innovation creates new wealth by the following four primary means, which can be practiced both internally and externally:

o Abandoning ongoing efforts to "make room" for innovation.
o Continuously seeking the opportunities found in change.
o Converting those opportunities into value for customers.
o Strategically allocating resources.

Key concepts in creating the future include the following:

- The *Silent Revolution,* which suggests the changes we're experiencing are significant but hard to perceive, and are condensing the timeline for innovation. Abandonment must occur frequently and rapidly, including everything about the business and not just its products.
- Seven varieties of opportunities must be considered in the context of new information, geography, and changing demographics. This context must be considered explicitly and focus on challenging the basic assumptions held by management about the business.
- The power of processes, bringing key resources into play, fostering disciplined decision-making and collaboration, and allocating resources are more important now than at any time in the past, and are growing in importance as information becomes more dynamic and impactful.
- Innovation in the *Lego World,* or the world of integrated solutions derived both internally and externally, is about building relationships and inventing white space. It is not about helping a product survive one more round of improvement.
- Connecting resources from externally derived sources has become a new competency required to create sustainable advantage.

The simplest definition of innovation is *the conversion of knowledge into economic value resulting from a human response to change in the present.* The literature is replete with information about innovation relative to methods and processes by which to innovate, many described in romantic and often magical terms. What are the primary tenets of innovation and how can they create sustainable economic value creation for the enterprise?

One very clear conclusion from the literature is that innovation is very situational, meaning that what works for one organization may not work for another. This conclusion is self-evident in that sustainable innovation is so uncommon, and implies that the enterprise must create an "innovation culture" that works over time for its evolving situation. You can't buy (e.g., consultants) or copy a solution. You need to invent it for yourself.

Nine Foundations of Successful Innovation

The following are nine foundations for successful innovation that must be recognized and adopted:
1. Innovation is hard work.
2. Innovation is both conceptual and perceptual.
3. Innovators must build on their strengths.
4. Innovation involves managed risk taking.
5. Innovation must be simple and focused.
6. Effective innovations start small.
7. Innovations must have economic and societal impact.
8. People innovate.
9. Innovation must be aimed at leadership.

Foundation #1: Innovation is Hard Work. Innovation requires knowledge and great ingenuity, which naturally results in some people being more innovative than others. Innovators rarely work in more than one area. Edison, for instance, only worked in the electrical field. Innovation involves talented people with a certain predisposition, working towards a common purpose. Innovation is very hard, focused, purposeful work, making very great demands in diligence, persistence, and commitment of the entire enterprise. If these are lacking, no amount of talent, ingenuity, or knowledge will matter.

Foundation #2: Innovation is Both Conceptual and Perceptual. Successful innovators look at both numerical data and qualitative information such as people's behavior. They use both sides of their brains concurrently. Critical to this imperative is that the innovator spends time with the customer in the environment where the innovation is to be employed. They combine thoughtful analysis with field exposure to customers and end users in determining definitions of value. Value and the receptivity to an innovation can be perceived, and perception becomes reality for those adopting the innovation. A key question the innovator must answer is this: *What does the innovation have to reflect so that people want to use it and see it fitting their opportunity?* Not answering this key question leads to an innovation that, while correct, is in the wrong form.

Foundation #3: Innovators Must Build on Their Strengths. Innovators may look for and analyze opportunities over a wide range but are driven to respond to those which play into their competencies. The successful innovator will ask, "Which of these opportunities fits me, fits my company, and leverages what we're good at and have shown capacity for in performance?" The opportunity must fit the temperament of the business and be a respected area of endeavor. For instance, most pharmaceutical companies consider innovation in cosmetics to be beneath them because they're in the business of saving lives. This "respect requirement" is needed for generating organizational commitment and passion for the hard work it takes to be successful. The innovation must make the innovators proud of their achievement.

Foundation #4: Innovation Involves Managing Risk. A common myth is that innovators are risk takers. In reality, successful innovators manage risk and avoid taking poor risks. One common attribute is that the successful innovator works diligently to avoid mistakes by analyzing situations carefully, taking educated risks with contingency plans, and constantly keeping in contact with their markets and customers.

Foundation #5: Innovation Must be Simple and Focused. Innovations must be simple and focused on doing one thing very well; otherwise, they confuse and eventually won't work. All innovations eventually run into trouble, and if such complications can't be fixed quickly enough, customer interest will be lost. All effective innovations are breathtakingly simple. The greatest praise of all is saying, "This is obvious. Why didn't I think of it"? In addition, the innovation must be directed toward a specific, clear, designed application with a specific need it satisfies and end result it produces.

Foundation #6: Effective Innovations Start Small. All successful innovation must start small and satisfy one specific need requiring little money, few people, and a small limited market. Successful innovations do not begin as grandiose adventures. Most innovations are initially barely "almost right" and must be evolved quickly to a near-perfect fit so they can be willingly adopted and create value. If the innovation is small and relatively simple, adjustments can be made quickly, with few people and little money. Global innovator 3M calls this the "Make a Little, Sell a Little" innovation process and has shown how it can be very effective and sustainable over decades. Key to this is managing expectations.

Foundation #7: Innovations Must Have Broad Socioeconomic Impact. Economic and societal impact is a case of *"I'll know it when I see it."* Put another way, these innovations are self-evident to those who are impacted by them, although they may not be conscious of it. Examples might include the zipper, dishwashing machine, and the vacuum cleaner.

Foundation #8: People Innovate. Innovation is clearly a "people game." While this may seem obvious, the ways in which human capital is employed are critical to the outcomes. Presuming a strategy is sound and there are adequate financial resources, the next focus is on the capabilities, alignment, and behaviors of the company's people. Supporting systems are also a priority because people without the proper tools and processes will fail.

Foundation #9: Successful Innovations *Must* Aim at Leadership. An innovation cannot be aimed at creating a large business, although some will achieve this. Instead, they must be focused at leadership in the given application. If leadership can't be achieved, then the innovation is probably not good enough to sustain itself in the market by being readily adopted. Innovations that fail to establish a leadership position only create opportunities for competitors, and are actually harmful to the enterprise. Leadership characteristics for the innovation must be well defined and targeted from the very beginning through good opportunity analysis.

What is needed are thought leaders skilled at gathering, disseminating and interpreting information about changes in the marketplace combined with a bias towards analysis on a deeper level. Clearly, a better competitive intelligence program will help. These kinds of analyses should then generate greater imagination in technical and marketing communities for satisfying customer expectations in unexpected and superior ways. Becoming more skillful in identifying *what* is required before the innovative *how* can be conceived.

Four Pre-Innovation Questions

The following four key questions must be answered before innovation can happen:
1. What do you have to abandon to create room for innovation?
2. How do you systematically find and analyze opportunities?
3. Is the innovation process disciplined?
4. Does the innovation strategy work with your business strategy?

The most elegant thinking on innovation comes from Peter Drucker. He teaches that truly sustainable economic value is derived from *purposeful innovation* – innovation that can be replicated and taught to a learning organization. Below is a fuller treatment of each of the key four questions preceding innovation:

Pre-Innovation Question #1: What must be abandoned to make room for innovation? This question is exceptionally difficult to answer because it mandates challenging the enterprise's current sources of value, (e.g., revenue and margin) often at their peak and just before their decline. However, clinging to the past almost ensures failure in the future. The following three key questions help determine what must be abandoned:

1. *If you weren't in this business today would you invest in it?* Kodak failed to answer the first question effectively. It hung onto traditional film while digital photography exploded around them. It was held captive by its past success and extensive capital employed. GE, on the other hand, challenged itself to be number one or two in its business, or have a way of getting there, or get out. Kimberly Clark in the 1970's moved away from its core offerings to challenge P&G in diapers and won. *Successful abandonment* requires a systematic approach where businesses and products are ruthlessly evaluated for fit with the future and long term value. This process must begin just as the business or offering is launched. Those that cannot offer viable strategies for creating future value must be "systematically abandoned" by being relieved of their best people and sold or harvested (more resources for innovation).

2. *What unconscious assumptions might constrain your business practices and limit your innovative thinking?* The most dangerous assumptions are those not explicitly or routinely challenged for validity. Often such assumptions are considered "enduring truths" until they damage the enterprise, often in a slowly corrosive way. The most critical assumptions are those related to the basic operations and economics of the business. Some questions to routinely ask and answer honestly include the following:

   a. Do our customers still obtain value from our offerings as they have in the past?

   b. Have our competitors changed their strategies? Are there new competitors from an unexpected source?

   c. Which variables impact our profitability and are we proactively managing them?

   d. Do macro-economic events impact our business asymmetrically? Is this a threat or opportunity?

   e. What new business models should we examine in light of systemic change forces like the Internet, alternative fuels, environmental regulations, and so on?

   f. Do we conduct routine sensitivity analysis on critical success factors impacting the enterprise?

3. *Are the Company's best people working on innovative opportunities or past problems?* An old medical proverb says, "There is nothing more expensive, nothing more difficult, than to keep a corpse from stinking." Most companies spend their best people's time, and significant sums of money, keeping old products from "stinking." The business must examine its portfolio of work regularly and ask who is working on projects that are of incremental value. If they are truly marginal they should be discontinued, but if they have incremental value then they should consume average, not exceptional, employees. Often urgent, but not necessarily important, short term problems such as complexity

reduction, cost management initiatives, and working capital projects consume the most innovative employees. Such work should be reserved for the 70% of employees who are average.

Pre-Innovation Question #2: How do you systematically find and analyze opportunities? The analysis of opportunities begins by identifying their sources. High-value opportunities come from the following seven sources, all of which involve change:

1. An organization's own *unexpected* success and unexpected failures, and those of the organization's competitors.
2. *Incongruities* in the business process (e.g., production, distribution, product positioning etc.) or customer behavior.
3. *Process* needs (e.g., getting LEAN).
4. *Market* disparities over time or geography (changes in industry structure).
5. Changes in *demographics.*
6. Changes in *meaning and perception.*
7. *New knowledge.*

Each source of opportunity must be carefully analyzed. This requires the organization to have a natural curiosity and disposition to understand observations on a deep level. It also requires the organization to invest financially, intellectually and behaviorally in systems of analysis and knowledge management. Each of the seven sources of innovation are more fully treated below:

The unexpected. An unexpected outcome, whether it is failure or success, denotes a major but poorly understood change force. These often defy conventional wisdom and are dismissed as aberrations. Smith-Barney, under Sandy Weill, grew rapidly in the institutional equity market when Drexel-Burnham-Lambert unexpectedly when bankrupt in 1989. Weill realized it was an opportunity to acquire entire departments at a steep discount. The key is that *the unexpected* denotes change that signifies opportunity for those who can see it as such. Unexpected events often come to the enterprise in the form of requests for products the firm does not supply but should. The entrepreneur always looks for opportunities.

Incongruities. An incongruity is the difference between what the customer wants and what the supplier thinks the customer wants. Often this results from suppliers looking at their customer's world from inside their firms rather than from the customer's view or that of the marketplace. Jet Blue became a profitable $1.3B airline by recognizing the incongruity between customers wanting a better flying experience (e.g., fresh food, wireless

Internet service, etc.), and being willing to pay for it, versus just a method for getting between places, as most airlines had concluded. A key source of innovation is where a high volume industry remains unprofitable.

Process vulnerabilities. *Process vulnerability* refers to some part of the workflow or operation that is missing, difficult, or not working at all, ultimately preventing users from embracing the offering. Scott's Lawn Care became very successful when it corrected the process vulnerability of using its grass seed product by providing the seed spreader. TiVo solved the problem of taping television programs made so painful by VCRs. Vulnerabilities in your firm's offerings offer opportunity to grow or a threat to lose business to a competitive offering that closes the gap.

Market disparities. This source of innovation is a mismatch between supply and demand that may be driven by economics, location or other characteristics. Prosthetics are just as necessary in the developing world as for more affluent countries. However, their costs are prohibitive if developed world economics apply. This reveals a disparity in demand (high in undeveloped countries) and supply (unavailable at an affordable price). The opportunity is for a prosthetic cost optimized relative to functionality to fill the demand in the less-developed world. Such an outcome has occurred in India, where a foot prosthetic was developed that can be manufactured at a cost of $45, whereas the developed world device costs thousands of dollars. A more obvious event is how the Internet has changed the leisure travel industry by allowing people to self-manage their vacations without involving a travel agent. Another example is cataract surgery in India cost $15 per eye vs. thousands of dollars in a developed country and the quality of post-operative outcomes are equivalent.

Demographic changes. A very visible and commonly discussed change force is the aging Baby Boomer generation in the US as well as aging populations in general. Places where young people dominate, such as in the Middle East, offer similar opportunities for growth. A simple example is the changing needs of the elderly for furnishings of all kinds to accommodate declining physical capabilities and the desire to be stationary for longer periods of time. Younger families with less disposal income offer another opportunity for attractive but affordable furniture that replaced "hand-me-downs" from parents to children.

New knowledge. A scientific break though is often associated with innovation in the minds of most people. However these kinds of innovations are slow to penetrate the market and become visible long before they have impact. In general a major new knowledge innovation requires

20-30 years before it has a true impact on the market place. Examples like transistors, digital cameras, X-rays etc. are obvious tools today but fit the "25 year rule." Bioengineering in general began with the discovery of DNA in 1953, progressed to laboratory recombination techniques in the 1970's, and finally drugs in the 1990s. The Internet and the explosion of, and accessibility to, knowledge may shorten the "25-year rule" in the future but in general many innovations take a long time and as such the ultimate benefactors are uncertain until commercialization begins. Xerox Corporation's investment in their world class R&D center named PARC invented nearly every major innovation used today in the information technology age but benefited very little from these investments. P&G, on the other hand, invented fluoride toothpaste in 1955, branded it Crest, and made huge amounts of money. Colgate did the same in 1997 with Colgate Complete using Triclosan.

Pre-Innovation Question #3: Is the Innovation Process Disciplined?
There are four key questions that reveal the elements of a disciplined process that converts ideas into practical solutions, thereby utilizing people most effectively. They are as follows:
a. Do your people brainstorm effectively? Are all worthy ideas and opportunities considered?
b. Do you match up ideas and opportunities?
c. Do you test and refine ideas based upon market response?
d. Do you deliver results by allocating resources, creating customers one at a time, and monitor progress externally?

Effective brainstorming requires exceptional listening skills, openness to new or unexpected ideas, and a focus on creating value for customers. Key is the ability to engage people of varying perspectives (e.g., diversity) on a common topic while retaining and embracing their differences.

The climate for the brainstorming activity must be results-oriented to create value for customers, respectful of everyone's ideas, discourage endless debate for its own sake, and have ground rules for encouraging constructive conversations. Some useful questions for the brainstorming team to consider are as follows:
1. Customer by customer, where are there possible problems and solutions that create value?
2. What would it take for us to seriously consider this idea?
3. What new and important need can we serve?
4. How can we use our core competencies in a new way?
5. How can we change the economics of this industry?

Do you match up ideas and opportunities? Will the idea respond effectively to a real world opportunity and is this opportunity significant enough to merit our best people? Minor modifications rarely yield significant value. True innovation must aim for leadership in satisfying a true meaningful unmet need. True innovations will do the following:

1. Change the customer's behavior by creating new utility.
2. Invent an entirely new business and not just a product.
3. Deliver unimagined value by solving an unmet need.
4. Deliver practical attributes while achieving leadership quickly.
5. Is often surprisingly elegant in its simplicity in use, satisfying one need.
6. Is speedy to market.
7. Is consistent with the organization's strengths.
8. Solve a problem in the present.

Do you test and refine ideas based upon market response? The concept of testing is simply proving that the innovation delivers the value expected in a way that is sustainable in the real world. Testing enables the innovator to rapidly improve the offering or fix it quickly once launched. Observing the customer using the innovation reveals which attributes are truly valuable. Sometimes the innovation is valued for what it doesn't require as much as for what it does.

Do you deliver results by allocating resources, creating customers one at a time, and monitor progress externally? Innovations don't deliver anything until they are executed in the market place with customers. To achieve leadership, the company must be aggressive but not foolhardy in addressing the market need. Because unexpected things happen, the innovator must have a living plan than can be adjusted to address what is experienced. The living plan begins with management committing adequate resources of the right quality so it can be put into action to deliver results. Innovations often require different skills than those effective to the existing business. Managing the future requires encouragement of ideas, however crude they may be, and management must answer the question: What does it take for this idea to be seriously considered?

Finally, management must recognize that innovations require different metrics focused on the opportunity, not on profitability. They must also protect the innovative investment from excessive overhead and "internal help" which can kill the effort. Management must also demand discipline and accountability at every stage of the innovative effort.

Pre-Innovation Question #4: Does the innovation strategy work with your business strategy? The final element of a successful innovation strategy is how well it fits with the business strategy. Key questions to answer include the following:

1. What is your company's target role or influence in defining the new markets?
2. What is the scope of the offering to this market?
3. How does your portfolio of opportunities fit with your business strategy?
4. Are you allocating resources where you should be making bets?

An effective business strategy embraces external realities and opportunities and provides the context to help ensure that every decision, priority, and allocation of resources is geared to value creation. The innovation strategy is the program of change that will create the company of the future.

What is your company's target role or influence in defining the new markets? The innovation strategy must articulate each opportunity in terms of your company's *influence* in defining the new market and target the *scope* of your offerings for playing in the defined white space. There are four basic approaches to defining influence and scope as follows:

1. First owner of the space.
2. The innovator who is the "space definer."
3. The niche player.
4. The last buggy whip provider.

First owner of the space is the company that provides the new market the *first offering* with the most integrated solution. Often this is a temporary position because it draws imitators who may bring more advantageous economics to the product or service. Long-term competitive advantage requires almost a monopoly like presence (e.g., Microsoft).

FedEx pioneered the express package delivery market and had the lead for 2 years before the USPS, DHL and UPS entered with lower cost to serve, forcing FedEx to reinvent itself.

In contrast, the *space definer* creates something that sets boundaries, defines the new space in some fashion, or executes an idea. Corning did this for high-speed light bulb production by inventing the machine that every light bulb manufacturer had to buy. GE may have owned the space but Corning defined it. When a space has been defined by an enterprise it creates opportunities for *niche players* to supply these leaders. Electronic Arts (EA) is a game designer for video games that change at an amazing pace.

They change with it, creating new game content to keep pace with device changes. Hardware manufactures define the space but EA provides an essential element – the game itself.

Finally there is the *last buggy whip manufacturer* who use innovation to incrementally improve the economics of their existing businesses. While viable over the short term, this strategy must be complimented with genuine innovation delivering new value to the market and customers. Many companies play in multiple spaces simultaneously but use a different strategy in each space. The pace of change today requires the enterprise to continuously adjust its innovation strategy and depend on strong linkages to external partners, including customers, complementors, and even competitors and other outside resources to help deliver value.

How does your portfolio of opportunities fit with your business strategy? An effective innovation strategy builds a portfolio that creates wealth and value tomorrow. But it must balance the following:
1. Innovation versus continuity.
2. Core capabilities versus new skills developed for tomorrow.
3. Defining new landscapes versus playing in existing ones.
4. Focus versus reliance on multiple businesses.

An example of expert alignment of innovation and business strategies is Corning Glass. From the mid-nineteenth century until the late 1990s Corning was a superb innovator in the use of glass and silicon. It lost its way with the telecommunication bust of 2000 but until then it invented many major devices from the CRT for televisions, to the catalytic converter for cars using its capabilities to make low cost but high performing devices from glass and ceramics. Corning's success stemmed from an unexpressed but consistent innovation strategy embracing the following elements:
1. Using invention and innovation to solve known customer problems.
2. Utilizing deep knowledge and know-how related to inorganic materials, especially glass and ceramics.
3. Exploiting a deep processing competency for converting sophisticated innovations into low-cost offerings.
4. Recognizing it was a technology company and not skillful as a marketer, something it acquires from its partners. In the process, Corning has become an expert in developing successful joint ventures.

Key to Corning's success and recovery from the near bankruptcy of 2001 was answering the key question: "What are we really good at and why?" and then acting on the answer.

Are you allocating resources to where you want to be making bets?
The answer might seem obvious, but unless you explicitly look and
proactively manage such resources, the answer may be surprising. Often the
urgent dominates the important in resource allocation decisions. This
happens due to fear of a short term consequence (allowing an even more
damaging long term consequence), lack of clear knowledge of where
resources are being used, poor alignment of operational plans to strategies,
lack of discipline, even tampering by senior management, among other
reasons.

Key to effective resource deployment is first recognizing where
resources are being used in the present. This requires an accurate portfolio
management system where people's time and company monies can be
tracked accurately and without threat. This resource management system
must be connected to the business and innovation strategies so the portfolio
being measured is legitimate. Once systems are in place, cultural norms of
behavior must support the strategies so employees are self-disciplined to
execute on sanctioned investments while having the courage and authority
to say "no" to unsanctioned work. Finally, the measuring system must be
flexible enough to adjust to necessary changes in the work portfolio so it's
kept valid.

Innovation Pitfalls

The following are a few important pitfalls that should be avoided:
1. Don't be clever.
2. Don't diversify.
3. Don't innovate for the future, just the present.

Don't be clever. Innovations must be handled by ordinary human beings to
be successful. If they're to attain any significant mass, they must be usable
by morons or near-morons. Incompetence is the only thing in great
abundance in the world. More simply put, the innovation must be
foolproof and battle-ready.

Don't diversify. This is the corollary to the third "do" of staying focused.
This focus must extend beyond just the technical community and embrace
everyone involved with making the innovation a success. Another way of
thinking about this is that the entire business must being working towards a
common purpose in order for the innovation to succeed.

Don't innovate for the future, only the present. To be successful,
innovations must achieve leadership in satisfying a current need. Future
needs might help the innovation grow in scale and impact, but if they

precede the market's readiness, they only pave the way for competitors. IBM successfully introduced the first business computer in 1953 via "Creative Imitation" by recognizing that a design developed by the University of Philadelphia fit an immediate market need. Edison is the classic example of innovating for the present. He waited *ten years* before tackling the light bulb, well after many others had begun, to be sure the infrastructure was there to support it. But then he focused *only* on the light bulb, allowing him to prevail in spite of starting late.

Becoming More Innovative – A Uniquely Human Event

Tactics mean doing what you can with what you have.
~ Saul Alinsky ~

Successful innovation requires a clear understanding of the context in which the innovator is dealing. With the advent of the Internet and large databases, the context that innovators experience is changing rapidly. There appear to be several very important variables impacting the context of innovation today, including negative quarter-power scaling relationships, shorter timelines to commercialization for web-enabled innovations, and connectedness that today is far easier to accomplish and has become a critical success factor. Finally, there are four elements to consider as follows:

1. Innovation is *fractal* – which means it looks the same no matter how close or far away you are from it. This suggests that all acts of being innovative have the same origins and are fundamentally similar and based on mutually beneficial cooperation more than brute competition.
2. Bigger is better in that the more people you have in the "innovative eco-system" the more likely you are to be innovative. With the Internet even small entities can have the advantages of scale.
3. Connecting ideas is better than protecting them, and the connections are what's key to breakthrough innovations. Good ideas want to connect, fuse, and recombine. Ideas "want to be completed" and then applied, not hidden.
4. The volume of data, growing exponentially, could impede innovation b encumbering the desired "collisions." The correct amount of data, colliding with the colliding with the appropriate force, at the correct time, is one of the secrets of successful innovation.

There are seven primary tactical elements of innovation:

1. The Adjacent Possible.
2. Liquid Networks.
3. The Slow Hunch.
4. Serendipity.

5. Errors.
6. Exaptation.
7. Platforms.

Combining these *seven* elements with the additional considerations of scaling power, critical mass, the impact of readily available information, and the fact that innovation is fractal, provides a framework from which to make innovation a discipline rather than a random occurrence. The common elements of innovation are applicable across any situation.

1. **Negative quarter-power scaling:** The larger and heavier the animal, the longer they live based on slower heart rate described by the following mathematical relationship: A cow, which is 1,000 times heavier than a woodchuck, lives 5.5 times longer. However, it seems every animal has the same number of heartbeats, but some use them at a slower rate. Slowing your heart rate increases your life. This scaling effect works for consumption, at the metropolitan level, but not innovation. Innovation has a positive quarter-power scaling. A city that is 10 times larger is 17 times more innovative, based on patents, R&D budgets, creative professions, inventors and so on. The conclusion is that the intimacy of a city multiplies the ability of ideas to build on each other and develop into innovations. People sharing information openly (information spill-over) facilitates innovation. The question then is how can this be encouraged in a corporate environment?

2. **The 10/10 rule has governed innovation timelines:** 10 years for a platform to develop and 10 years for it to reach a mass market. However, The web has reduced this for some innovations by making development and adoption much faster. YouTube has a 1/1 development/adoption ration, whereas HDTV was more the lithe traditional 10/10.
   - The more an innovation does the faster it will be adopted. HDTV made regular TV better. YouTube enabled people to use movies as never before.
   - City and Web are alike in facilitating information sharing.

   a. **What if innovation is fractal**, meaning it looks the same no matter how close or far away you are from it. Innovation has the same origins and is fundamentally based on mutually beneficial cooperation more than brute competition.
      - Pre-competitive development within the auto industry for emission control systems. We get the best of everyone's knowledge so the air is cleaner for everyone.
      - Connecting ideas is better than protecting them, and the connections are the key to breakthrough innovations. Good

ideas want to connect, fuse, and recombine. They want to complete each other more than compete, using as a lifeboat to return home. Mission control quickly assembles a "tiger team" of engineers to hack their way through the problem.

Neonatal incubators from spare car parts

In the year following the 2004 tsunami, the Indonesian city of Meulaboh received eight neonatal incubators from international relief organizations. Several years later, when an MIT fellow named Timothy Prestero visited the local hospital, all eight were out of order, the victim of power surges and tropical humidity, along with the hospital staff's inability to read the English repair manual. Assembling "nerdbots" from found objects, like ideas, are connecting seemingly random pieces creating something new. Mr. Prestero and the organization he cofounded, Design That Matters, had been working for several years on a more reliable and less expensive incubator for the developing world. In 2008, they introduced a prototype called the NeoNurture.

It looked like a streamlined modern incubator, but its guts were automotive. Sealed-beam headlights supplied the crucial warmth; dashboard fans provided filtered air circulation; door chimes sounded alarms. You could power the device with an adapted cigarette lighter or a standard-issue motorcycle battery. Building the NeoNurture out of car parts was doubly efficient because it tapped both the local supply of parts and the local knowledge of automobile repair.

You didn't have to be a trained medical technician to fix the NeoNurture; you just needed to know how to replace a broken headlight. The NeoNurture incubator is a fitting metaphor for the way that good ideas usually come into the world. They are, inevitably, constrained by the parts and skills that surround them.

Innovation insights

1. Innovation is about taking available resources (materials, knowledge, and capabilities) and cobbling them together to create new uses and sources of value. Question: What are your core competencies and resources?
2. While anything is possible, past innovations must enable future ones by using the past as a bridge to the future. Babbage's mechanical computer was limited because modern electronics didn't yet exist. Question: What success can be built upon?
3. Basic research provides "The Platforms" for future innovations by expanding the knowledge base to build upon.
4. Specialization is required to build on the "spare parts" from past innovations. For the industrial organization this means a minimum scale is required for innovation to be possible.

5. Processes, like Stage Gates, must enable learning while not becoming end points. They're role is in facilitating action when faced with imperfect knowledge and learning by using intelligent, thoughtful experimentation.

Liquid Networks: The Goldie Locks Approach

Liquids are a perfect analogy, given that gases have too much chaos and solids too little chaos for ideas to collide with enough energy to create an innovation. Innovation prospers when ideas can serendipitously connect, recombining with other ideas, leading to wealth-creating insights. It then seems illogical, even strange, that the study of innovation over the past two centuries has pursued the exact opposite argument, building walls between ideas erected with the explicit aim of encouraging innovation. These walls go by many names: Intellectual property, trade secrets, proprietary technology, top-secret R&D labs. But they all share an assumption that in the long run, innovation will increase if you put restrictions on the spread of new ideas, because those restrictions will allow the creators to collect large financial rewards from their inventions. And those rewards will then attract other innovators to follow in their path.

By contrast, liquid networks have the ability for making new connections – all ideas in the same liquid phase encouraging collisions between ideas with sufficient energy to form new and innovative concepts. Organizations need to build these elements into their organizational designs, physical space, management practices, information systems, rewards practices etc.

Successful liquid networks facilitate recombining what already exists by having scale (enough things to recombine), are plastic in adopting whatever form is required to be innovative, and are user friendly, encouraging people to explore new combinations.

Gutenberg press. The printing press is an example of a "combinatorial" innovation. All of the key elements—the movable type, the ink, the paper and the press itself— were developed separately well before Johannes Gutenberg printed his first Bible in the 15th century. Pi Sheng, a Chinese blacksmith, invented movable type in the 10th century with the press itself adapted from a German screw press used for wine.

Double-entry accounting. One of the essential instruments of modern capitalism appears to have been developed collectively in Renaissance Italy. Now the cornerstone of bookkeeping, double-entry's innovation of recording every financial event in two ledgers (one for debit, one for credit) allowed merchants to accurately track the health of their businesses. First codified by the Franciscan friar Luca Pacioli in 1494, it had been used for at least two centuries by Italian bankers and merchants.

More innovation insights

Leaders need to create working conditions that facilitate the flow and collision of ideas creating new combinations that solve important problems creating value. Innovations occur when a community acts together to create something beneficial to all within it. Balancing chaos and order involves getting the physical working environment right. Open offices and closed offices both inhibit innovation. Space must be reconfigurable or available to suit the purpose at hand. Physical infrastructure can inhibit liquid networks from flowing together. MIT building 20 in WWII was reconfigurable on demand because it was temporary to be thrown out after the war. Microsoft's building 99 was designed to be reconfigurable to spur innovation.

- Cultures need to do the same with leaders "walking the talk" and stimulate innovation by their actions. Leaders need to balance the demands for data with calculated risk-taking.
- Firms need to strategically design their organizational structures to foster deep relationships within the company (e.g., marketing, sales, manufacturing) and with external parties (e.g., customers, academics, competitors, partners) to help liquid networks function effectively.
- Marketplaces are like cities where information collides, creating new forms which allow for the connection of seemingly unrelated ideas.
- Living lab studies of science groups showed that most insights and discoveries occurred as the result of group meetings and informal conversations, not physical time alone in the lab doing experiments. Lab meetings and face-to-face encounters generally promote innovation if the climate is conducive (e.g., non-threatening).

The Slow Hunch: Ideas take time to develop

Over time these hunches need to be preserved until they can be "completed." Hunches need to collide with each other sometimes in one person's mind and sometimes among various individuals.

Darwin's theory of natural selection

Another surprising truth about big ideas is that even when they seem to be individual flashes of genius, they don't happen in a flash, though the people who have them often subsequently claim that they did. Charles Darwin always said that theory of natural selection occurred to him on September 28, 1838 while he was reading Thomas Malthus's essay on population; suddenly, the mechanism of evolution seemed blindingly straightforward. Yet Darwin's own notebooks reveal that the theory was forming clearly in his mind more than a year beforehand. It wasn't a flash of insight. It was a slow hunch. And on the morning after his alleged eureka moment, was Darwin feverishly contemplating the implications of his breakthrough? No. He busied himself with some largely unconnected rumination on the sexual curiosity of primates.

The 9/11 attacks

Ken Williams noticed interest in flight schools by potential Islamic radicals and wrote a report that was filed and never recognized. Concurrently, Zacaria Moussaoui enrolled in the Pan Am International Flight Academy in St. Paul, MN. FBI arrested Moussaoui but couldn't get courts to allow them to look at his computer, which outlined the 9/11 attacks. Two missed hunches that needed to find each other, and if they'd been connected perhaps the 9/11 attack would have been prevented. A tool for connecting slow hunches is DEVONthink, an artificial intelligence tool that allows you to put information into a database that then associates these hunches, connecting the seemingly unrelated dots.

Innovation insights

- Most ideas begin as incomplete hunches that need to collide in a liquid matrix like a city or the Internet, becoming "completed" and yielding an insight. The missing pieces may reside in the head of another person.
- *Blink* by Malcolm Gladwell describes the power of the instant hunch driven by knowledge in our subconscious mind. Often hunches are slow to develop, fragile, and often lost. The hunch owner needs to keep the hunch alive for long periods of time to become significant revelations.
- Slow hunches need to be kept in the mind for long periods, which requires the discipline of documenting them for later review. The "Commonplace Book" used to be routine for English scientists. The modern notebook and idea book play the same role, but a tool like DEVONthink makes capturing and relating these ideas much easier.
- Free time for researchers (3M allows 15% and Google has a 20% rule) must be facilitated by the organization's structure, work space design, information flows, and risk tolerance to manage the chaos-order ratio.

Serendipity

This means a "happy accident" or "pleasant surprise" is finding something good or useful while not searching for it. The word was voted one of the ten English words hardest to translate in June 2004 by a British translation company. However, due to its sociological use, the word has been exported into many other languages.

Synchronicity. Is the experience of two or more events that are apparently causally unrelated or unlikely to occur together by chance, yet are experienced as occurring together in a meaningful manner? It was first described in this terminology by Carl Gustav Jung, a Swiss psychologist, in the 1920s. The concept does not question, or compete with, the notion of causality. Instead, it maintains that just as events may be grouped by cause, they may also be grouped by meaning. A grouping of events by meaning need not have an explanation in terms of cause and effect.

Innovation insights

- Dreams can reveal new connections of hunches or experiences that escape the conscious mind when the brain uses existing chemicals – GABA – and acetylcholine-releasing cells that fire the brain stem indiscriminately during REM sleep. This stimulates the brain to randomly colloid memories, which might connect into a revelation, such as Kekule's discovered the cyclic structure of benzene from a dream.
- Often the more disorganized your brain operates the smarter the person is because the brain is acting chaotically while the person is conscious.
- Serendipitous discoveries often involve exchanges across traditional disciplines needing unlikely collisions leading to discoveries.
- How does one stimulate serendipity?
  - o Feed your mind many different kinds of information – read, listen, and experience various situations for continuous learning.
  - o Go for a walk, take a shower – do something that allows your subconscious- conscious mind to colloid and make connections.
  - o Make time available for your mind to wander.
  - o Write down ideas and hunches, recorded them in a database that can be searched by an AI program like DEVONthink.
- Can the Web facilitate serendipity or hinder it? It depends.
  - o If the chaos of the Web can be managed, it becomes a huge source of information for the mind to use and connect. Filters help this if they aren't too restrictive. Balance is key.
  - o Using RSS feeds can bring information to anyone on demand.
  - o The Web drives us to "look everything up" as in the past we wrote everything down to stimulate serendipity.
- A dichotomy is that protecting innovation for financial gain (e.g., patents, trade secrets etc.) inhibits serendipity in the short-term.
- Organizations maximize idea communication within their organizations by breaking down barriers and creating environments where ideas are constantly running in the background for people to digest and connect. Use idea exchanges – both formal and informal.

Errors: A Special Gift to Ourselves

Errors often create a path that leads you out of your comfort zone making you challenge your assumptions.

"...error is needed to set off the truth, much as a dark background is required for exhibiting the brightness of a picture.
~ William James ~

Innovation insights

- Transforming error into insight is the key function of a conversation like the lab meeting, group meeting, or other forum where data is critically assessed. This forces those who are observing the error not to dismiss it as "noise."
- Free-associating is integral to connecting unrelated dots, but most people associate things that are common to many – herd mentality.
- Very creative people tend to have more varied thoughts when asked to freely associate, and when people are exposed to inaccurate information they're more creative because they're not bound by their past knowledge.
- Good ideas are more likely to emerge from environments with a certain amount of noise and error – managing the chaos.
- Noise, meaningful errors, makes people more innovative because we're forced to rethink our biases.
  - Innovative environments thrive on "useful mistakes." In environments that are too quality-focused (6 Sigma, TQM, etc.), innovation is retarded by eliminating useful errors.
  - Better to "fail faster and learn" vs. controlling the process extensively.
  - Errors are endlessly diversified whereas facts are uniform and narrow – less likely to lead to new connections.

Exaptation and Diversity: Legos in Action

Combinatorial innovation is building on past innovations to create new solutions or combining two or move innovations into a new innovation. Gutenberg combined the wine press from ancient Greece and Rome with movable type invented in China and his metallurgy training to create metal dyes that led to the printing press. Bird feathers evolved from Sarcopterygii fins – first to swim, then walking on land as an auto-pod, and eventually a bird that could glide and then fly. Exaptation requires the following:

- Critical mass of individuals who are interested in the same thing and something that's not mainline culture – it's a change.

- Diversity in the critical mass is required to fertilize idea and knowledge transfer.
- The context, or place, where diverse people meet has to be conducive to knowledge and information transfer leading to connections.
- Connections need to be sufficiently high-energy so that the collisions create new substances. This requires the people involved to have a critical level of passion for the topic.

The diversity needed is variation of professions and disciplines, not race or gender, and focused on the breadth of their networks and kinds of acquaintances they had.

Innovation Insights
- The most creative individuals had the broadest social networks that extended beyond their organizations with people from diverse fields.
- Diverse horizontal networks were 3 times more innovative than vertical networks.
- Entrepreneurs that build bridges outside their "islands" were able to borrow from these external environments lead to exaptation.
- Emphasized the strength of weak ties (*Tipping Point*[31] argument).
- Information from weak ties must come from a different context.
- One idea-space migrates to another idea-space through these long distance connections, and in the new environment they have unanticipated properties leading to a breakthrough.
- Once connected, these remote ideas become quasi-autonomous to make sense.

Apple is a model of forcing weak connections within their "fortress" and making different perspectives clash, leading to exaptation. They avoid the linear product development approach of handing the project off from research to development to manufacturing where each manages to achieve only 80% of the desired value and in the end the final offering is marginalized. Apple does concurrent or parallel production, making all areas interact at the same time.

Individuals who have multiple projects ongoing concurrently tend to be more innovative than those who only work on one thing and finish it completely. This variation helps open the innovator's mind to new connections. This allows the mind to survey "multiple boxes" at once vs. thinking outside the box. Working within multiple boxes allows the mind to borrow from one context and use the learning's in another.

---

[31] Gladwell, Malcolm. *Tipping Point,* Hachette Book Group, 2007.

Platforms: Building on the Past, Creating the Future

Platforms are basic discoveries that reveal new truths that can be broadly applied in many different contexts to create value via innovation. The beaver is an eco-system engineer that builds a basic platform – a dam – that serves to alter the entire forest around them as follows:

1. Woodpeckers live in the dead trees.
2. Wood ducks and geese settle in abandoned beaver lodges
3. Herons and kingfishers and swallows enjoy the artificial ponds where fish are easily caught.
4. Frogs, lizards and slow-water species like dragon flies, mussels and aquatic beetles all benefit from the altered eco-system.

Sputnik leading to GPS as a platform:

1. Scientist at Applied Physics Lab (APL) noticed that Sputnik made a recurring sound.
2. They thought that they could use the Doppler Effect to calculate Sputnik's speed.
   - Doppler Effect - It is commonly heard when a vehicle sounding a siren or horn approaches, passes, and recedes from an observer. The received frequency is higher (compared to the emitted frequency) during the approach, is identical at the instant of passing by, and is lower during the recession.
   - A manager at APL asked if they could calculate a receiver on the ground if you knew the exact orbit of the satellite. Could it be used to track submarines? The inverse use of the Doppler Effect on tracking Sputnik led to the creation of GPS, a huge military invention made public by President Reagan in 1983 for the greater good of society after the tragic loss of a Korean airliner due to faulty ground-based tracking systems.
3. APL had a culture and leadership team to connect hunches. These leaders created environments where different kinds of thoughts could productively collide and recombine.

All platforms come as stacks built one upon another over time and look like an archeological dig. Check out data.gov for how the federal government is trying to make connections possible by exposing its data leading to new platforms. Access to emerging platforms can dramatically reduce the cost of innovation via exaptation. Emergent platforms derive much of their creativity from the inventive and economical reuse of existing resources. In a city this is real estate. Old buildings are continuously reused as new small businesses and places where artists thrive because they're cheap but still useful. An example of reuse is dumping old rail cars into the oceans to create new fish beds where these otherwise useless vehicles find new and dramatic sources of value. A more complex example is a coral reef where thousands of species reclaim and reuse waste from one species as the starting material of another.

Innovation insights

- Learn to reuse technologies in new ways to solve new problems. This saves time and money and enables you to build upon the past learning's to get faster value.
- The denser the environment is with *refuse*, and the more collaborative it is for mutual benefit, the more innovation you'll get.
- *Recycling* is a key ingredient of innovation.
- The Web, and your internal proprietary databases, is "a vast junkyard" of stuff waiting to be recycled into new forms that solve important problems that become major innovations.
  a. Tweets.
  b. DEVONthink.
  c. Google.
  d. Facebook.
  e. Linked-In.

Tricks of the Trade

Becoming an effective innovator is an apprenticeship program, meaning that new innovators learn under the tutelage of experienced innovators. Often these experienced innovators have learned tricks of the trade that can be cataloged and shared. One such master innovator, Stephen M. Schapiro, has published some of these trade secrets in his book, *The Little Book of Big Innovation Ideas.*[32]

Cultural Characteristics

- *Get the knowledge workers doing knowledge work.* This means that the knowledge workers focus on high-value tasks and off-load transactional, repetitive and administrative tasks to others. The greatest value of outsourcing is its ability to leverage and organization's human capital to do more valuable work.

---

[32] Shapiro, Stephen, M. *The Little Book of Big Innovation Ideas*, InnoCentive Edition, 2009.

- *Create a chief laziness officer.* The goal of this person is to do the minimum amount of work. But, be certain that that work is the most important work to be done. The objective of the chief laziness officer is to implement the 80/20 rule, which suggests that 80% of the value can be obtained from 20% of the work if the work is properly focused. Their role is to ask hard questions such as the following:
  1. What do you do that is non-value added?
  2. What do you do that others should do?
  3. What work can others actually do?
  4. What work can be automated?
- *Hire people you don't like.* Creativity comes from tension, giving rise to differing viewpoints and differing ways of solving problems. On your team, surround yourself with people who think differently than you. Choose people with different analytical, creative, and personality styles. Welcome the creative tension that is inevitable.
- *Be aware of the performance paradox.* Goals are necessary, but paradoxically, sometimes trying to achieve your goals may prevent you from actually achieving them. Goals increase stress and fixate the innovator on the future rather than the present. It's been found that improved concentration, combined with intellectually challenging tasks, enables the knowledge worker to be self-motivated, where achieving the goal overtakes the personal interest of the endeavor. This forces the innovator to focus on achieving the desired end result and not the specific metrics.
- *Watch out for confirmation bias.* This simply means that you will often look for and interpret information in a way that supports your beliefs without verifying that the observation is accurate. This is especially dangerous when the data involved is unstable and "noise" can be interpreted as real.
- *Lead with why and what, not how.* This means that innovative leaders direct their teams by focusing on why the innovation is important, what problem it solves, and what value it creates without being be focused on how that solution will actually be made available. Separating the *why* in the work from the *how* allows you to think creatively about the opportunity without being too narrowly focused, driven by the company's processes and biases.
- *Design from the outside in.* While this seems obvious, innovators often do not consider how the customer is going to interact with their business and their design from the customer's perspective. A companion trick of the trade is to improve your customer's business by enhancing their processes and walking in their shoes to understand how the customer defines value.

- *Focus on content and context.* Only people innovate, and people are motivated by the tasks they are doing and why they are doing those tasks. Getting employees to understand why their jobs matter drives internal motivation to achieve the objective for its own sake, rather than for personal gain.
- *Distinguish causality from correlation and coincidence.* In the era of *big data* it is difficult to make good decisions because often one cannot distinguish between causality, correlation, and coincidence. Causality is direct outcome-influence that can be identified and measured; correlation is aligned with an outcome from causality, and coincidence is unrelated to the outcome. Causality provides meaningful information that can be used to improve decision-making efficacy while correlation and coincidence have the opposite impact, leading to poor decision quality.

The Innovation Process

1. *Diverge and then converge.* The first step in the innovative process is to create a list that identifies as many possibilities as conceivable, using the imagination of the team, while deferring judgment on any of these concepts. Once the list of possibilities has been collected, then the innovator team needs to make a choice based on a set of criteria such as value and relevance, quality, feasibility, and customer desire.
2. *Evaluate the best ideas.* Establish a set of criteria that allows the team to evaluate the ideas and make them in a numerical fashion, allowing for a prioritized list to emerge. The system can be as simple as a 1 to 5 rating system and the categories might include pragmatism, creativity, value, sustainability, and adaptability. This system allows for the conversion of qualitative information into semi-quantitative data to be force-ranked.
3. *Build it, try it, and fix it.* One of the biggest barriers to success is analysis paralysis. Rather than trying to analyze, design, build, test, and deploy an innovation, it is better to iterate by building it, making it available to the customer who tries it, and then fixing the flaws so that the next generation will be more attractive. Failing quickly facilitates learning quickly and, ultimately, being successful.
4. *Use collaboration tools and open innovation.* This happens when many people allow their ideas to collide with sufficient force to change the composition. It can be enabled by the Internet and vast volumes of data. These kinds of collisions should be more easily encouraged, leading to faster outcomes. Combining collaboration tools with a mindset of looking outside of the corporation for ideas in the form of open innovation is superior to either of these alone. Deploying processes that encourage both collaboration and open innovation drastically improve the innovative output of the organization.

5. *Establish an innovation owner.* A good innovation owner focuses on *what* and *why* rather than *how*, is respected within your organization for getting results, is determined, confident, energetic, persistent, and thick-skinned, is empathetic to, and especially adept at, handling human concerns, is innovation-oriented and knowledgeable, devoid of any personal agenda, and able to grasp the big picture while being especially attuned to the customer's perspective. This kind of leader is rare and needs to be cherished by the organization.

6. *Create an innovation library.* This is a repository of all kinds of resources that can stimulate creative thinking, including books, DVDs, uploaded information, audio programs, and so on that stimulate innovative people to connect unrelated concepts that, when combined with collaboration and open innovation, become sources of solutions.

Creativity Techniques

1. *Unlearn the bad habits that stop creativity.* People are at their most creative around age five in that they are smart enough to ask a question but not to have an answer. For example, 1,600 five-year-olds took a NASA creativity test to select innovative engineers and scientists. 90% of the children scored in a highly creative range. Five years later the same children were retested and only 30% of the 10-year-olds were rated highly creative. At age 15, just 12% were highly creative, and the population in general at age 25 has only 2% of the adults as highly creative. Creativity is, therefore, not learned, but rather unlearned. Education focus is on regurgitation of facts rather than gathering new experiences, which stifles creativity and innovation.

2. *Avoid "Yeah, but…" statements.* When engaged in a conversation about innovation and looking for a meaningful solution to a problem, be sure to answer questions in ways that contribute and build upon what has been previously offered rather than invalidating by identifying what's wrong. Becoming skeptical too early in the process destroys creativity and limits the options available to come up with an innovative solution.

3. *Find value in wild ideas while looking for analogies to connect unrelated dots.* This approach works well because it allows you to think without constraints. The wild ideas open the mind to solutions that would be otherwise missed. Asking questions like, "What is this like?" rather than "What does it mean?" helps a person connect something new to something familiar, allowing them to understand the new observation. This associative process leverages past experiences.

4. *Bust assumptions.* First surface any assumptions, then challenge the assumption and think opposites. When someone says, "We always do it this way," they should be asked, "What if we did it the opposite way?"

5. *Use the 7Rs Process.*

- *Rethink* is asking why questions to challenge assumptions and current realities.
- *Reconfigure* is asking what can be eliminated, revised, or done differently.
- *Resequence* is asking "when" questions around when something needs to be done or eliminated.
- *Relocate* are questions challenging "where" an activity occurs.
- *Reduce* questions explore how frequently (how much, how often) inactivity needs to occur.
- *Reassigned* is about how the performers of the process work, the people carry out the tasks. It involves coming up with new answers to questions that begin with, "Who carries out this activity? Who could else possibly do it effectively?"
- *Retool* focuses on technologies and competencies that enable work to be done. It looks for answers to questions that begin with *how*, such as health and technology transforms process.

Using the 7Rs Technique for asking these seven types of questions (Why? What? When? Where? How often? Who? and How?) and looking for new answers, workers will find themselves stimulated to come up with fresh approaches to old problems, and occasionally with completely new ones.

Stephen Shapiro breaks innovation into three parts: The *culture*, the *processes*, and the *creativity*, where carefully managing each will lead to greater innovation across any enterprise. Combining these insights with the historical context gives you a road map to becoming more innovative.

Chapter 3 Summary

A simplistic definition of innovation is responding to change by converting knowledge into economic value. Innovation is very situational, meaning that what works for one organization will likely not work another – it needs to be invented. Successful innovation requires the following:

- Analysis and hard work within the confines of what the organization does well (its core competencies).
- It can be used by ordinary people and must be simple to use.
- Creates sustainable economic value derived from purposeful utility.
- Can be replicated, taught, and utilized by an educated customer base.
- Focuses on attaining a leadership position in its application.
- It embraces everyone involved with making the innovation a success.
- Focuses on the present.

- Its introduction is aligned with the market's ability to adopt it for use.

Innovations that occur in an isolated activity are the exception not the norm since good ideas can, and do, come from anywhere and these need to be used to "complete" hunches that people leading to answers to complex problems. Networks enable innovation through connection of unrelated ideas and data with sufficient energy to create new forms and utility. Open environments encouraging the sharing, and connecting, of ideas is where innovation can take hold easily. Closed systems like industrial R&D functions inhibit innovation, and those organizations bent on highly structured process like Stage Gates, TQM, 6 Sigma are the worse off.

There are seven primary tactical elements of innovation: The Adjacent Possible, Liquid Networks, The Slow Hunch, Serendipity, Errors, Exaptation and Platforms which when combined with the additional considerations of scaling power, critical mass, the impact of readily available information, provides a framework from which innovation becomes a discipline rather than a random occurrence.

Academic research is a large source of early platform concepts but someone in the firm needs to connect these to the marketplace. This holds for the web and enhanced flows of information making basic research more useful but needs more available. In addition, the web has reduced the cost of sharing ideas to zero. The metaphor for a platform is the coral reef or rain forest where collaboration is spontaneous and essential. Competition for resources is everywhere but so is a marvelous biodiversity. This complex environment thrives because of collaboration among species allows for the recombination of materials into innovative forms.

The human version of the coral reef is the remixing and sharing of information in a collaborative format allowing connection of remote concepts in the correct context to create value. Connections are more valuable than protection. You may not be able to turn your company into a coral reef, but you can create comparable environments on the scale of everyday life; in the workplaces you inhabit; in the way you consume media; in the way you augment your memory.

Becoming an effective innovator is an apprenticeship program, meaning that new innovators learn under the tutelage of experienced innovators. Often these experienced innovators have learned "Tricks of the Trade" that can be cataloged and shared and segmented into three categories: *culture*, *processes*, and *creativity*. Carefully managing each will lead to greater innovation across any enterprise. Combining these insights with the historical context from *Brand New* gives the average person a road map to becoming more innovative, which includes the following:

1. Go for a walk.
2. Cultivate your hunches.
3. Write everything down but keep your folders messy.
4. Embrace serendipity.
5. Make "generative" mistakes and learn from them.
6. Take on multiple hobbies.
7. Frequent coffeehouses and other liquid networks.
8. Follow the links.
9. Let others build on your ideas.
10. Borrow, recycle, reinvent.
11. Build your tangled bank.

Chapter 3 Critical Questions

1. How do you define innovation?
2. What are different types of innovation? Innovation is more than whiz-bang technology; consider different strategic intents (e.g., create a new category, extend current business) or innovation mechanisms (e.g., new product, distribution channel, marketing approach).
3. How do I spot opportunities for innovation? Go to the source: the customer you hope to target.
4. Which customers should I target? Look beyond your best customers to those who face a constraint that inhibits their ability to solve the problems they face in their life.
5. What should I look for? As Drucker said, "the customer rarely buys what the business thinks it sells him;" look for a job-to-be-done, an important problem that is not adequately solved by current solutions.
6. How should I look? Start with deep ethnographic research; avoid focus groups!
7. How do I come up with an idea? Remember the Picasso line "good artists copy, great artists steal." Seek to borrow ideas from other industries or geographies.
8. What is disruptive innovation? An innovation that transforms a market or creates a new one through simplicity, convenience, affordability or accessibility.
9. What is the best way to disrupt a market? Embrace the power of trade-offs. Seek to be just "good enough" along historical performance dimensions but introduce new benefits related to simplicity or affordability.
10. What does "good enough" mean? Performance above a minimum threshold to adequately solve a customer's job to be done; sacrificing performance along traditional dimensions can open up new avenues to innovate.

11. What is a business model (and how do I innovate one)? How a company creates, captures, and delivers value; codifying the current business model is the critical first step of business model innovation.
12. How can I "love the low end"? Build a business model designed around the low-end customer's job-to-be-done.
13. How do I know if my idea is good? Let patterns guide and actions decide; remember Scott Cook's advice that "for every failure we had we had spreadsheets that looked awesome."
14. How can I learn more about my idea? Design and execute "high return on investment" experiments to address critical unknowns.
15. How can I get other people behind my idea? Bring the idea to life through visuals and customer testimonials.
16. How long does it take new businesses to scale? Almost always longer than initial projections; be patient for growth and impatient for profits.
17. Why is innovation so important? The "new normal" of constant change requires mastering perpetual transformation.
18. Why is innovation so hard? Most organizations are designed to execute, not to innovate
19. What feature can you create that's missing in someone else's product?
20. Where can you disrupt significant cost areas in physical goods?
21. How can you digitize a physical element, action, or experience – or digitize all three?
22. What steps can you take to create a service out of your strongest / most prevalent support capability?
23. How can you inject a completely emotional experience into what you do?
24. Ever thought about ways to digitize a service?
25. How is it possible to smooth demand for inefficient / difficult to provide capabilities?
26. What would it take to turn in-person interactions into remote interactions?
27. How can you digitize scarce resources to put them in more places simultaneously?
28. What could you do to help push the biggest player in your desired market to leave the marketplace?
29. If the most prominent player in your market did go away, what opportunities would it open up? Who are your influences? Academics like Clayton Christensen and Vijay Govindarajan, leading-edge innovative companies like Procter & Gamble and Cisco Systems, and thoughtful writers like Michael Mauboussin and Bill James.
30. How do I encourage innovation in my organization? Stop punishing anything that smells like failure, recognizing that failure is often a critical part of the innovation process.

31. What is "the sucking sound of the core?" The pull of the core business and business model that subtly influences new ideas so they resemble what the organization has done before.
32. What is an innovation "safe space"? An organizational mechanism that protects innovators from the sucking sounds of the core.
33. How should I form and manage innovation teams? Keep deadlines tight and decision makers focused.
34. What is in a good innovation strategy? Overall goals, a target portfolio for innovation efforts, a mechanism to allocate resources to achieve that portfolio, and clearly defined goals and boundaries for innovation.
35. What is the best way to manage an innovation portfolio? Make sure you correctly capture current activities and measure and manage different kinds of innovations in different ways.
36. What does 'prudent pruning' mean? Recognizing that destruction is often a critical component of creation.
37. What role should senior executives play in innovation? A big one.
38. How can I personally become a better innovator? Practice – innovation is a skill that can be mastered.
39. How can I find more resources for innovation? Shut down "zombie projects" those are a drain on corporate resources.
40. How can I more quickly turn good ideas into good businesses? Remember what Edison said – genius is "1% inspiration and 99% perspiration;" get ready to sweat.
41. How have the more innovative companies such as Google, Apple, Procter & Gamble, Amazon.com, Cisco Systems, Godrej & Boyce and General Electric scaled innovation?

Chapter 4: Leadership

We try to value each person individually at Southwest and be cognizant of them as human beings…we value you as people aside from the fact you work here.
~ Herb Kelleher ~

This chapter considers leadership and norms of behavior for connecting ideas in the information age. While many innovative techniques withstand the test of time, new tools and methodologies are constantly emerging. The roles of leadership, inquiry, conflict, and change management remain standards of any innovative construct. Two new change forces, the availability of vast amounts of data and role of the individual, are considered in the context of modern organizational designs and how people do work as sources of sustainable competitive advantage, especially in light of the advent of new knowledge and tools such as social media platforms. Given the tools available, innovators are improving many age-old concepts such as the role of leadership, ability to inquire, and managing the conflict that comes from change effectively.

If you're going to lead innovation successfully, your passion must be for both leadership and innovation. Anything short of this will fail. You must live and breathe innovation and the desire to innovate through people. Perhaps the most challenged leaders will be older executives who are trying to adapt to the age of the knowledge worker in the developed economies.

Passion begins with having *purpose*, the reason why something exists or is done, made, or used. The context surrounding purpose gives it meaning and successfully leading innovation requires the leader to define their purpose and recognize the context in which they'll achieve it. Often, the purpose for leading innovation is to create wealth useful in making the world a better place. Such innovations must be merged with a theoretical understanding of the process if innovation is to be sustainable.

You do this by reading widely on innovation and leadership and applying it to real life, everyday situations in an iterative fashion – also known as the scientific method. What is your purpose and context for leading innovation? Are they theoretical or pragmatic, strategic or tactical, inspiring or mundane? If your purpose and context are latent and unexpressed, this will retard your ability to achieve the results you want. Answering these questions is critical to success, and then you must remain loyal to your purpose and context while being consistent within it.

Leadership has been extensively studied and discussed during the past 50 years. However, never has this discipline faced such change as it does now with the advent of the electronic age, massive changes in work content, and the prospect of a dramatically changing workforce. These change forces, combined with the ever-increasing scrutiny of the CEO, have created a premium on proven leadership capability. Given the critical importance of leadership, a discussion of the topic must begin with an actionable definition of what a leader does.

A leader is a person whose continuous insights are so compelling, that followers will subordinate their self-interests, for what the leader wants them to do.

Historically, executive leadership skills could tolerate weaknesses in basic capabilities without significant consequences since the work force was skilled doing defined tasks while not very expectant, attrition was manageable, and the pace of change was modest. With all of these characteristics changing radically, today's executive must possess exemplary leadership skills just to be competitive.

The impact of poor leadership is likely to be pronounced, more immediate, and can quickly be fatal. From the plethora of leadership characteristics easily found in the literature, seven stand out as timeless and especially relevant today as follows:

1. Integrity – Keep your word, tell the truth, and don't play favorites.
2. Vision – Explain why the team's activities are important.
3. Competence – Demonstrate skill in some aspect of business.
4. Decisiveness – Make sound, defensible decisions in a timely fashion.
5. Humility – Acknowledge that you don't know everything.
6. Persistence – Don't give up easily, but know when to cut your losses.
7. Team building and maintenance – Show that "It's all about the people."

Leadership, according to Peter Drucker, is lifting a person's vision to higher sights, the raising of a person's performance to a higher standard, the building of a personality beyond its normal limitations. The definition of innovation is the specific act of responding to and exploiting changes by endowing resources (e.g., people) with a new capacity to create wealth. Innovation is hard work, and leading innovation even harder still, but there is no alternative to sustained success, especially in today's current economic climate. In the end it's all about finding ways to make people successful.

Critical to success is that everyone involved in the innovation process must have purpose, passion, and courage. This simply means that you, as the leader, must want to do it with all your being. It must drive your existence. However, even the most effective leader of innovation must deal with the fact that things beyond your control will impact your destiny. But when innovation is successful, it doesn't get any better, and it's *fun!*

Tomorrow the definition of strong leadership will be *collective leadership;* given that leaders will also be followers, taking pride in standing up to one group while kowtowing to another. The image of the strong leader as someone who projects strength of personality and individuality, as critical characteristics, is often an illusion. Granted, under certain circumstances, a strong personality of the leader may be required for dealing with crisis situations, such as war. This kind of leadership style, however, will be the exception rather than the norm in the future, especially as the world becomes more globalized and economically integrated. A military approach to conflict resolution must evolve to a more nuanced form of economic warfare requiring leadership trained in the skill of persuasion for getting parties to agree on win-win solutions to complex problems.

A more appropriate description of a future leader will be as *redefining* or *transformational. Redefining leadership* means stretching the limits of what's possible and radically altering the agenda in a positive direction. Often, redefining leaders both as individuals and collectively in a group, seek to move the center in their direction, redefining what the center is rather than simply accepting the conventional view of the middle ground at any particular time. Examples of redefining leaders are Franklin D. Roosevelt with his New Deal, Lyndon B. Johnson with his Great Society, and England's Margaret Thatcher.

By contrast, transformational leaders are the rare people who make a still bigger difference. A *transformational leader* is one who plays a decisive role in changing the entire system, whether national or even internationally. The focus is on systemic change that is for the better, rather than the worst. Examples of transformational leaders, especially in revolutionary roles, are people like Vladimir Lenin in Russia, Joseph Broz Tito of Yugoslavia, and Mao Zedong of China and Fidel Castro of Cuba.

Revolutionary transformational leaders tend to create transformation through force, rather than persuasion, with a rare example being Mikhail Gorbachev, an exceptional transformational leader, who used persuasion to lead the Soviet Union to end the Cold War in the early 1990s.

Leadership can be like the weather, much discussed, but not necessarily deeply understood in a useful manner. What are the essentials of leadership that a person can grasp and use routinely to generate value? Are leaders are born or made? This has been debated for decades, often positioning leadership as a genetic endowment. In reality, leadership is a skill that must be developed and cultivated while forever being evolved to fit changing circumstances. Ultimately "Situational Leadership" will become the norm where everyone will be both leaders and followers.

Situations in the future will clearly be more complex than those of the past and should unequivocally put to rest the concept of "The Great Man" leader who is omnipotent in both intellect and strength to resolve any issue. In its place will be the concept of collective leadership, where the leader relies extensively on resources external to themselves to make good decisions, especially where time is limited and the stakes are high.

The new definition of sustainable leadership will be a person who has neither power nor patronage to dispose of but who inspires large numbers of people to act on behalf of the enterprise. Leadership, provided by an emergent or rising political party, by a group or by an individual, will be commonplace. It is the readiness of others to embrace the message and take part in the movement that defines the effectiveness of such leadership. Two examples are the Indian struggle for independence from British imperial rule, led by Mahatma Gandhi, and the American civil rights leader Dr. Martin Luther King, Jr. Both of these leaders chose the path of nonviolence, showing the world that peaceful resistance could introduce profound transformational change.

An important point is that effective leadership is very contextual, and what is effective in one context can be disastrous in another. Hence, the idea of "Situational Leadership" will become much more the norm, and leaders must understand the context in which they find themselves, know their few areas of strength and supply resources to fill their gaps.

Everyone must think of themselves as leaders. If we're all leaders, and leadership roles are situational, then what behaviors are essential to effective leadership? Personal leadership, and the accountability that comes with it, can be frightening, but also invigorating if the leader has the correct mindset. Successful leadership, within an ethical and legal framework, is the height of human achievement because it mandates helping others do what they couldn't do alone for the good of all. Leadership is something everyone should embrace and aspire to because it makes the world better.

Leadership Essentials

Leaders, chosen because they were skilled individual contributors, often fail because the exact skill that made them successful, working alone, is counter to the necessary inclusion and collaboration require of a modern leader. Mastering the core leadership capabilities requires the following:

- Leading by example (I lead by example).
- Getting results alone *and* through people (I make things happen).
- Leveraging diversity within the workforce (I win with people).

Leadership Essential 1: I Lead by Example. Leadership is first and foremost a state of mind fueled with an educated point of view. "I'm a leader" can be a question, or a statement. For real leaders, it's a statement of who they are without reservation. *I'm a leader!* versus *I'm a leader?*

Leadership demands that the leader lead with their actions as well as their words. While communication is critical to leadership, non-verbal communication speaks volumes more than what we say. The adage *actions speak louder than words* is especially true for leaders.

A subtle reality that many new leaders don't recognize is that leaders are visible at all times and not just when they're with their followers. Leaders being constantly observed and are all watched carefully by those led and those who are just observers. It is critical for leaders to be fully aware of their every action, including body language, the times you start and leave work, the way you dress, the manner in which you speak and address people, who you socialize with, what you eat for lunch, and so on. This visibility demands that we're aware of and in control of our attitudes. Attitude is a difficult term but can be defined as follows:

- A manner, disposition, feeling, position, etc., with regard to a person or thing; tendency or orientation, esp. of the mind: a negative attitude; group attitudes.
- A position or posture of the body appropriate to or expressive of an action, emotion, etc.: a threatening attitude; a relaxed attitude.

Attitude is not a quantitative expression. It is a feeling or emotional state, and often not consciously recognized by the individual but readily recognized by others. As a leader you must manage your attitudes in a conscious manner so you project the view you want given the situation. It is imperative that the leader's attitude is real and appropriate for the situation. Leaders are human and not always happy or positive because situations don't always warrant that frame of mind. Leaders fail when their behavior is insincere. What kind of attitudes do great leaders possess? Fortunately, there aren't too many attitudes to master, but because they can be both opposing, required, and practiced concurrently, they present the leader with a unique challenge of keeping two opposing concepts in the mind. Attitudes of great leaders are as follows:

1. Visionary but pragmatic.
2. Optimistic but challenging.
3. Humble but confident.
4. Persistent but realistic.
5. Empathetic but accountable.

Leading by example, while displaying a genuine attitude that fits the situation, is the first and most important, leadership essential.

Leadership Essential 2: I Make Things Happen. Leaders are decisive and manage risks. They have a "can-do" attitude and act with energy and purpose. Leaders take initiative to get things done through people and by themselves. Being indecisive is fatal to a leader, sometimes immediately, but more often eventually. It is corrosive to the leader's reputation and frustrating to those who follow. Leaders don't always need to be right, nor should they expect to be since they are human, but they must know how to make decisions while managing risk.

With experience, and the proper use of skills like effective inquiry, leaders can be right more times than not, and when they're wrong the key is to admit the error and correct it. Leaders know to let go of negative history and put all their energy into the future. Lamenting the past or holding grudges against people inhibits the leader from addressing the future.

My interest is in the future because I am going to spend the rest of my life there.
~ Charles F. Kettering~

Leaders have power that is required for successful leadership, but abuse of that power to punish people for past indiscretions will destroy the leader's credibility in the eyes of many, eventually bringing failure. Leaders display three forms of discipline in their organization: Disciplined people, disciplined thought, and disciplined action. Discipline is a core skill of great leaders, often missing from those leaders with average skill. Being undisciplined isn't a fatal flaw, but often results in a much less effective leader, especially when managing a crisis. Some observations about the value of being disciplined are as follows:
1. When you have disciplined people, you don't need hierarchy.
2. When you have disciplined thought, you don't need bureaucracy.
3. When you have disciplined action, you don't need excessive controls.

Disciplined leadership provides the enterprise with a basis from which to achieve exceptional results from employees who are otherwise average. Leaders push for quick decisions. Speed is a great differentiator, especially in today's world where information and change happen so quickly. Some observations about the value of speed are as follows:
- You will never have enough information to be 100% certain.
- Taking extra time to be 100% certain increases risk.

It's better to act too quickly than to wait too long.
~ Jack Welch ~

A good plan executed right now is better than a perfect plan executed next week.
~ George Patton ~

The key point is the leader sets the pace of action and therefore must be predisposed to act quickly but intelligently. This requires the leader to be learning-agile, capable of building a learning organization, and valuing and rewarding rapid, intelligent decision-making at all levels. Leaders listen attentively and have a clearly communicated vision.

- They don't just send out information and facts.
- They simplify and make it easy to understand. They have a "teachable point of view."
- They speak that point of view clearly.

Leadership Essential 3: I Win with People. Leaders value and build a diverse workforce, tapping into the unique contributions of each individual. They are inclusive. Leaders know that no matter how great their vision, or the company's technology or implementation, to be successful they must utilize the skills of every employee. Diversity within the workforce is critical to success in the present business climate.

Diversity must be considered broadly since every human being is different, and these differences are a huge source of advantage if they're recognized and utilized. Diversity takes many forms as follows:

- Race.
- Gender.
- Educational background.
- Family experiences.
- Physical capabilities.
- Spiritual outlook.
- Ethnic origin.

The point here is that the leader must recognize all forms of diversity within their organizations and use them fully. The value of diversity is that it enables the leader to see a situation from as many vantage points as possible. A person's background and experience frame how they look at events and what they conclude from these observations. Collecting many distinct observations provides the leader with points of view they could never achieve alone. However, harnessing diversity is difficult.

Organizations reflect the societies around them, including prejudices, such that valuing diversity will not happen spontaneously. It is up to the leadership team. Once diversity has been embraced, effective use depends on recognizing the kinds of teams required for a given situation. Simply deploying the diversity of the enterprise is a challenge all unto itself.

Eleven Leadership Derailers

Continually managing the seven leadership characteristics and the three essentials is a must to remain effective. They are subject to decline, especially when executives are under stress or they're "overused." Strengths devolving into weaknesses, known as *derailers*, can derail an executive's career, causing significant harm to their organizations. The top 11 derailers with their misused strengths are as follows:

1. **Arrogance,** defined as always being right and everyone else being wrong, is confidence gone awry. Confidence is essential to any executive-level role but is vulnerable to success, especially over a period of time whereby the executive becomes to believe they are invulnerable.

2. **Melodrama** is always being the center of attention. While presence is critical for a leader, especially in times of crisis, melodrama drowns out important feedback that the executive requires to lead effectively.

3. **Volatility** exhibited in wild mood shifts, damage trustworthiness and destabilizes leadership. An executive who is too predictable is at risk of manipulated but unstable behavior engenders fear and loss of confidence by those being led.

4. **Excessive Caution**, or the unwillingness or inability to make timely decisions is nearly always fatal for senior executives. Decisiveness is a critical skill for any executive, especially when information is lacking and situations are ambiguous. Excellent judgment and making correct decisions a majority of the time while facing ambiguity is expected.

5. **Habitual Distrust**, or focusing on the negatives of any situation, often combined with an unhealthy skepticism. The negative viewpoint often involves direct suspicion of colleagues, which destroys trust. Habitual Distrust is the misuse of critical thinking and proper due diligence that is so critical with senior-level jobs.

6. **Aloofness,** or detachment, is being disengaged and disconnected from the organization and its employees. Leaders need a certain degree of separation from the workforce to remain objective. However, "being known" conveys confidence and trust. Leaders cannot be trusted if they're unknown as a person.

7. **Mischievousness** leaders view the rules as "suggestions" for them personally. They generate excitement and a passionate following since this kind of leader is often optimistic, energetic about the future and appears as a fearless risk taker. Risk Management is a critical skill for all executive leadership. A mischievous leader can often be insensitive to consequences of their decisions and take unhealthy risks for their firms.

8. **Eccentricity**, the cousin of mischievousness, is being different for the fun of it, versus for a cause, making leader appear weird. Tolerating eccentric leaders is possible if they remain effective, which the case in a

rapidly changing environment is rarely. Eccentric leaders fail to recognize the importance of being respected, making them ineffective over the long term and driving their followers away especially during difficult situations.

9. **Passive Resistance,** or silence mistaken for agreement, is a very destructive leadership trait that undercuts trust and confidence in the executive's actions. With this derailer, the leader often seems to agree to one action and then takes another behind the scenes. Transparency and honesty have become hallmarks of modern leadership with the advent of Sarbanes-Oxley and recent corporate malfeasance.

10. **Perfectionism,** described as doing the little things right but the big things wrong, can afflict the executive who has deep technical or operational skills. Today's business environment requires the executive mindset must be that "good enough" is all the firm can afford. An average plan executed in a timely fashion well is much better than a perfect plan executed too late.

11. **Eagerness to please** is preferring popularity to respect. Respect is a key for every senior leader to acquire to be effective over long periods of time. Being likable often leads to promises not kept, as too many commitments being made leading to under delivery. This causes a credibility gap and loss of confidence in the executive. Confidence and trust are two of the key currencies of senior leadership.

There are a plethora of additional skills beyond the previously listed leadership essentials, but in their absence, the more sophisticated skill of inquiry has unlimited utility and longevity.

Inquiry-Driven Leadership

Most leaders are unaware of the amazing power of questions, how they can generate short-term results and long-term learning and success. It's often considered rude, inconsiderate or intrusive from an early age to ask questions, especially challenging ones, be it at home, school or at church. Rewards come for having answers, not questions. A growing number of leaders recognize that a learning organization is better able to adapt to changes and respond to the opportunities these changes present when questions are at the root of learning.

Leaders who don't ask questions miss opportunities that in some cases lead to disaster. The Titanic sank, in part, because planners failed to raise reservations about its design and the steel used to build it. Similarly, the Challenger space shuttle disaster was avoidable if the engineers would have questioned the outside temperature at the time of launch. They knew the O-rings we're unreliable below 53° but allowed the launch to occur when the temperature was 36° because they were fearful of raising the issue since the launch was already well behind schedule. A final example is the Bay of Pigs invasion, where group-think led to disaster despite many having doubts. After all, if everyone agrees, they must be right and I'm wrong.

There are many ways questions, and a questioning culture, can add meaningful value to an organization or a project. Beyond preventing disasters, they force you to face reality and can be the ultimate leadership tool. Great leaders ask great questions to get things done. Great leaders tend to listen first, speak last, and inquire always. The best thing to strengthen leadership is to ask questions while encouraging others to do the same in safety. The world is changing at an unprecedented pace, with knowledge doubling every 5 years. In dealing with this reality, leaders...

- Can't know enough.
- Must aggregate the knowledge of their people through inquiry.
- Multiply the IQ of the enterprise.
- Use inquiry to drive decision-making but without relying on consensus.

Where consensus provides comfort, conflict yields excellence, but only if it's constructive, and constructive conflict can only take place where there is a trusting environment. By creating a question-friendly environment, leaders are building the trust that can lead to excellence in decision-making and strategy development. Inquiry-driven leadership is an underutilized capability that can positively impact the enterprise by shaping its purpose, vision and values, empowering its employees, and affecting its overall sustainability. People are educated not to ask questions but provide answers, which is diametrically opposed to human nature, which is naturally curious. Through careful analysis and practice, leaders can learn to use inquiry as a powerful tool in becoming more effective, creating learning organizations that are self-sustaining in a very dynamic business climate.

Asking Questions is Difficult

Why do people have so much difficulty asking questions? After all, humans are curious by design and have survived by adapting to our environment, a process enabled by questioning. There appear to be many reasons for this with four standing out as follows:

- We desire to protect ourselves.
- We are often in a rush.
- We lack the skills in asking or answering questions.
- We find ourselves in a culture that discourages questioning.

Protecting ourselves. People often avoid asking questions to preserve self-image and the image they have in the eyes of others. Basically, they want to avoid "looking dumb" since the leader is expected to know everything. If you don't have the answers, it's better to remain silent and not affirm your "ignorance." This is especially so in organizations where not having the answers erodes trust and confidence. To overcome this fear, you must develop confidence and courage, the first step of which is to admit you *don't* know everything, and no one else does either. Becoming educated is the goal of asking questions. Leaders lead by example, showing that they don't know everything, but are willing to be educated by others and that they're learning-agile. To achieve this, leaders must earn the respect of their teams by asking insightful questions while helping others finds the best answers.

Being rushed. Rapidly changing environments require employees to find answers quickly. The electronic age exacerbates this reality with tools like e-mail, compressing the time to think from days to minutes. This fixation on speed has led to a serious decline in decision quality and overall outcomes. We just don't take the time to get the best answer. By asking questions, we slow down the pace and increase the quality of the result. Time will always be important, but redoing work because the first decision was incorrect or inadequate wastes time. Beyond quality, asking questions and sharing information builds a shared responsibility and commitment to the outcome. The courage to pause and reflect on issues allows the leader to legitimatize the fact that the team may not know what to do. Poor action is often worse than no action, and the willingness to address ignorance, confusion, and risk by inquiry is at the heart of great leadership and great outcomes.

Lacking skill. Employee inquiry is often unwelcomed given they're expected to have answers and often lack leaders skilled in the practice of inquiry. Without role models, the power and benefit of skilled inquiry is lost on most firms. Hence, firms end up reinforcing ineffective inquiry skills. Often, when inquiry does occur, it elicits a defensive response because the question can appear as threatening. Ineffective questions lead to detours, missed goal, and costly mistakes. Today's leaders must break this cycle. Asking good questions requires two critical skills: Knowing *what* question to ask (not all questions are created equal) and knowing *how* to ask them.

Culture discourages inquiry. Your environment or culture determines in large part your personal behavior. In some corporate cultures and with some bosses, it would be taboo and dangerous to ask too many questions, especially questions that might rock the boat or cause someone to lose face. People thus become afraid to ask questions. American culture drives people towards a "rush to action" since contemplation and reflection are considered are signs of weakness. Corporate cultures that avoid bad news reinforce this. Bad news must travel faster and farther than good news, and oftentimes new ideas are not allowed to occur in organizations since they might conflict with existing norms, established mental models, or ways of doing things. Questioning leaders have the task of confronting these assumptions without evoking defensiveness or anger. They must be able to surface and test mental models and basic assumptions of colleagues. Asking questions that are challenging requires risk, occasional conflict, and instability because addressing the issues underlying problems may involve upending deeply entrenched norms. Questioning leaders are confident and willing to challenge beliefs and assumptions.

Confronting inquiry discomfort. Dealing with the issues of fear, time pressure, lack of skills, and discouraging culture requires leaders to reevaluate the climate of their organizations. The simplest path forward is making the organizational climate conducive to teaching as the best way to achieving sustainable results. This transition, while not easy or quick, will be rewarding. The classroom approach converts the leader into a facilitator helping the team define problems and develop solutions. As the team becomes more capable, the leader's role becomes easier with better decisions and more insightful strategies developed and executed.

Creating a question-friendly culture. Effective inquiry begins with cultivating and using a question-friendly culture. The best way to consider this definition is with descriptors. A question-friendly culture is a sharing culture, sharing values, responsibility, ideas, problems, and ownership. It is focused on *we*, rather than *you* or *I*. Questions asked by leaders transform the organization as they can evoke the images of what employees hope to create, and of the value and behaviors desired by their people. People in a questioning culture have the following six hallmarks:

- Are willing to admit, *I don't know.*
- Go beyond allowing questions; they encourage questions.
- Are helped to develop the skills needed to ask positive questions.
- Ask empowering questions and avoid disempowering questions.
- Emphasize the process of asking questions and searching for answers rather than finding the "right" answers.
- Accept and reward risk-taking.

Ultimately, the critical success factor for creating and sustaining a question-friendly culture are leaders willing to lead by example.

Benefits of a Questioning Culture

There are many benefits of a questioning culture on organizational effectiveness, such as the following:

- Improved decision-making.
- Greater adaptability to change.
- Higher motivation and morale.
- Stronger ream work.
- Enhanced innovation.

These organization benefits extend and create benefits for the individual around the following:

- Greater self-awareness.
- Greater self-confidence.
- Better conflict management.
- Stronger overall leadership.

Improved decision-making and problem-solving. Questioning helps people gain perspective and understand the perspectives of others. As they see issues and problems from different points of view, they gain an appreciation for their complexity – and also expand the range of possible solutions. By their nature, questions help us think clearly, logically, and strategically while helping us view each other as resources. These same questions help us gather necessary information from which to make better and more insightful decisions leading to faster and more effective problem-solving. The inquiring leader recognizes that the most effective problem-solving begins by first diverging through the use of inquiry, and only then using questions that create a converging and narrower focus.

Inquiring leaders using "triple-loop learning" or learning that delves into the culture and mindsets which get to the root causes of the problems. This approach of asking *why* five time or more helps leaders avoid solving the wrong problem. Dialogue and debate, engendering trust in the decisions being taken, supports a learning organization. This process reduces the chances of solving the wrong problem and avoids disasters as previously described by getting to root causes, using the broadest available knowledge to reveal options, and empowering employees to act with conviction.

Greater adaptability to change. The business world is undergoing an ever-increasing pace of change. When faced with change people focus on what they're going to lose more than what they may gain. The more people feel that they make a difference; the better they will feel about what they're doing. By posing the right questions, and engaging staff in the pursuit of a response, effective leaders gain more than just buy-in to change. Effective leaders serve as the catalyst for change and give their followers the opportunity to exert some control in determining their future. Questions will enable staff to be more aware of how they contribute to the organization's goals, thereby generating greater commitment to those goals.

Greater self-confidence. Organizational cultures that encourage curiosity and questions help people develop themselves. People who ask questions have more self-confidence as they see the people they question show appreciation and respect for the questioner. When a non-threatening environment for questions is a daily reality, people become even more comfortable with them, know their strengths better, and are more self-assured. Not responding openly and honestly to employee questions erodes self-confidence, the powerful catalyst for generating results. Employees who feel confident to manage risk and act on the behalf of the organization will contribute more to the decision-making process and be accountable for their actions. When leaders responsible for developing strategy and making critical decisions embrace a safe haven for questions, they multiple their capability to deliver results.

Stronger leadership. Jim Collins, in his book *Good to Great* (HarperCollins, 2001), reports his discovery that leaders of great companies are both very humble and very persistent. In his description of *Level 5 Leaders*, he observes that successful leaders of companies recognized that the title of leader does not make one a source of all wisdom. In fact, the best leaders are often the best students, always willing to learn, asking and promoting inquiry as a major source of continual learning. Questioning leaders tend to be more modest and more effective, which is a hallmark of great leadership.

The Art of Asking Questions

Grasping the art of questioning can lead to impressive results. Asking inappropriate questions closes off learning. Even when we work hard to make sure we ask great questions, we can undermine the process by asking questions carelessly. Great questions occur by blending the science and art of inquiry. A question asked at the right time in the right manner with the right person is just as important as the content of the question itself.

Great questions are empowering, selfless and supportive, insightful and challenging, and when asked effectively create learning and demand listening. Poor questions are disempowering, clever in such a way to deceive those involved, and often judgmental, destroying learning and progress. At their root, great questions have several common elements as follows:

- They challenge taken-for-granted assumptions.
- They enable people to better view the situation.
- They cause people to explore their behaviors.

- They are opening ended to elicit discussion.
- They generate courage and confidence.
- They lead to positive and powerful action.

There are several types of great questions, including the following:
- Empowering – focus on positive outcomes.
- Open-Ended – asking why (five times)
- Explorative – have you thought of...?
- Affective – how do you feel about...?
- Reflective – what do you think of...?
- Probing – describe this in more detail...
- Fresh – why must it be this way...?
- Clarifying – what specifically do you mean by...?
- Analytical – why has this occurred...?

There are two general classes of inquiry: Those that *empower* and those that *disempower*. Empowering questions encourage thinking constructively about solutions, build self-esteem, create trust, and invite discovery. They're based on respecting the individual being questioned, are genuine in their nature, and do not accuse but inquire. Disempowering questions are judgmental, focus on blame, close off options and learning, and often attack self-esteem either directly or indirectly. The differences between empowering and disempowering inquiry can be subtle. It takes practice and skill to ask empowering questions, especially under pressure. Observe body language to see if your questions are empowering and disempowering.

Disempowering Questions	Empowering Questions
Blaming	Responsibility
Either/thinking	Both/thinking
Defends assumptions	Questions assumptions
Debates	Dialogues
Win-lose outcomes	Win-win outcomes
Protective	Curious

Leading questions are also unhelpful. They often have an answer within the question, such as, "Don't you agree that...?" They compromise people, yielding a no-win situation. Asking multiple questions without giving the person questioned a chance to respond makes people appear ignorant and destroys self-esteem. Other unhelpful questions are those asking to prove a negative. How do I know this new product won't cause two-headed fish to appear in 20 years? Again, it creates a no-win situation.

Asking Great Questions Effectively

Asking great questions effectively demands that the leader use a process, becoming skillful with experience. Since many times the leader will find themselves in varying situations, they must be flexible in applying the process or technique they're most comfortable with, such as the following:

- Frame the question and manage your mindset.
- Be deliberate.
- Show sincerity.
- Actively listen.

The most critical part of the process is the framing of the questions and how we think about the encounter. Successful inquires begin with the leader being in a learner mindset supported by a careful analysis of the situation. A learning mindset is accepting, thoughtful, inquisitive, flexible, adaptive, and curious. A judging mindset, on the other hand, is reactive, self-righteous, blaming, defensive, protective, and diametrically opposed to effective inquiry. Equally important is for the leader to have their body language and words aligned. Negative body language will override a positive verbal tone. Once the leader has established the winning mindset, they must frame the situation of the person being questioned. The leader must answer questions in the following ways:

- What's going on in the person life?
- Are there other challenges being faced by the work group?
- What is the business experiencing?
- Are there any meaningful external conditions to consider with customers suppliers etc.?

Beyond the context the leader must decide on the timing, location, and environment for the questions to be asked:

- Should we meet in the morning or later in the day?
- Use my office or a more neutral place?
- Are formal or casual surroundings best?

When an inquiry session is expected to be difficult, an even more formal process should be considered. This would involve the following:

- Breaking the ice – make small talk and ask permission to discuss the topic with the employee.
- Set the stage – open yourself up and offer some self-disclosure showing a concern relative to the impending conversation.
- Ask what you want – use empowering questions, actively listen and avoid being defensive.

- Listen attentively – keep eye contact, parrot back what you're hearing to affirm understanding, do not interrupt.
- Follow-up – if actions are required after the conversation, be sure they are documented and responded to in a timely fashion.

Effective inquiry is an acquired skill learned by *doing* more than from study. Role-playing is a useful tool for especially important events like investigations, negotiations, and serious performance issues. Sometimes the role-play can be videotaped for analysis. If conditions warrant, having a third party as an observer can be helpful, providing the employee involved in the inquiry is aware of the fact in advance. Fortunately, once skillful at effective inquiry, one rarely loses the skill.

Using Inquiry to Shape Strategy

When leaders shape corporate vision, purpose, and strategy, their focus must turn outward, and the questions they ask must go far beyond the company's walls. Questions involving corporate strategy are questions about how the organization relates to the world around it, such as what markets it competes in, what customers it serves, what alliances it pursues, how it produces its products and services, and how it relates to the community and stakeholders. Vision and values looking outward and informed by the perspectives of outside stakeholders become relevant to the challenges the firm encounters. People can become entrapped in the organization's accumulated knowledge and established procedures. Leaders must periodically question the collective wisdom of the organization. In today's world of rapid change, this kind of introspective analysis must occur almost continuously.

Example Questions

Questions about Vision, Values and Purpose

Questions useful in guiding vision, values, and purpose are simple in content but difficult to answer. Questions like the following are straightforward but exceptionally expansive.

- Image: What will the future look like if we're successful?
- Values: What do we stand for?
- Goals: What do we want our people to focus on?
- Ethics: Are we behaving in a legal, fair and ethical manner?
- Actions: What needs to be done?
- Metrics: How will we measure results?

When employees answer these questions, the organization develops meaningful and actionable responses. In a disempowering environment the answers will all emanate from the top and be myopic at best. Once questions on the company's vision, values, and purpose have been answered, questions about strategy, or how to approach the vision and live our values so we achieve our purpose, can follow.

Queries about Strategy – Bringing a new perspective

- What are our aspirations?
- Where will we play?
- How will we win?
- What capabilities do we need?
- What do we want to keep?
- What do we want to change?
- What are we afraid to do?
- How do we begin?
- Who do we involve?

Asking *why* five times will bring clarity and reveal the root cause of the issue being considered. In addition, leaders responsible for strategy must realize how the process is iterative and never complete. Continuous improvement is the essence of good strategy since it recognizes the world is constantly changing. Today's business climate is so highly integrated and networked that internal inquiry is barely the beginning of the process for strategy development. Those entities involved in our value network, such as customers, suppliers, and communities must all weigh in on strategy.

Questions for Customers

Customer-centricity has become a prerequisite for success and even survival in today's market place. Despite this reality, it's interesting how few employees have ever met a customer or even recognize their critical role. In questioning customers, leaders must endeavor to learn what is wrong as well as right. Improving through customer inquiry, the enterprise develops a sustainable competitive advantage. Questions for customers are as follows:

- Why do you do business with us?
- Why do you do business with our competitors?
- How and when did we make it hard to do business with us?
- What will you need from us in the future?
- What one thing would you change with my organization?
- What should we do differently?
- How can we most effectively thank you for your business?

Following customers, suppliers, partners and other participating third parties become critical. These questions differ from those asked of customers, but must be integrated, yielding a complete picture.

Queries for Suppliers and Partners

- What's our relationship vision?
- How should we work together?
- What challenges are we likely to face?
- How will manage conflict?
- How will handle surprises?
- How will we deal with breakdowns in trust?
- Who will be involved in the relationship?
- What will we learn from each other?
- What will we teach each other?

Finally, but by no means least important, are inquires of the communities in which the enterprise operates because the enterprise exists only by their discretion. All levels of community relationships must be managed proactively through well-developed inquiry.

Queries for the Community

- How do you feel about our company?
- What can we do to help make our relationship better?
- Is there something we should stop doing?
- What do you want us to start doing?
- What sort of information would you like about the company?
- What will we learn from each other?
- What will we teach each other?

Norms of Behavior

A *norm*[33] is a group-held belief about how members should behave in a given *context*. Norms have two dimensions: How much behavior is exhibited and how much the group approves of that behavior.

The critical element is the context within which the norm of behavior is found. For example, the norms of behavior for an English monastery are different from the Viking horde about to pillage that same monastery. The monks in the monastery would expect their members to be kind, loving and

---

[33] http://en.wikipedia.org/wiki/Norm_%28social%29

Christ-like in their behaviors, whereas the Vikings would expect an entirely different kind of behavior that one need not describe. Vikings are unlikely to be very successful as monks and vice versa. The same applies to innovation and innovators along with their norms of behaviors. The paradox is many technical professionals are taught they need to be independent when in reality innovation requires collaboration.

Hence, many technical professionals have developed norms of behavior unfit for being successful innovators. The first step in correcting this is for technical professionals to recognize this paradox and accept they need to now build on their strengths of being independent and also become collaborative. The key message is not to abandon their autonomy but to use it constructively and not exclusively. An innovator's norms of behavior for becoming collaborative includes the following:

1. Forget old resentments; use private discussion to resolve conflicts.
2. Invite each other in.
3. Directly express your needs (or as a spokesperson for your group's needs) to each other. Make time for and be willing to engage each other when asked.
4. No public attacks of each other or each other's groups. Give public support, reserving critical comments for private discussion.
5. Honest discussion of issues and become trustworthy.
6. Confront problems with each other (or each other's groups) directly with each other.
7. If at an impasse, bump it up to next level (No "running to father" unless you have already cleared it with the other individual.).
8. Next level can intervene whenever they see fit.
9. Respect each other's opinions, abilities, and needs. Demonstrate it.
10. Reduce competition between groups (we're all in this together).
11. See what others miss by connecting unrelated dots.
12. Be "Realistically optimistic" but not naïve. Skepticism is okay, but cynicism is not.
13. Be curious about your teammates projects and contribute.
14. Be willing to accept ideas but evaluate their value.
15. Be open and engaging.
16. Be respectful but direct.
17. Be data-driven.
18. Be complimentary in public and critical in private.
19. Try to have fun.

Holding two opposing concepts in one's mind concurrently is a prescription for insanity, but also for excellence. The most innovative people recognize the need to be *both* independent *and* collaborative.

Chapter 4 Summary

Leadership uses the organizations resources for making good decisions and is recognized as critical to yielding successful outcomes. Often, leaders are chosen not because they're skilled leaders but because they were skilled individual contributors. Basic leadership capabilities can be developed once the essential skills are recognized and a defined. The key "Leadership Essentials" are obvious, albeit not trivial, to master.

Unfortunately, from an early age we are discouraged from asking questions, especially challenging ones, as they are considered rude, inconsiderate, or intrusive. A growing number of leaders recognize that a learning organization is better able to adapt to changes.

Inquiry-based leadership is an under-utilized capability that can positively impact the enterprise by shaping its purpose, vision, and values, empowering its employees, and affecting overall sustainability. People are educated not to ask questions but provide answers, which is diametrically opposed to naturally curious human nature. Through careful analysis and practice, leaders can learn to use inquiry as a powerful tool in becoming more effective, creating learning organizations that are self-sustaining in a very dynamic business climate. Inquiry is the adhesive that binds otherwise unrelated communities together so they can collaborate, which is a critical behavior for innovation to flourish.

Chapter 4 Critical Questions

Individual Leadership – Defining a Leader
1. What does it mean, to you, to be a leader?
2. What does being an "effective" or "successful" leader mean to you?
3. What defines a person of character?
4. What does being a leader of character mean to you?
5. Think of someone you admire, a role model. What qualities do you admire about this person(s)?
6. How can you develop these qualities?

Facing Challenges as a Leader
1. What has been the biggest test of your leadership ability?
2. What have you learned as a result of his challenge?
3. Do you confront issues of injustice? When do you? When do you not?
4. How do you handle it when you've done something wrong?
5. What are you afraid of? Does that fear impact what type of leader you are?
6. What risks have you taken recently? How did they turn out?
7. What did you learn about yourself by taking the risk?

Finding a Balance

1. What are four things you absolutely want to incorporate into your time each week?
2. How many of these things did you do in the last week? Are you keeping what's important to you at the forefront?

Managing Stress

1. What do you anticipate being the most common sources of stress in the particular leadership role you will be taking on (or considering)?
2. What causes you stress? Do you have a safe, effective outlet for managing and relieving stress?
3. Do you know where and how to seek help should stress become unbearable?
4. How do you prioritize?
5. What strategies do you plan to use to cope with these sources of stress?

Values, Morals, and Ethics in Leadership

1. What ethical or moral issues do you anticipate encountering in your leadership role? How well prepared do you think you are for dealing with these issues?
2. What has being fair mean to you? And how do your actions back up that belief?
3. Who do you know on campus who really treats others with fairness? Is being fair always the best approach?
4. Why or why not?
5. How do I lead from my core values? What changes can I make to lead more consistently from my values?
6. What is one thing you have a passion for?
7. What are you doing to incorporate this into your role as a leader?
8. Would you agree or disagree with the following statement?
9. "For humans to be truly happy, they have to find meaning in their lives at comes from recognizing they must make a commitment to something larger than themselves, such as humanity, the natural world, or something that transcends human existence."

    _____ Agree

    _____ Disagree

    What is the reasoning behind your agreement or disagreement with the previous statement?

Working with Others

1. What does being a good follower mean to you?
2. What does it mean to be a team player?
3. Do you fit your own definition?

Your Personal Leadership Style

1. As you contemplate your own leadership passion, vision, and purpose, consider:
   a. If I had all the time in the world, how would I spend it (don't let potential boundaries stifle your thoughts)?
   b. Where do I get, or what gives me, energy and motivation?
   c. What do I really care about (people, organizations, relationships, human issues, social issues, etc.)?
2. What was I most proud of this week?
3. What gifts and talents do you bring to your role as leader?
4. What inspires and motivates you?
5. What is one thing you've learned in the last 24 hours that you can adapt to your leadership life?
6. How will you do it? Why is it important?
7. How are your leadership skills best being used today? How will they best be used in the future?
8. Do you think emotional self-awareness is important for wellness and personal success?
9. Why?
10. Where am I headed?
11. Who do I really want to be?
12. How do I truly see myself? If you're a "work in progress," what does that mean?
13. What are you striving for?
14. How does access to higher education make you who you are today?

Chapter 5: Career Development

Today knowledge has power. It controls access to opportunity and advancement.
~Peter Drucker~

More and more people in the workforce, and most knowledge workers, will have to manage themselves. They will have to place themselves where they can make the greatest contribution. They will have to learn to develop themselves. They will have to learn how to stay young and mentally alive during a fifty-year working life. They will also have to learn how and when to change what they do, how they do it, and when they do it.

Knowledge workers are likely to outlive their employing organization. Even if knowledge workers postpone entry into the labor force as long as possible, such as staying in school into their late twenties to get a doctorate, they are likely to live into their eighties. And they are likely to have to keep working, even if only part-time, until they are at least seventy- five or older. The average working life, in other words, is likely to be fifty years, especially for knowledge workers. But the average life expectancy of a successful business is only thirty years, and even that is optimistic in today's turbulent times. Those that do survive will change their structure, the work they are doing, the knowledge they require, and the kind of people they employ.

Self-Management Questions for 21st Century Workers

History's greatest achievers, the Napoleons, Leonardo da Vincis and Mozarts, have always managed themselves. Today we consider them the rarest of exceptions, far outside the boundaries of normal human existence. Now, even people of modest abilities will have to learn to manage themselves. Knowledge workers facing drastically new demands must ask themselves questions such as the following:

1. What are my strengths?
2. How do I perform?
3. What are my values?

4. Where do I belong?
5. What is my contribution?
6. How do I take relationship responsibility?
7. How do I plan for the second half of my life?

Most people think they know what they are good at. They are usually wrong. People know what they are *not* good at more often, and even then people are more often wrong than right. And yet, you can only perform with your strengths. You cannot build performance on weaknesses, let alone on something you cannot do at all.

For the great majority of people, knowing their strengths was irrelevant as recently as a few decades ago. People were born into a job and into a line of work. The peasant's son became a peasant. If he was not good at being a peasant, he failed. The artisan's son was similarly going to be an artisan, and so on. But now people have choices. They have to know their strengths so that they can know where they belong.

There is only one way to find this out, and that is through *Feedback Analysis*. Whenever you make a key decision, and whenever you perform a key action, write down what you expect will happen. Nine months or twelve months later, compare the results to your expectations.

This is by no means a new method. An otherwise obscure German theologian invented it in the 14th century. Some 150 years later, Jean Calvin in Geneva (1509-1564), the father of Calvinism, and Ignatius Loyola (1491-1556), the founder of the Jesuit Order, quite independent of each other, picked up the idea and incorporated it into their rules.

This explains why these two new institutions (both founded in the same year, in 1536) came to dominate Europe in just thirty years. Calvinism was rooted in the Protestant north while the Jesuit Order took to the Catholic south. By that time, each group contained so many thousands of members that most of them were ordinary rather than exceptional. Many of them worked alone, if not in complete isolation. Many of them had to work underground and in constant fear of persecution. Yet very few defected. The routine feedback from results to expectations reaffirmed them in their commitment. It enabled them to focus on performance and results, and then on achievement and satisfaction.

Within a fairly short period of time, maybe two or three years, this simple procedure will tell you first where you strengths are, and this is probably the most important thing to know about yourself. It will show you what you do or fail to do that deprives you of the full yield from your strengths. It will show you where you are not particularly competent, and it will finally show you where you have no strengths and cannot perform. Repeated use of this process over centuries has yielded some important conclusions as follows:

Concentrate on your strengths by placing yourself where your strengths can produce performance and results.

Work on improving your strengths. The feedback analysis rapidly shows where you need to improve skills or acquire new knowledge. In today's free information age, making these corrections is easier than ever before in history.

Eliminate arrogance. The feedback analysis soon identifies areas where intellectual arrogance causes disabling ignorance. Far too many people, and especially people with high knowledge in one area, are contemptuous of knowledge in other areas, or believe that being "bright" is a substitute for true knowing. The feedback analysis, however, soon shows that a main reason for poor performance is simply not knowing enough, or is the result of being contemptuous of knowledge outside your own specialty.

Mathematicians are born. But almost everyone can learn trigonometry. The same holds true for foreign languages and many other major disciplines, whether history, economics or chemistry.

First-rate engineers tend to take pride in not knowing anything about people because human beings are much too disorderly for the good engineering mind. Accountants also tend to think it unnecessary to know about people. Human Resources people, by contrast, often pride themselves on their ignorance of elementary accounting or of quantitative methods altogether. Brilliant executives who are being posted abroad often believe that business skill is sufficient, and proceed to dismiss learning about the history, the arts, the culture, and the traditions of the country where they are now expected to perform, only to find that their brilliant business skills produce no results.

One important action conclusion from the feedback analysis is to overcome intellectual arrogance and work on acquiring the skills and knowledge needed to make your strengths fully productive. It is also important to remedy any bad habits, whether they are things you do or fail to do, that inhibit effectiveness and performance. They quickly show up in the feedback analysis.

The analysis may show, for instance, that a planner's beautiful plans die without proper follow-through. Like so many brilliant people, you may believe that ideas move mountains. In reality, it's bulldozers that move mountains. The ideas show where the bulldozers have to go to work. The most brilliant planners far too often stop when the plan is completed. But that is when the work really begins to find the people to carry out the plan, explain the plan to them, reach them, adapt, and change the plan as it moves from planning to doing, and eventually decide when to stop using the plan.

The analysis may also show that a person fails to obtain results because of a lack of manners. Bright people, especially bright young people, often do not understand that manners are the "lubricating oil" of an organization.

It is a law of nature that two moving bodies in contact with each other create friction. Because human beings are nearly always in motion, when two come into contact with each other there will always be friction. That is when the lubricating oil of manners enables these two moving bodies to work together, whether they like each other or not. Simple things like saying "please" and "thank you," and knowing a person's birthday or name, and remembering to ask after the person's family, can go a long ways towards making work more successful. If the analysis shows that brilliant work fails again and again as soon as it requires cooperation by others, it probably indicates a lack of courtesy or manners.

Feedback analysis also shows where you should *not* try to do anything at all. It shows the areas that in which you lack the minimum capacity needed, and there are always many such areas for everyone. Most people lack even one first-rate skill or knowledge area, and everyone has an infinite number of areas in which they have no talent or any chance to become even mediocre. In these areas you should not take on work, jobs, or assignments.

One key is to waste as little effort as possible on improving areas of low competence. Concentrate on areas of high competence and high skill. It takes far more energy and far more work to improve from total incompetence to mediocrity than it takes to improve from first-rate performance to excellence, and yet most people, teachers, and organizations concentrate on moving from incompetence to mediocrity. Put that energy and those resources into boosting a competent person into a star performer.

Defining Individual Performance

How Do I Perform? This question is as important as the one about strengths, possibly even more important. Few people actually know how they get things done. Most do not even know that different people work and perform differently. One reason for this is rooted in the homogeneity of schools, where there is often only one right way to learn for everyone. To be sure, this was out of necessity in cases where classes had as many as 40 children in them. The homogeneity was the result of striving for efficiency. The result is adults assuming there's only one way to do work as well.

As with your strengths, how you perform is individual. It is personality. It is a "given," just as what a person is good at or not good at is a "given." It can be modified, but it is unlikely to be changed. Just as people get results by doing what they are good at, people also get results by performing how they perform. Feedback analysis may indicate there is something amiss in how you perform, but rarely identifies the cause.

Am I a reader or a listener? The first thing to know about how you perform is whether you are a reader or a listener. Yet very few people even know that that such a distinction exists or that very few people are both. Even fewer know which of the two they themselves are. It's something you must know about yourself.

When he was Commander-in-Chief of the Allied Forces in Europe, General Dwight (Ike) Eisenhower was the darling of the press, and attending one of his press conferences was considered a rare treat. These conferences were famous for their style, for Eisenhower's total command of whatever question was being asked, and for his ability to describe a situation or to explain a policy in two or three beautifully polished and elegant sentences.

Ten years later, however, President Eisenhower was reviled by his former admirers. They considered him a buffoon. They complained he never addressed the question asked, but rambled on endlessly about something else. He was constantly ridiculed for butchering the King's English in his incoherent and ungrammatical answers. Yet Eisenhower had owed his brilliant earlier career in large measure to a virtuoso performance as a speechwriter for General MacArthur, one of the most demanding stylists in American public life.

Eisenhower apparently did not realize that he himself was a reader and not a listener. When he was Commander-in-Chief in Europe, his aides made sure that every question from the press was submitted in writing at least half an hour before the conference began. As long as that happened, Eisenhower was in total command. When he became President he succeeded two listeners, Franklin D. Roosevelt and Harry Truman. Both men knew this and both enjoyed free-for-all press conferences. Roosevelt knew himself to be so much of a listener that he insisted that everything first be read out loud to him, and only then would he look at anything in writing. When Truman realized after becoming President that he needed to learn about foreign and military affairs, neither of which previously interested him, he arranged for his two ablest Cabinet members, General Marshall and Dean Acheson, to give him a daily tutorial which each delivered in a forty minute spoken presentation, after which the President asked questions. Eisenhower, apparently, felt that he had to be like his two predecessors. Most of the time he never even really heard the question the journalists asked, and he was not even an extreme case of a non-listener.

A few years later, Lyndon Johnson destroyed his presidency because he was a listener, although he didn't know it. Johnson's predecessor (John F. Kennedy), who knew that he was a reader, had assembled a brilliant group of writers as assistants, such as Arthur Schlesinger, Jr (the historian) and Bill Moyers (a first-rate journalist). Kennedy made sure that they first wrote to him before discussing their memos in person. Johnson kept these people as his staff, and they kept on writing. He never apparently understood one word of what they wrote. As a senator, Johnson was superb. Above all else, congressmen must be listeners.

Only a century ago very few people, even in the most highly developed countries, knew whether they were right-handed or left-handed. Left-handers were forced to suppress their left-handedness. Few actually became competent right-handers, most of them ended up as incompetent no-handers and with severe emotional damage such as stuttering.

But only one of every ten human beings is left-handed. The ratio of listeners to readers is more like fifty-fifty. Yet, just as few left-handers became competent right-handers, few listeners can be made, or can make themselves, into competent readers, and vice versa.

The listener who tries to be a reader will suffer the fate of Lyndon Johnson, while the reader who tries to be a listener will suffer the fate of Dwight Eisenhower. They will not perform or achieve.

How do I Learn? The second thing to know about how you perform is to know how you learn. Schools everywhere are organized on the assumption that there is one right way to learn, and that it is the same way for everybody. Nothing could be further from the truth.

Many first-class writers (Winston Churchill is but one example) do poorly in school, and they tend to remember their schooling as pure torture. This is because first-rate writers do not, as a rule, learn by listening and reading. They learn by writing. Since this is not the way the school allows them to learn, they get poor grades. To be forced to learn the way the school teaches is pure torture for them.

Beethoven left behind an enormous number of sketchbooks, yet he himself said that he never looked at a sketchbook when he actually wrote his compositions. When asked, "Why then, do you keep a sketchbook?" he is reported to have answered, "If l don't write it down immediately I forget it right away, if I put it into a sketchbook I never forget it, and I never have to look it up again."

Alfred Sloan built General Motors into the world's largest automotive company and for sixty years the world's most successful manufacturing company, conducting most of his management business in small and lively meetings. As soon as a meeting was over, Sloan went to his office and spent several hours composing a letter to one of the meeting's participants, in which he brought out the key questions discussed in the meeting, the issues raised, the decisions reached and the problems uncovered but not solved. "If I do not sit down immediately after the meeting and think through what it actually was all about, and then put it down in writing, I will have forgotten it within twenty-four hours. That's why I write these letters."

A chief executive officer who, in the 1950s and 1960s, converted what was a small and mediocre family firm into the world's leading company in its industry, was in the habit of calling his entire senior staff into his office, usually once a week, had them sit in a half-circle around his desk, and then talked at them for two or three hours. He very rarely asked these people for their comments or their questions. He argued with himself about various business issues of the company. He always took three different positions on every one of these issues: One in favor, one against, and one on the conditions under which such a move might make sense. He needed an audience to hear himself talk it out. Successful trial lawyers learn the same way, as do many medical diagnosticians. There are probably half a dozen different ways to learn. Some people who learn by taking copious notes like Beethoven, but Alfred Sloan never took notes, nor did the CEO mentioned.

There are people who learn by hearing themselves talk. There are people who learn by writing. There are people who learn by doing, and in an informal survey of professors in American universities who successfully publish scholarly books of wide appeal, I was told again and again, "To hear myself talk is the reason why I teach; because then I can write." Of all the important pieces of self-knowledge, this is one of the easiest to acquire.

When you ask people, "How do you learn?" most of them know it. But when you then ask, "Do you act on this knowledge?" few do, and yet to act on this knowledge is the key to performance, and to not act on this knowledge is to condemn oneself to non-performance.

To ask "How do I perform?" and "How do I learn?" are the most important first questions to ask, but they are by no means the only ones. To manage yourself, you have to ask: "Do I work well with people, or am I a loner?" If you find out that you work well with people, you then ask: "In what relationships do I work well with people?" Some people work best as subordinates. A prime example is the great American military hero of WWII, General George Patton. He was America's top troop commander. Yet, when he was proposed for an independent command, General George Marshall, the Chief of Staff and the most successful talent recruiter in American history said, "Patton is the best subordinate the American Army has ever produced, but he would be the worst commander."

Some people work best as team members, some people work exceedingly well as coaches and mentors, and some people are simply incompetent to be mentors. Another important thing to know about how you perform is whether you perform well under stress, or whether you need a highly structured and predictable environment.

Are you a big-fish-small-pond or little-fish-big-pond? Few people work well in both situations. Again and again, people who have been very successful in a large organization such as General Electric or Citibank, flounder miserably when they move into a small organization, while people who perform brilliantly in a small organization flounder miserably when they take a job with a big organization. Which is right for you?

Do I produce results as a decision maker or as an adviser? A great many people perform best as advisers, but cannot take the burden and pressure of being the innovation leader. A good many people, by contrast, need an adviser to force them to think, but then they can make the decision and act on it with speed, self-confidence, and courage. This is one reason why the number-two person in an organization often fails when promoted into the top spot. The top spot requires an innovation leader who often puts a trusted adviser in the number two spot, but that doesn't automatically make the person right for the number-one spot. They often know what the decision should be, but cannot handle the decision-making responsibility. Do not try to change yourself. It is unlikely to be successful. Instead work hard to improve the way you already perform and try not to do work of any kind in a way that simply doesn't work for you.

What Are My Values? To be able to manage yourself, you have to know what your values are. In respect to ethics, the rules are the same for everybody, and the test is a simple one called the *mirror test.*

As the story goes, the most highly respected diplomat of all the Great Powers in the early years of this century was the German Ambassador in London. He was clearly destined for higher things, at least to become his country's Foreign Minister, if not the German Federal Chancellor. But in 1906 he abruptly resigned. King Edward VII had then been on the British throne for five years, and the diplomatic corps was going to give him a big dinner. The German ambassador, being the dean of the diplomatic corps, had been in London for close to fifteen years and was to be the chairman of the dinner. King Edward VII was a notorious womanizer and made it clear what kind of dinner he wanted. After serving dessert, a huge cake was going to appear, and out of it would jump a dozen or more naked prostitutes as the lights were dimmed. The German ambassador resigned rather than preside over this dinner. "I refuse to see a pimp in the mirror in the morning, when I shave."

This is the mirror test. What ethics requires is to ask yourself: "What kind of person do I want to see when I shave myself or put on my makeup in the morning?" Ethics mean a clear value system that doesn't vary much from workplace to workplace. Ethics constitute just one part of an organization's value system. If you aren't aligned to the organization's ethics and value system, you'll be doomed to frustration and nonperformance.

A brilliant and highly successful human resources executive found herself totally frustrated after her old company was acquired by a larger one. She received a big promotion into doing the kind of work she did best. Part of her job was selecting people for important positions. She deeply believed in hiring people from outside the company only after exhausting all inside possibilities. The company in which she now found herself, however, believed in looking externally first, "to bring in fresh blood." There is something to be said for both ways, and a mix of both is probably best, but they are fundamentally incompatible, not as policies but as values.

They bespeak a different view of the relationship between organizations and people; a different view of the responsibility of an organization to its people and in respect to developing them; a different view in what is the most important contribution of a person to an enterprise, and so on. After several years of frustration, the human resources executive quit, at considerable financial loss to herself. Her values and the values of the organization simply were not compatible.

Similarly, whether to try to obtain results in a pharmaceutical company by making constant, small improvements or by occasional, highly expensive and risky "breakthroughs" is not primarily an economic question. The results of either strategy may be largely the same. It is at root a conflict of values, between a value system that sees the contribution of a pharmaceutical company to help the successful physician to do better what he or she already does well, and a value system that is "science" oriented.

It is also a value question whether a business should be run for short-term results or for "the long run." Financial analysts believe that businesses can do both simultaneously. Successful businessmen know better. To be sure, everyone has to produce short-term results. But in any conflict between short- term results and long-term growth, one company decides in favor of long-term growth while another company decides in favor of short-term results. Again, this is not primarily a disagreement on economics. It is fundamentally a value conflict regarding the function of a business and the responsibility of management.

One of the fastest-growing pastoral churches in the United States measures success by the number of its members. It believes that how many people join and become regular churchgoers is what matters. Another pastoral church, on the other hand, believes that what matters is the spiritual experience of people. It will ease out members who join the church but who do not eventually enter into the spiritual life of the church.

This is not a theological difference, but a difference in values. One of the two pastors said in a public debate, "Unless you first come to church you will never find the Gate to the Kingdom of Heaven." The other answered, "No. Until you first look for the Gate to the Kingdom of Heaven, you don't belong in church."

Organizations have values, as do people. To be effective in an organization, your own values must be compatible with the organization's values. They do not, however, need to be the same. They must be close enough so that they can coexist. Otherwise, you will be both frustrated and unable to produce results.

There rarely is a conflict between your strengths and the way you perform. The two are generally complementary. But there is sometimes a conflict between your values and your strengths. What you do well may not fit with your value system.

Where Do I Belong? The answers to the three questions about strengths, performance and values should enable you to decide where he you belong. This is not a decision that most people can or should make at the beginning of their careers.

To be sure, a small minority knows very early where they belong. Mathematicians, musicians or cooks, for instance, are usually mathematicians, musicians or cooks by the time they are four or five years old. Physicians usually decide in their teens, if not earlier. But most people, and especially highly gifted people, do not really know where they belong until they are well past their mid-twenties. By that time, however, they should know where their strengths are. They should know how they perform. And they should know what their values are. Where you belong is any place that aligns with those three items. They also reveal where you don't belong.

Successful careers are not "planned." They are the careers of people who are prepared for the opportunity because they know their strengths, the way they work, and their values. Knowing where you belong makes mediocre people into outstanding performers.

What Is My Contribution? To ask, "What is my contribution?" means moving from knowledge to action. The question is not "What do I want to contribute?" It also is not, "What am I told to contribute?" It is instead, "What *should* I contribute?" This is a new question in human history. Traditionally, the answer was a given. It was given either by the work itself or it was given by a master or a mistress, as was the task of the domestic servant. Until very recently, the advent of the knowledge worker is changing this, and fast. The first reaction to this change was to look at the employing organization to give the answer. *Career Planning* is what the personnel department was supposed to do in the 1950s and 1960s for career employees, and it's still that way in Japan. But nowadays everyone has to be their own career planner. That's why you have to learn to ask, "What should my contribution be?" Only then should you ask, "Does this fit my strengths? Is this what I want to do? Do I find this rewarding?"

The best example is the way Harry Truman repositioned himself when he became President of the United States, upon the sudden death of Franklin D. Roosevelt at the end of World War II.

Truman had been picked for the Vice Presidency because he was totally concerned with domestic issues. For it was then generally believed that with the end of the war, the U.S. would return to almost exclusive concern with domestic affairs. Truman had never shown the slightest interest in foreign affairs, knew nothing about them, and was kept in total ignorance of them. He was still totally focused on domestic affairs when, within a few weeks after his ascendancy, he went to the Potsdam Conference after Germany surrendered. There he sat for a week, with Churchill on one side and Stalin on the other and realized, to his horror, that those foreign affairs would dominate, and that he knew absolutely nothing about them. He came back from Potsdam convinced that he had to give up what he wanted to do and instead had to concentrate on what he had to do, that is, on foreign affairs. He immediately recruited General Marshall and Dean Acheson as his tutors.

Within in a few months he was a master of foreign affairs and he, rather than Churchill or Stalin, created the postwar world with his policy of containing Communism and pushing it back from Iran and Greece; with the Marshall Plan that rescued Western Europe; with the decision to rebuild Japan; and finally, with the call for worldwide economic development.

By contrast, Lyndon Johnson lost both the Vietnam War and his domestic policies because he clung to "What do I *want* to do?" instead of asking himself "What *should* my contribution be?" Johnson, like Truman, had been entirely focused on domestic affairs. He too came into the presidency wanting to complete what the New Deal had left unfinished. He very soon realized that the Vietnam War was what he had to concentrate on. But he could not give up what he wanted his contribution to be. Splintered between the Vietnam War and domestic reforms, he lost both.

One more question has to be asked to decide what your contribution should be: *Where and how can I have results that make a difference?* The answer to this question has to balance a number of things. Results should be hard to achieve. They should require "stretching," but they should be within reach. To aim at results that cannot be achieved, or can only be achieved under the most unlikely circumstances, is not being ambitious. It is being foolish. At the same time, results should be meaningful. They should make a difference. And they should be visible and, if at all possible, measurable.

A newly appointed hospital administrator asked himself the question, "What should be my contribution?" The hospital was highly prestigious, but had been coasting on its reputation for thirty years, becoming mediocre. The new hospital administrator decided that his contribution should be to establish a standard of excellence in one important area within two years.

He decided to concentrate on turning around the Emergency Room and the Trauma Center, which was big, visible and sloppy. The new hospital administrator thought through what to demand of an Emergency Room, and how to measure its performance. He decided that every patient who came into the Emergency Room had to be seen by a qualified nurse within sixty seconds. United States and within another two years the whole hospital had been transformed. The decision "What should my contribution be?" thus balances the following three elements:

- What does the situation require?
- How could I make the greatest contribution with my strengths, my way of performing, and my values, to what needs to be done?
- What results have to be achieved to make a difference?

This then leads to the action conclusions of what to do, where to start, how to start, and what goals and deadlines to set.

Throughout history, few people had any choices. The task was imposed on them either by nature or by a master and so, in large measure, was the way in which they were supposed to perform the task. But so also the expected results were given. To "do one's own thing" is, however, not freedom. It is license. It does not have results. But to start out with the question "What should I contribute?" gives freedom in responsibility.

How Do I Take Relationship Responsibility? Very few people work by themselves and achieve results beyond a few great artists, a few great scientists, and a few great athletes. Most people work with other people and are effective through other people. That is true whether they are members of an organization or legally independent. For you to manage yourself requires taking relationship responsibility, and there are two parts to it. The first part is to accept the fact that other people are as much individuals as your are, which means that they too have their strengths, their ways of getting things done, and their values. To be effective, you have to know the strengths, the performance modes, and the values of the people with whom you work. This sounds obvious, but few people pay attention to it.

Typical are people who, in their first assignment, worked for a man who is a reader. They were trained in writing reports. Their next boss is a listener. But these people keep on writing reports to the new boss, the way President Johnson's assistants kept on writing reports to him because Jack Kennedy, who had hired them, had been a reader.

Invariably, these people have no results and their new boss thinks they are stupid, incompetent, and lazy, and they become failures. All that could have been avoided by taking stock of the boss to answer the question, "How does he or she perform?"

Bosses are not a title on the organization chart or a "function." They are individuals and entitled to do the work the way they do it. And it is incumbent upon the people who work with them to observe them, to find out how they work, and to adapt themselves to the way the bosses are effective. There are bosses, for instance, who have to see the figures first, like Alfred Sloan at General Motors. He himself was not a financial person but an engineer with strong marketing instincts. But as an engineer he had been trained to look first at figures.

Three of the ablest younger executives in General Motors did not make it into the top ranks because they did not look at Sloan, they did not realize that there was no point writing to him or talking to him until he first had spent time with the figures. They went in and presented their reports. Then they left the figures. But by that time they had already lost Sloan.

Readers are unlikely ever to become listeners, and listeners are unlikely ever to become readers. But everyone can learn to make a decent oral presentation or to write a decent report. It is simply the duty of the subordinate to enable the bosses to do their work. And that requires looking at the bosses and asking, "What are their strengths? How do they do the work and perform? What are their values?" In fact, this is the secret of "managing" the boss.

You do the same with all the people you work with. Each of them works their own way and not your way. And they are entitled to work in their way. What matters is whether they perform, and what their values are. The first secret of effectiveness is to understand the people with whom you work and on whom you depend, and to make use of their strengths, their ways of working, and their values, for working relations are based as much on the person as they are on the work.

The second thing to do to manage oneself and to become effective is to take responsibility for communications. After people have thought through what their strengths are, how they perform, what their values are, and especially what their contribution should be, they then have to ask: "Who needs to know this? On whom do I depend? And who depends on me?" And then you go and tell all these people, but in the way in which they receive a message, such as a memo to readers, or by talking to listeners.

When consultants start to work with an organization, they are often first told of all the "personality conflicts" that exist. Most of them arise from the fact that one person does not know what other people do, or does not know how other people do their work, or does not know what contribution other people focus on, and what results they expect. And the reason that they do not know is that they do not ask, and therefore are not told.

This reflects human ignorance less than it reflects human history. It was unnecessary until very recently to tell any of these things to anybody. Everybody in a district of the medieval city plied the same trade; there was a street of goldsmiths, and a street of shoemakers, and a street of armorers. In Japan's Kyoto, there are still the streets of the potters, the streets of the silk weavers, the streets of the lacquer makers.

One goldsmith knew exactly what every other goldsmith was doing; one shoemaker knew exactly what every other shoemaker was doing; one armorer knew exactly what every other armorer was doing. There was no need to explain anything. And those few people who did things that were not "common," the few professionals, for instance, worked alone, and also did not have to tell anybody what they were doing.

Today the great majority of people work with others who do different things. For example, If a marketing vice-president came out of sales and knows everything about sales but knows nothing about promotion and pricing and advertising and packaging and sales planning and so on, then it is incumbent on the people who do these things to make sure that the marketing vice-president understands what they are trying to do, why they are trying to do it, how they are going to do it, and what results to expect.

If the marketing vice-president does not understand what these high-grade knowledge specialists are doing, it is primarily *their* fault, and not that of the marketing vice-president. They have not told her. They have not educated her. Conversely, it is the marketing vice-president's responsibility to make sure that every one of the people she works with understands how she looks at marketing, what her goals are, how she works and what she expects of herself and of every one of them.

Even people who understand the importance of relationship responsibility often do not tell their associates and do not ask them. They are afraid of being perceived as presumptuous, inquisitive, or stupid. No so. Whenever anyone goes to their associates and says: "This is what I am good at. This is how I work. These are my values. This is the contribution I plan to concentrate on and the results I expect to deliver," the response is always, "This is very helpful. But why didn't you tell me earlier?" The same appreciation emerges when you ask others about themselves.

In fact, knowledge workers should request of people with whom they work, whether as subordinates, superiors, colleagues, or team members, that they adjust their behavior to the knowledge workers' strengths, and to the ways the knowledge workers work. Readers should request that their associates write to them, and listeners should request that their associates first talk to them.

Organizations are increasingly built on trust. Trust does not mean that people like one another. It means that people can trust one another, which presupposes that they understand one another. This makes taking relationship responsibility both a necessity and a duty.

How Do I Plan for the Second Half of My Life? For the first time in human history, individuals can expect to outlive organizations. This creates a totally new challenge: What to do with the second half of your life?

You can no longer expect that the organization for which you work at age thirty will still be around when you are sixty. But forty or fifty years in the same kind of work is much too long for most people. They deteriorate, get bored, lose all joy in their work, "retire on the job," and become a burden to themselves and everyone around them.

Exceptions to this are often found among great artists. Claude Monet (1840-1926), the greatest Impressionist painter, was still painting masterpieces in his eighties, and working twelve hours a day, even though he had lost almost all his eyesight. Pablo Picasso, (1881- 1973) was perhaps the world's greatest Post-Impressionist painter, similarly painted until he died in his nineties, even inventing a new style in his seventies. The greatest musical instrumentalist of this century, the Spanish cellist Pablo Casals (1876-1973), planned to perform a new piece of music and practiced it on the very day on which he died at age ninety-seven. But these are the rarest of exceptions, even among the greatest achievers.

Neither Max Planck (1858-1947) nor Albert Einstein (1879-1955), the two giants of modern physics, did important scientific work after their forties. Planck had two more careers. After 1918, aged sixty, he reorganized German science. After being forced into retirement by the Nazis and at the age of ninety, he started once more to rebuild German science after Hitler's fall. But Einstein retired in his forties to become a "famous man."

There is a great deal of talk today about the "mid-life crisis" of the executive. It is mostly about boredom. At age forty-five, most executives have reached the peak of their business career and know it. After twenty years of doing the same kind of work, they are good at their jobs. But few are learning anything new, few are contributing anything fresh, and few expect the job to ever become a challenge again.

Manual workers who have been working for forty years are physically and mentally tired long before they reach the end of their normal life expectancy or even traditional retirement age. They are quite happy spending ten or fifteen years doing nothing, playing golf, going fishing, engaging in some minor hobby and so on. But knowledge workers are not "finished." They are perfectly capable of functioning despite all kinds of minor complaints. And yet the original work that was so challenging when the knowledge worker was thirty has become a deadly bore when the knowledge worker is fifty. Performing another fifteen or twenty years of work is a mind-numbing proposition. Managing yourself will increasingly require preparing oneself for the second half of one's life. There are three potential scenarios:

The career change. The first is actually to start a second and different career, as Max Planck did. Often this means just moving from one kind of an organization to another. Typical are the middle-level American business executives who in substantial numbers move to a hospital, a university, or some other nonprofit organization, around age forty-five or forty-eight, when the children are grown and the retirement pension is vested. In many cases they stay in the same kind of work. The divisional controller in the big corporation becomes, for instance, controller in a medium-sized hospital, but there are also a growing number of people who actually move into a completely different line of work.

Increasingly, for instance, students in American Protestant theological seminaries are forty-five rather than twenty-five years old. They made a first career in business or government, some in medicine, and then, when the children are grown, moved into the ministry.

In the United States there are a fairly substantial number of middle-aged women who have worked for twenty years, say in business or in local government, that have risen to a junior management position and now, at age forty-five and with the children grown, enter law school. Three or four years later they then establish themselves as small-time lawyers in their local communities. There will be many more such second-career people who have achieved fair success in their first job and have substantial skills. They need a community, and the house is empty with the children gone. They may need the income, but above all they need the challenge.

The parallel career. The second answer to the question of what to do with the second half of your life is to develop a parallel career. A large and rapidly growing number of people, especially people who are very successful in their first careers, stay in the work they have been doing for twenty or twenty-five years. Many keep on working forty or fifty hours a week in their main and paid job. Some move from busy full-time to being part-time employees, or become consultants. But then they create for themselves a parallel job, usually in a non-profit organization, and one that often takes another ten hours of work a week. They get involved in the administration of their church, for instance, or the presidency of a local civic organization or human service agency, or serve on the local school board and so on.

Social entrepreneurs. The third scenario is those who become "social entrepreneurs." These are usually people who have been very successful in their first profession, as businessmen, as physicians, as consultants, or as university professors. They love their work, but it no longer challenges them. In many cases they keep on doing what they have been doing all along, though they spend less and less of their time on it. But they start another, often a nonprofit, activity.

Bob Buford has authored two books about preparing for the second half of life. Having built a very successful television and radio business, Buford still keeps on running it. But he also started and built a successful nonprofit organization to make the Protestant churches in America capable of survival. Now he is building a second, equally successful organization to teach other social entrepreneurs how to manage their own private, nonprofit ventures while still running their original businesses. But there is also the equally successful lawyer, legal counsel to a big corporation, who has started a venture to establish model schools in his state.

There is one requirement for managing the second half of one's life: To begin creating it long before one enters it.

When it first became clear thirty years ago that working life expectancies were lengthening very rapidly, many observers believed that retired people would increasingly become volunteers for American nonprofit institutions. This has not happened. People who don't begin to volunteer before the age of forty tend to never start. Similarly, all the social entrepreneurs I know began to work in their chosen second enterprise long before they reached their peak in their original business.

There is another reason that managing one's self will increasingly mean that the knowledge worker develops a second major it interest, and develops it early. No one can expect to live very long without experiencing a serious setback in one's life or in one's work.

There is the competent engineer who at age forty-two is passed over for promotion in the company. There is the competent college professor who at age forty-two realizes that she will stay forever in the small college in which she got her first appointment and will never get the professorship at the big university, even though she may be fully qualified for it. There are tragedies in one's personal family life, the breakup of one's marriage, the loss of a child or spouse.

That is when a second major interest, and not just another hobby, can make all the difference. The competent engineer passed over for promotion now knows that he has not been very successful in is job. But in his outside activity, for example, as treasurer in his local church, he has achieved success and continues to have success. This will be increasingly important in a society in which success has become important.

A knowledge society expects everyone to be "successful," but it is clearly impossible for everyone to succeed, which means some will fail. Therefore a second area, whether a second career, a parallel career, a social venture, or a serious outside interest, offers an opportunity for being a leader, for being respected, and for being a success.

The changes and challenges of managing yourself may seem obvious compared to the changes and challenges discussed in earlier chapters. And the answers may seem to be self- evident to the point of appearing naïve.

Nothing could be further from the truth. Managing yourself is nothing short of a revolution in human affairs requiring new and unprecedented things from the individual, and especially from the knowledge worker, for it demands that each knowledge worker think and behave like a CEO.

It also requires an almost 180-degree change in knowledge workers' thoughts and actions from what most people, even of the younger generation, still take for granted as the way to think and the way to act. Two deeply embedded false assumptions are that *organizations outlive workers* and *most people stay put.* The present reality is quite the opposite.

Workers are likely to outlive organizations, and the knowledge worker has mobility. The emergence of knowledge workers who both can and must manage themselves is transforming society.

Career Progression Process: The Technical Ladder[34]

Addressing the topic of the dual career path for technical professionals is very company and situation dependent. Various models can be found depending on the size of the company, the industry sector, the kinds of technical professionals involved and so on. Given this diversity I've chosen to focus on the chemical industry as an example of the framework involve in designing, implementing and managing a success career progression process facilitates recruiting, hiring, development and retention of technical professional. This topic has taken on greater significance with the emergence of the self-managed knowledge worker as the basis for the 21st century.

Job satisfaction is a very individual emotion. What makes one employee feel happy and successful will not have the same effect in another. Perceptions are very different, and jobs have very distinct requirements, responsibilities, rewards, and headaches. Employers want to capitalize on diverse skills, talents, and expertise in a range of functions and levels to support their businesses.

Recognizing both employee and corporate needs, companies have developed compensation and career systems that they hope will attract, retain, and motivate employees. Many companies have adopted the so-called dual career ladders or tracks. Companies design these to provide career paths for professionals separately from those for managers or administrators.

While ladders are often found in organizations where research is highly visible or strategically important career progression is important even in start-ups since highly skilled employees expect to receive appropriate recognition for their contributions. In firms with large R&D investments

[34] Thayer, Ann, M., Volume 76, Number 44 CENEAR 76 44 1-80 ISSN 0009-2347

the dual career track is part of the strategy giving opportunities for technical professionals to be recognized for their accomplishments without having to abandon their disciplines. Further, technical professional migrating to managerial roles often leads to unacceptable outcomes since their education doesn't prepare them for this role. The idea that the best technologist will also the best manager or administrator has been proven wrong more times than correct. In almost every case demoting a manger back to a role as a technologist is painful and embarrassing for all involved and is avoidable. The dual career track helps mitigate this risk.

The dual approach enables a technical professional to move up the scientific track and be paid at an equivalent level to a supervisor or a manager while remaining a really excellent scientist, bringing value through innovation, ideas, and scientific leadership. This level of leadership is every bit as demanding as that involved with leading people in non-technical activities. It's leading the effort around ideas, technology, or intellectual capital rather than a manager of people with the administrative activities. Both are required and leveraging each employee's strengths giving the firm the best value. Hence, developing an effective career progression process, be it a formal dual track system or something less formal is critical.

In the chemical and pharmaceutical industries, career ladders have been in place for at least 15 to 20 years, and the approach has evolved and gathered support with time. Many employers initially created ladders for technical or research employees, and some still use them only in this area.

Many companies have put ladders in other functions, such as engineering, manufacturing, finance, human resources, legal, and marketing areas. This approach not only provides for employee growth in different functional areas, but also allows employers to adjust pay scales independently to be competitive with the broader market for different jobs. This enables meeting both what the company needs and what the individual needs or wants.

So how do members of the chemical industry accomplish this, as an example for what is involved, and how do they avoid common pitfalls? Today, most successful companies have adopted some form of career progression process. Examples from Air Products, Eli Lilly, DuPont, Philips Petroleum and Pfizer are instructive.

Air Products & Chemicals is an example among many chemical and drug producers with very similar outlooks toward having a ladder system. They believe a primary driver is to provide opportunities for career growth for practicing scientists and engineers. They didn't want to have to move people into management roles to afford them that career growth where they may fail and, even if successful, the firm has lost a hard-to-replace specialist.

Years ago, Eli Lilly saw a trend where people who had excellent scientific skills were stepping away from research to pursue administrative work because there wasn't an opportunity for them to grow along technical paths. They were losing good scientists over to administration and probably had people doing work that wasn't as much to their 'calling.' That's when they put in our first generation ladder. It's important to recognize that career ladders need to be refreshed to keep current with the market on salaries and to align with the technical skills the firm requires.

A fallacy is the academic view of tenure applied to members of the technical ladder. A technical professional must keep their skills relevant and advance as their field moves forward. "Retiring on the job", after reaching a high rank as a technical leader, must be known as unacceptable. In short, getting demoted on the technical ladder must be a real possibility.

DuPont has recognized that beyond employee preferences, the dual career ladder is recognition that employees have certain strengths creating value for the firm. By providing parallel routes a technical professional can choose whichever one is suitable for them as well as suitable from a business perspective. Although the exact details and mechanics vary from company to company, career ladders have some common features.

The first is the opportunity for employees to be in salary grades or on "rungs" equivalent to their colleagues on another ladder. Companies also offer similar reward possibilities such as stock options, bonuses, and profit-sharing incentives. Most ladders usually are open to employees at all degree levels. Realistically, most ladders--technical, professional, or management-- are best viewed as pyramids, because the number of positions decreases as the levels increase.

On the way up, management and technical/professional ladders can have the same number of rungs although the number of steps depends on a business' need and the company's need for that function and for that grade level. Firms need to be up-front with employees about the reality of this and the basis for decisions and criteria for advancement. Skill requirements, metrics and duration are the key variables influencing advancement on any ladder and must be clearly and consistently communicated and adhered to.

The top technical level may be as high as a vice president. Others' ladders run to upper-level technical positions that are equivalent to a director or general manager. Ladders are more successful when senior technical staff report to senior, rather than lower-level, managers. Many technology-based companies have chief technical officers or senior vice presidents for R&D, but these jobs generally are on the management ladder.

Employees usually have the chance to move between ladders--for instance, starting in research and then becoming a research manager. Other technical employees may make more dramatic shifts, moving onto ladders in product development, marketing, or another area. Yet most ladders don't start or split from the lower salary grades until after the first few levels. The logic is that it probably takes that long for either the corporation or the individual to recognize what direction they want a career to go. Employees are unlikely to distinguish themselves on either a technical or managerial basis until they have been with a company for about five to seven years. It's noteworthy that executive management positions—those approaching president or chief executive—are filled most often by individuals who come up the management ladder.

A survey of the biographies of top executives at major chemical companies finds that most have undergraduate degrees in an engineering field, often supplemented with an MBA; possibly time spent in a technical area or manufacturing; followed by stints in sales, marketing, or finance and in jobs with increasing business and management responsibilities. If a technical professional aspires to executive management they need to accept at some stage they'll have to abandon their discipline. The reality is that technology advances so quickly that a manger or executive can't stay competent if they're not working at it full time. However, in highly technical businesses, having executives who understand the nuances of technical disciplines is a real advantage.

If a technical professional aspires to executive management, they need to recognize that these jobs require experience in functions that generate the near-term, present value of a company, such as in manufacturing, marketing, and sales. Although human resources managers generally agree that movement up the management ladder can occur faster than on the technical side, they offer disparate reasons for when it happens, why it happens, and whether it will continue. One driver is the business need for managers that may be in greater demand than the availability of qualified people making technical professional attractive candidates to move into these non-technical roles. Generally it's easier for a technical professional to develop the business skills than a non-technical business manager to learn the technology. This trend seems dominate as organizations are becoming very complex, with the number of people and projects expanding, creating an inherent need for managers. This trend may accelerate as Baby Boomers begin retiring over the next 10 years.

Several trends are reducing the need for managers while concurrently increasing the opportunities for technologists to have impact as individual contributors:

1. As companies move to flatter organizational designs to facilitate information flows the spans of control, the number of people reporting to a manager increases creating fewer management jobs.
2. Attractive technical career paths drains candidates, who would otherwise be attracted to management jobs, can be satisfied staying as technologists.

3. Self-managed knowledge workers will reduce the firm's needs for managers, potentially increasing the value of individual technologists.
4. Management jobs are bound by quotas – you only need so many creating more qualified candidates than roles.
5. Technical roles are not bound by quotas – as long as a technologist is qualified they can advance their career.
6. Technical roles are becoming more impactful as firms rely on innovation to impact company performance.
7. Despite this situation, researchers may find themselves spending more time in the same jobs. Movement on professional ladders requires demonstrated competency in a role for some period of time measured in years.
8. "The flash in the pan" technologist flying up the technical ladder is unlikely being limited by benchmarks for advancement.

Advancing on the technical ladder requires ability, competencies, and performance on the job, things not truly measurable six months. However a person with the right skills could move more rapidly up the managerial ladder because of the individual was in the right place at the right time when a position opens up and a replacement is needed.

Successful ladder systems will formally recognize the difference in cycle times required to deliver results from different job functions. R&D plays an important role but you may not see the visible manifestation over the short term – "quarter to quarter" – as a firm's performance tends to be measured.

In marketing, for example, you can put together and execute a program that might have substantive results within a year. Human resource managers must address these issues by clearly defining objectives for success in different jobs. At Pfizer's employees understand these discrepancies as they relate to what are in fact "different jobs." Pfizer notes that "the job content is different, and the jobs have different markets. On the scientific ladder, you are promoted more on your accomplishments than your scope of responsibility change.

On the managerial ladder, the scope of responsibility change is quicker and dramatic as you grow in your career. Although ladder-based compensation systems may lead to expectations that all career paths are created equal, in actuality, jobs will have different dynamics, impact, and visibility. According to the American Chemical Society's Career Services Department, management positions are actually higher risk jobs, with a greater level of unemployment, than technical positions.

What companies say they are offering through dual ladders is the "opportunity" for being compensated fairly in the career one chooses. Company managers emphasize that they carefully evaluate and compare compensation between ladders to make it equitable.

Still, anecdotal evidence, and a pending lawsuit filed by two 3M scientists, suggests that some employees believe they are not treated fairly. Surveys, such as one conducted annually by ACS, also show that managers earn more on average than researchers at equivalent times in their careers. However, the ACS data are not comparing pay for scientists and managers by salary grade, but by time, and do not consider whether individuals reach the same salary grade at identical times in their careers.

Within salary grades, human resource managers stress that individual performance still determines exact pay levels. And, they add, companies frequently tie compensation to performance on teams or projects and to business impact or performance. The nature of how things get done in the workplace is changing so Human Resource leaders have tried very hard to link rewards supporting the culture the firm desires to develop and drive behaviors in the workplace.

Aligning with a firm's "Norms of Behaviors" are critical for how employees determine their "fit" to the firm impacting their ability to succeed. "Fit" is like what makes a marriage successful – the individuals in the relationship value each other's differences. Importantly employees need to fit the firms they join since the firm isn't going to change to "fit" them. "Fit" is often the unspoken "tie breaker" as to why one individual advances faster than another of seemly equivalent abilities. Another way of thinking about "fit" is it's not only what you get done—the results but how you go about it—the behavioral side.

Ladders are part of what many companies call "competency-based pay" systems. These systems define criteria, competencies, abilities, or objectives for each step on the ladder that they then share with employees so that they know what it takes to advance. It spells out what the expectations are in greater detail and communicates value, which traditional job evaluations did not do well enough and didn't facilitate the growth of competency.

A career ladder recognizes that employees who stay within a function can contribute more over time allowing them to be rewarded accordingly. In defining job competencies, most companies have, for example, created very specific requirements to reach the upper technical level. Criteria vary but may include combinations of scientific expertise (recognized internally and often externally), unique accomplishments, publication or patent records, major effects on or contributions to a business or organization, and key product or process developments.

Companies are finding that having a clear mission for the most senior people makes the role productive and useful. Companies are using great care not to compensate somebody hundreds of thousands of dollars per year if the role is not going to be gainfully applied. Beyond measurable competencies the insight, opinions, and experience of these individuals can often be used to create substantial gain for a company.

Senior staff, titled as advisers, fellows, or scientists, apply their knowledge as internal consultants, links to research outside, technology planners and acquirers, and mentors or leaders for developing scientists and technologies. Many companies also name just a handful of people to these top positions.

The credibility of the technical career ladder is dependent on maintaining agreed quality of those individual occupying the highest levels. It's critically important that the technical career ladder doesn't become the "dead manager's ladder" in that a once promising technologist who fails in management, and because of their pay scale then receives a title very senior on the technical ladder.

However some companies emphasize the flexibility that ladders give in starting and moving employees through suitable career paths, which may involve reclassifying employees if they move between ladders. The key is the business need and how best it will be served by having this person in the managerial or technical track. Critically, a move from the managerial ladder to the technical ladder needs to be justifiable to those on both.

Firms recognize that most senior scientists are leaders, and they need the title, the recognition, and the equality of the senior managerial ladder to enable them to lead scientific professionals. Senior technical staff will often supervise research projects, laboratories, or groups requiring some of the same skills of senior managers especially in the emerging work place where knowledge workers will command greater responsibility and accountability. Further companies are giving their most senior scientists more freedom to pursue research interests, namely, their desired career and that which got them to the top in the first place, while now calling upon them to play active and strategic roles.

In high technology companies, be it pharmaceuticals or information technology, scientists named to upper-level positions will do so via a panel or peer review group, where future managers demonstrate their technical capabilities in advance of receiving their first management position.

Often the highest level of the technical ladder is the title of research fellow award for work that had significant economic promise for the firm. Additionally, many scientists who had become world experts in a technology could also be promoted to research fellow as a career reward.

In some cases a research fellow will be assigned a set of functions where they provide technical leadership. This puts a strategic value on the positions clarifying their true roles and how the firm expects them to add value. For example an expert in a certain technology would be required to partner with a business unit where that technology is core to the unit's success be it maintaining profitability, growing market share or keeping a position it has acquired.

Fellows can be responsible for leadership in research and technology such as identifying and developing new technologies; cultivating external technical relations; and identifying, mentoring, advancing the company's core technologies, keeping the company highly competitive, and developing technical leaders from among younger staff. Key is that the fellow title does not award the technologist for living in an ivory tower and doing academic research. Their effort must increase the firm's shareholder value.

Most Human Resource executives say that ladder systems are attractive in recruiting. There is no question that graduate school in and of itself doesn't prepare anybody for a managerial job and there is an anxiety among graduate students and postdocs that to be recognized in a company means that they are going to have to give up research to take a promotion. Having a viable fellows program refutes that concern immediately.

Dual career ladders are also important in later career development as well. Recent graduates are often interested in a professional job using the skills they learned as students. However, later in their careers, they may see the management ladder as attractive and desire to transition. This needs to be possible if the professional has developed the appropriate skills by managing projects and project team.

Critical to any successful career is the person understands and can communicate what they want, and don't want, and why. This is how the "Aligning Employee Performance "section describes doing. How do employees describe in writing their wants and needs and how they align with the firm's objectives. Managers must be candid with employees so they have realistic goals. For example, an entry-level person with a bachelor's degree may aspire to being the CEO in a firm that has a history where CEOs have advanced degrees.

The employee needs to appreciate what they may need to do to become qualified for consideration. If obtaining the advanced degree isn't reasonable then aspiring to be CEO may not be either. The sooner these kinds of disconnects are recognized he better. However, human resources managers note that the choice is not entirely in an employee's hands and companies will work to identify roles for an individual before making a commitment. Options to alter career paths, or jump ladders depend on interest, ability, performance, and job needs within a company. Annual performance discussions are usual practice, as are review systems that provide career guidance.

Every employee must have candid discussions with their managers about their strengths, weaknesses, and career aspirations and the organization's needs to determine how these desires fit the firm's needs. Some firms have introduced very specific discussions of performance and potential with employees at two, four, and nine years, and every five years after that.

When employees make those decisions on which ladder to pursue their careers they must make them with a lot of knowledge about what it is that they want to do with their life and what they want to do on a day-to-day basis. People measure their careers more than just from a compensation perspective. People are very happy when they've been given the opportunity to make decisions about their careers.

Building the Global Career Ladder

Case for Change: Why Global Career Ladders Were Created[35] [36]

Often a complex global company uses job titles that can be dramatically different throughout the world. This issue is most clearly evidenced when planning developmental expatriate assignments. Often the need for greater title consistency is highlighted as talent is shared and redeployed across businesses and regions. There was no "level playing field" to ensure that a scientist, process engineer or production manager, for example, had the required background, experience level and an expected level of contribution regardless of which business the employee worked for or where the employee was stationed.

Using periodic employee surveys shows that significant portions of the population felt that promotions frequently did not go to those most deserving. The career ladders marked an effort to provide clarity around the central question: "What do I need to do to get to the next level in my career?" A global career ladder can be specifically designed to answer this fundamental question, and once implemented can be used to gauge employees' readiness for promotion. Global Career Ladders are designed to support these guiding principles:

- Establish acceptable career band and position hierarchy structures to be used by all businesses across all regions.
- Set consistent job standards.
- Establish position requirements and uniform guidelines for recruitment.
- Facilitate consistent standards and expectations for performance.
- Provide job-relevant examples of the required knowledge, skills, abilities and behaviors an employee must demonstrate for a period of time to be considered for promotion.
- To serve as lasting policy, supporting the corporate culture while incorporating sound market principles.

---

[35] Oliva, Paul, V., World at Work, Third Quarter, 2009

[36] Conway, James M. 2000,"Managerial Performance Development Constructs and Personality Correlates." *Human Performance.* January: 23-46.

How the Global Career Ladders Were Built

After comparing external technology markets and the firm's current job family hierarchies, compensation was mapped showing the firms positions to established benchmarks in the market place. This is done primarily through participation in closed and industry wide compensation surveys.

Title and Band Structures. Ladder project teams' initial charter was to review titles currently used across the globe and propose consensus title and career-band structures that translated well across businesses and regions. While developing job-family hierarchy and career-band structures sounds fairly straight forward, each project team had to take cultural sensitivities and prevailing regional practice into account. Absent the discipline of pre-existing ladder, differences in how titles are used across global regions were found. For example, the title of "manager" is most often used for those who have direct reports, conduct performance reviews and have salary-planning responsibilities in North America. However, in Europe and Asia-Pacific regions, manager titles can often be used for senior-level individual contributors who may provide task direction to a small group of employees, but do not have performance- management or salary-planning responsibilities. And while "director" titles are commonly used for second-level manager positions in North America, in the United Kingdom and some Asia-Pacific countries, "director" can often mean "board member."

Project-team members were encouraged to conduct informal focus-group studies by testing proposed ladder structures with their senior managers and trusted peers as a check of face validity. In other words does this proposed ladder structure make sense? On a number of occasions, changes were made at this early stage incorporating good suggestions along the way. The solicitation of Titles and career band proposals should be solicited provided a vehicle to reestablish senior-management support and buy-in. In this manner, global consensus could be reached fairly early on in the development process.

Part of the challenge in building job-family hierarchies and career-band structures that incorporate regional input from throughout the globe is that project- team members must define what constitutes standard practice for agreed jobs.

Title and career-band structure proposals often met with compromise in terms of what various professional levels across regions were called; so some degree of flexibility was incorporated into the proposed-title structures for individual contributor roles. For example, in North America the title of "strategic account manager" described sales professionals who are relationship managers with a portfolio of large national accounts, whereas the equivalent role in Asia-Pacific was titled "key account manager." The team held fast to a set of principles or corporate expectations regarding what the requirements would be to be called a "manager." These included the following:

- Managers must have professional-level direct reports.
- Managers must be responsible for conducting performance reviews of their direct reports.
- Managers must have salary-planning responsibility for their direct reports and must make merit increase recommendations during the annual common review date process.

Employees were free to have business cards printed with titles they deemed necessary (within reason: they could not adopt the title of COO or CEO for example), for it was recognized that customers sometimes had certain expectations regarding the effectiveness of company representatives based on title. This was more often the case for primary client-facing jobs in sales and technical service.

New Application for Constructs. Once agreement was reached on title and career-band structures, the next phase of development involved identifying constructs. Subject Matter Expert (SME) project team members working with human resources acted as informal focus team leaders and they would obtain agreement from senior managers that an acceptable title structure and job family hierarchy had been reached. These senior managers were ultimately impacted by the ladder and would ultimately become stakeholders. Constructs are knowledge, skills, abilities or attributes that elicit observable behavior. For the company's purpose, constructs were defined as clusters of knowledge, skills, abilities and behaviors an employee needs to perform a job successfully and to an expected level of performance. The selection criteria identifying constructs were differentiating positions within each career band in a meaningful way and were considered critical competencies to be considered for promotion.

Drawing from a number of sources, including assessment center research and behavioral inventories, project-team members identified constructs that were aligned with the ICI's "Success Factors." The ICI "Success Factors" were generic constructs consisting of functional competencies and core behaviors identified as critical to success at ICI. Once constructs were identified, project teams modified them to differentiate the positions in a meaningful way within a career band. As a consequence, constructs naturally evolved across career bands. The following example illustrates a progression as an employee moves up the career bands for communications-related constructs:

1. Written and verbal communication skills (first career band)
2. Presentation skills (second career band)
3. Influencing skills (third career band)
4. Organizational impact (fourth career band).

The emphasis shifts from an ability to effectively communicate with one's peers and managers to the outcomes of effective communication such as influencing departments and levels of management to ensure allocation of required resources. While ascending the career bands, the "bar gets higher" in terms of the required level of competency and supporting behaviors to be successful. Once constructs were identified and modified, project teams spent the next four to eight months on weekly global teleconferences (approximately 90 minutes) developing competency statements describing expected level of performance for each job on the ladder.

The constructs were never intended to be an exhaustive list of every task and duty. Rather, constructs and their supporting competency statements were specifically designed to address the central question: What Do I Need to Do to Get to the Next Level in My Career?

What Are The Global Career Ladders?

Constructs Profiles and Career Band Definitions. The global career ladders consist of two core documents: "Constructs Profiles" and "Career Band Definitions." The "Constructs Profiles" document is a career-development tool used for categorizing jobs based on the knowledge, skills, abilities, and behavioral competencies employees need to be successful on the job and to demonstrate they're ready to be promoted. The process for developing the "Constructs Profile" document is described in the preceding section, and is unique to the company's global career ladders, representing a new application of constructs (See Figure 1 on page 80).

The "Career Band Definitions" document captures experience and education requirements, duties and responsibilities and the primary role of the positions within a career band. Band definitions were most often developed around the end of ladder development phase. This makes sense given that jobs were being defined during the constructs-development process and it is easier to describe roles that are well defined.

Links to Compensation. Through participation in closed-industry and industry wide surveys, the compensation department found fairly robust benchmark comparisons of the company's ladder positions to the market. Consistent with the corporate culture, the career ladders had more levels than generally recognized in the market. Therefore, the company developed hybrid pay range structures based on the 25th, 50th and 75th percentiles of the market from benchmark positions immediately above or below the company's positions. Pay-range structures developed for the United States and Canada were regional (e.g., New York City Metro, Southeast, Central and California), to mirror the location of the plants and businesses. For Europe, Asia-Pacific countries and South Africa, a combination of local surveys and widely recognized survey vendors were used to develop market-based pay range structures, using a similar approach as described in this paper. Drawing from the author's previous experience developing broad banding and establishing market-based pay ranges associated with this initiative, range spreads gradually increase moving up the career bands, and there is considerable overlap in band ranges.

Global Career Ladder Implementation – Job Slotting Process. The company's HR community was routinely updated on the progress of career ladders during their development. In some cases, they were participants during informal focus group testing of title and career-band structures, or in the case of the Global Sales Ladder, HR directors also participated on the project team with SMEs. The first phase of implementation was the job-slotting process. To kick off the job-slotting process, a detailed instruction memorandum was prepared and distributed to high-level managers in the business functions as well as their supporting HR director or manager, with attachments containing the ladder documents and a spreadsheet with employees to be slotted. The job-slotting process was orchestrated as a partnership between HR and senior managers. Initially, this was a spreadsheet exercise downloaded from the company's Global Human Resource Information System (GHRIS). However, obtaining senior-manager input and alignment across global regions left a confusing trail of spreadsheets and an inability to identify which spreadsheet had the latest job-slotting assignments. Later, a customized Lotus Notes database was used to ensure changes made to job-slotting assignments reflected the latest amendments.

Targeted Presentations and Town Hall Meetings
Communication plans were carefully developed in alignment with the culture of the business units targeted for implementation. In regions with more formal management protocols (e.g., China, Japan, Singapore, South Korea and Thailand), there was a strong preference for tiered rollout by level of management; thus targeted presentations for the intended audience were developed. For example, the author might have conducted a presentation with senior managers only, then HR directors and HR managers would deliver a presentation specifically targeted to line managers, and finally town hall meetings would be conducted for those slotted on the

ladder. In the case of businesses functions with a less-formal style (e.g., production management, engineering, and sales in North America), town hall meetings were conducted with managers and their direct reports who were slotted. At the end of town hall meetings, copies of the ladder documents were distributed to attendees. Project team members were present at line manager and town hall meetings to answer questions from employees. Enlisting visible support from the SME project team helped reinforce buy-in and credibility of the ladder. Once town hall meetings were completed, managers individually met with their direct reports within one- to two-week timeframes to communicate where they were slotted and why. In the rare case of a disagreement, this would be further discussed with their supporting HR manager or director as well as the next-level functional manager.

Corporate News Service Article. Corporate Communications interviewed project team members and sponsoring senior executive managers to develop an article for publication on the company's electronic communications system or intranet portal. This paper's author had input on the article. The articles would be posted around the same time as town hall meetings were conducted.

Intranet Posting. With each ladder rollout, intranet Web pages were developed with a branded look and feel (See Figure 3), and posted on the U.S. And global HR intranet portals under the heading "Personal Development." The intention was to make the global career ladders readily available to employees and their managers. Deploying Global Career Ladders on the company intranet HR portals helped build the case for ladders to be developed for job families not addressed at that time.

Global Career Ladder Features

Promotion Requirements for Individual Contributors. To be considered for promotion to individual contributor career-ladder roles, an employee must:
- Meet education and experience requirements.
- At a minimum, must be performing their current job responsibilities consistently and to an expected level of performance.
- Consistently demonstrate 80 percent of the required constructs at the next-level position for a period of six months or more.

If an employee meets all three criteria, he/she can be considered for a promotion within the same career band. Promotions to the next career band are based on organizational need in addition to meeting all the previously listed requirements. If an opportunity does not currently exist for an employee being considered for promotion to the next career band, the employee must consider transferring to another business unit or moving to a new location with an open position, or wait until an opportunity opens in his/her business unit.

Promotion Requirements for Managers. While the promotion requirements for manager roles are highly similar to those for individual contributors, organizational need also comes into play for promotions to the next-level position within the same career band in addition to the next-level career band.

Individual Contributor versus Management Career-Path Choice. In comparing NSC ladder positions to market, it was discovered that high-level individual contributors in technology and sales disciplines can earn just as much as their first-, second- and third-level management counterparts. Mirroring market- pay practice, ladder pay range structures have a fork or "Y," where high-level individual contributor roles have considerable overlap with the market-based pay-range structures of their management counterparts. By eliminating career plateau for high-level individual contributors, compensation was removed as a primary motivation to become a manager. Should an employee choose to pursue a management career path, management ladder roles emphasized managerial skills by incorporating constructs such as "problem resolution/decision-making/decision support," "coaching/mentoring," "people development" and "organizational development." Thus readiness for promotion in manager roles was strongly linked to demonstrating required managerial competencies. This sent a powerful message that if an employee decided to pursue a management career path, he/she must care about developing his/her subordinates and managing his/her people in the manner he/she would like to be treated. Thus, employees could be tested in a management role and if they did not succeed, they could be returned to an individual contributor role with an equivalent pay range structure and a good technical resource did not leave the company. This feature of the career ladders helped foster an improved pool of managers as well.

Greater Clarity Means More Career Choices

To repeat a central issue, the primary purpose for which global career ladders were designed was to address the fundamental question: "What do I need to do to get to the next level in my career?" To this end, the ladders provide specific examples of the competencies required, thus clarifying what employees need to demonstrate to be considered for promotion. Removing career plateaus for individual contributors and creating parallel career ladders where it makes sense to do so gives employees more freedom to pursue new career paths. Employees can choose individual contributor or manager roles, or decide to try related disciplines such as research and development, technical service or engineering without fear of being penalized for trying something new. Improved clarity around what it takes to get promoted, coupled with increased career choices, enables employees to pursue a chosen career path because it is what they like to do and they are good at.

Keys to Global Career Ladders Success

The success of global career ladders was defined by their ongoing use in the various businesses and regions, impacting selection, performance management and succession planning. Career ladders were developed and implemented globally across firm for the following areas:

- Research and development (individual contributor roles)
- Engineering (individual contributor roles)
- Technical service (individual contributor roles)
- Technology management (manager up to vice-president level for research and development and technical service)
- Engineering management (manager up to vice-president level)
- Production management (production supervisor to plant general manager)
- Global sales ladder (individual contributors to vice president, sales)
- Supply chain/logistics ladders (individual contributors to group manager)
- Customer relations
- Logistics, inventory/production planning and control
- Procurement
- Supply chain management
- Warehousing, transportation and distribution

Senior Management Buy-in

To help make the case for career ladder projects, the author sought sponsorship from senior executives who were key stakeholders in their ultimate success; they in turn helped win the approval of the company's CEO at the time of the project's development. The CEO challenged HR to make the ladders global, which, in turn, led to an expanded methodology involving the creation of regional teams from Europe, Asia-Pacific and South America representing the four specialty chemical businesses. Having successfully developed and implemented a truly global career ladder for research and development, technical service and technology management, the author was surprised when the CEO made it a "corporate focal point" for 2005 to develop engineering and production management career ladders. Successful completion and delivery of the 2005 "Corporate Focal Points" created demand and senior executives were soon lining up to request and sponsor Global Career Ladders supporting their respective areas.

Supporting the Corporate Culture

Often the first attempt at career ladders are unsuccessful even though the model mirrored market practice. The designed model was not a good fit for the corporate culture. Focus-group surveys were routinely conducted in the research and development community and this resource provided a better handle on developing an approach that supported the needs of research and development professionals.

Eliminating position levels was not an option for it was perceived as a huge takeaway. Focus-group survey results pointed to an expectation by research and development professionals in individual contributor roles of being promoted every two to three years. While this expectation was out of sync with market practice, it was clear that the solution must have no perceived takeaways while ensuring market competitive pay; the way to resolve this quandary was to create more job levels than the market. For example, while the market generally recognizes six individual contributor levels for research and development: entry, intermediate, career, specialist, master and fellow levels; the firm's research and development ladder had 13 position levels within five career bands.

The lesson learned: Wed market practice to corporate culture. This approach was taken for all ladders afterwards for it fostered the perception that global career ladders meant no takeaway while providing managers with proactive tools to maintain competitive pay based on a pay-for-performance approach to salary management.

A Carefully Planned and Orchestrated Communication Campaign

HR professionals have all, at one time or another, probably worked hard on a new policy, procedure, tool or initiative only to have it collect dust sitting on a shelf as senior management buy-in was not secured, or the communication plan wasn't thorough enough or well executed.

The thoroughness and attention to detail paid in developing communication plans and their targeted delivery are as important to the successful launch of corporate-wide HR initiatives as the compelling reasons for doing them, the quality/relevance of the tools and instruments behind them. Every communications channel available was used, from targeted presentations delivered in town hall and one-one-one meetings to corporate news service articles and brochures for job candidates.

Ladder Champions

In addition to the using all communications channels available, it was recognized that getting the HR community to embrace using the ladders was another key to their ongoing success. HR directors and managers championed the ladders, ensuring that they were vetted through tangible HR processes; the ladders success was attributable in large part to their support. Once implemented, the ladders impacted selection, performance management, capability reviews for promotions, salary planning and succession planning

A Proven Formula for Success

During the course of the first few ladder projects, the evolving well-organized process ensured successful completion, implementation and ongoing utilization; this enabled human resources to track progress as the ladders were begin built and when completion could be expected. The ladder development process is summarized as follows:

1. Enlist senior-executive management sponsorship.
2. Appoint a subject matter expert project team.
3. Kick off meeting/process orientation.
4. Develop job-title and career-band structures.
5. Conduct focus group testing of proposed job title and career bands.
6. Identify constructs.
7. Develop "Constructs Profile" document.
8. Develop "Band Definitions" document.
9. Convene global meeting with project team members to review ladder documents.
10. Develop communication plan.
11. Conduct job slotting.
12. Communication campaign.
13. Targeted presentations.
14. Corporate news service article.
15. Town hall meetings.
16. Intranet deployment.
17. Revise as necessary to ensure ladders reflect current practice.

Maintaining Relevance of Global Career Ladders

The global career ladders were designed to serve as lasting policy: The tool had to be kept relevant to the businesses and to current business practices. So from time to time, subject matter experts were reconvened to amend or suggest additional improvements. Such efforts reassured employees that the global career ladders continued to be relevant and can be used with confidence.

Aligning Employee Performance

It's not what you achieve, it's what you overcome. That's what defines your career.
~Carlton Fisk~

Aligning business goals to talent goals starts with a company's strategic plan. All successful businesses have a clear understanding of their strategy. The strategy is then reflected in business goals that align to the strategy. This requires management commitment at all levels since all managers not only have to develop the business goals but also have the ability to develop a clear line of sight from those business goals to employees goals. These plans are living, breathing documents that are revised when and if the business plans change. While technology will help facilitate, manage, and report progress, it starts with a committed management team and a solid process for execution. Senior management needs to articulate the corporate strategy and create the environment to drive that strategy down through the business. Management must align business goals with the strategy and create accountability and responsibility in the execution of those goals.

Purpose

The purpose of this technique is to align the business strategy of the corporation with an employee's preferences and skills leading to superior outcomes for both. The key concept is that defining and aligning an employee's desires (e.g., "likes and dislikes"), their capabilities, and job assignments to yield higher employee and company performance. In addition, such alignment increases employee morale, loyalty and development.

Career Coaching is a practice designed to align the corporation's objectives with an employee's performance and development over time. Successful career Coaching helps the employee increase their value to the corporation while increasing their job satisfaction and increasing retention rates.

The outcome from this process may vary depending on the situation but in all cases it should involve a clear understanding between employee and Coach of what the employee's like and dislikes, their strengths and developmental areas, and how these align with business strategy. This understanding is then documented in ways that are actionable using existing performance management processes. The complete process comprises four phases.

- **Phase 1:** The employee defines their likes and dislikes and strengths and developmental areas with the assistance of the career Coach. The Coach should be independent of the employee's management line.
- **Phase 2:** The Coach and employee then review this analysis in the context of employee's current or proposed role using a formal job description. The Coach keeps the employee's Manager updated.
- **Phase 3:** The Coach then assesses the analysis with the employee's direct Manager in the context of the department, divisional and corporate strategic objectives and annual operating plan (AOP). This requires a working knowledge of how the function fits within the business strategy and AOP.
- **Phase 4:** The employee and Manager (with or without the Coach) then create a Personal Growth Plan using the analysis in defining the employee's future role and metrics for measuring performance. The overall process can be seen in Figure 6.

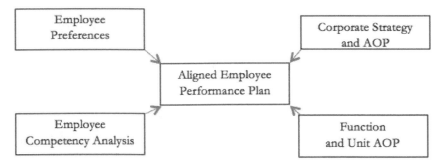

Figure 6. Aligning Employee Development with Business Strategy

Critically, the Coach and employee's manager must be aligned on the outcomes of the process before it is implemented. The Coach's role is not to replace the manager but offer an objective and teachable point of view for all parties involved. This level of transparency and understanding underpins the trust required for an employee to being an effective innovator.

Roles and Responsibilities. The process has two distinct phases: *Discovery* of the employee's preferences and *aligning* them with the business strategy and objectives. The employee leads the discovery phase, with the Coach and then engages the Manager who defines alignment. The entire process can be completed with a few one-hour meetings, although initially both the employee and Coach will likely find the process will take somewhat longer.

The Coach's role is to facilitate the employee's discovering their preferences, strengths and development areas while identifying growth opportunities. The Coach must be open-minded and listen intently during the process and not be biased. This is one reason the Coach and Manager should be different in the beginning. While the Coach in this role is providing support for the employee they must always remember that they are representing the organization during these discussions.

The Coach should not have responsibility for evaluating and measuring the employee's performance if an accurate understanding of the employee's preferences is to be obtained. This may most easily be achieved by having a Coach not responsible for directly supervising the employee to facilitate the discovery phase. The Coach can be another Manager who is open-minded about the employee.

Once the employee's preferences have been defined the Manager must assess the employee's skills triangulating the recognized preferences and skills with the Function's and Corporation's business objectives. This phase requires the direct supervisor to participate in the process.

The employee's role is to be open and honest with their Coach about their likes, dislikes, interests, skills and developmental areas, as well as the underlying rationale for these positions. It is important that they are willing to receive feedback and insights from the Coach in an open-minded way. The employee must do most of the work in assembling the starting preferences, answering the Coach's questions honestly to discern their true profile.

Coach – Employee Relationship

For this process to be effective it is important that a relationship develops between the Coach and employee. There are two key elements of the relationship: trust and acceptance. The greater the trust between the employee and Coach the more he or she can utilize the Coach as a sounding board, taking advantage of the Coach's feedback. For example: In order for the Coach to be effective they must have the employee's best interests in mind while representing the needs of the corporation. Honesty for the Coach is critical.

The more accepting, as opposed to being critical and judgmental, the Coach is of the employee, the more likely are they to help achieve a successful outcome. The Coach will be ineffective if they bring preconceived concepts to the process. This unbiased point of view is why the Coach is desired for this process over the employee's manager.

Phase 1: Discovering Employee Preferences (Likes and Dislikes) and Strengths and Developmental Areas. Phase 1 of this process involves getting to a comprehensive overview of like, dislikes, strengths and developmental areas. This provides the foundation for subsequent stages of this process. This phase can take 6-8 hours with the majority of time being spent during interviews between employee and Coach.

Prepare list of 3-5 likes and 3-5 dislikes. (Requires approximately 1 hour if employee has good understanding of themselves, otherwise they may need to spend additional time reading, completing exercises etc.)

It is important that the *employee* spends some time to understand what is really important to them. They should be open and honest about what they like and what they don't like. If the employee is struggling to define what they like and what they don't like there tools that may provide assistance. Most career related books have a chapters or exercises to help to define interests. Example (Like): Knowledge Transfer – Love being able to share learning, absorbing knowledge and sharing it with others through training/practice, applying past experiences, current learning's to new situations, sharing ideas, learning from others. Example (Dislike): Dealing with Ambiguity – Dislikes not understanding where I stand relative to direction of business. Dislikes getting mixed messages regarding the direction in which things are moving. Interview employee to get further information regarding likes and dislikes *(Requires approximately 4 hours).*

In this part of the process the *coach's* role to ask probing questions to get to the essence of what is important to the employee. Questions should also be designed to help distinguish key matches/mismatches between role and employee interests. For example: The employee likes interacting with people. Some sample questions from the coach:

1. When problem solving do you like working in groups/working alone?
2. Do you like working with people you know or people you don't know?
3. Why and under what circumstances?
4. What type of people do you enjoy working with? Why?

Strengths/Developmental Areas (Requires approximately 2 hours). This step should be completed using the standard tools and processes if available and sanctioned by the company. Standard method/testing are available online or this can be done by inquiry by the Coach. When completing the exercise keep in mind the competencies most important to your current role and/or next role (1-2yr).

*   Both the Coach and the employee should have a good understanding of the definitions of the competencies.
*   Coach and employee record their individual assessment on the tally sheet separately to avoid one assessment biasing the other.
*   A discussion occurs where assessments are compared.

There are four outcomes to look for during this discussion as follows:

- Both agree the description is a strength.
- Both agree the description is a developmental need.
- Employee thinks a description is strength but Coach thinks it is a developmental need (blind spot).
- Employee thinks a description is a developmental need but Coach thinks it is strength (hidden strength).

This is an opportunity for Coach and employees to have an open discussion. It is important that reasons and insights are shared regarding 3 and 4 so that each understands the others position. The top three strengths and top three developmental needs are identified for incorporation into the Personal Growth Plan (PGP).

Phase 2: Aligning the Employee's Preferences, Strengths and Developmental areas, are aligned with their role and the function helping achieve the company's annual plans. It is important to understand if there are any major mismatches between likes and dislikes and what it will take to fulfill role responsibilities in meeting the business objectives defined in the annual and quarterly performance plans. Phase 2 consists of two steps, using the information in phase 1 to create a personal growth plan and reviewing current role in context of likes and dislikes for any key mismatches/opportunity areas relative to desired business objectives. This phase should take (2-4 hours).

Draft Personal Growth Plan (PGP) based on identified developmental areas (2-3 hours). A personal growth plan is created focusing on three key areas for development as outlined during Phase 1. This should be documented in the standard format. Critical to a successful PGP is defining who is going to support in the development of this competency. This may be the Manager, a colleague who is stronger in this particular skill, a mentor or some other person/team. Each development area plan should be described with the following elements:

Specific Competency/Development Goal for Growth. Describe competency being developed and any specific related goals. It is important that the employee understand their motivation to improve their skills in this area. Likewise they should understand any obstacles/barriers to accomplishing the objective and potential solutions to overcoming these barriers. The key components of the PGP are:

1. Identify and document the development area clearly,
2. Define specifics tasks and actions required for improvement,
3. Identify the metrics for measuring progress,
4. Establish review dates.

Example of Development Area – Planning. Planning – Improve planning skills, creating and following plan. Learn to accurately scope out length and difficulty of tasks and projects. Learn to anticipate and adjust for problems and roadblocks.

Tasks/Actions to be completed. This section should describe specific actions to be taken to meet goal. *Create project plan and timeline for pilot and implementation of a tool for managing unsolicited technology proposals.*

Metrics. It is sometimes difficult to focus on many development areas at once. This section should describe when focus will be on this area and any key milestones that can be used to measure progress. *Plan with key elements around scope and objectives, timelines, action plans etc. has been created and reviewed by project leader by end of Q1.*

Review Dates. It is important that periodic review and or key milestone are built into the plan normally quarterly.

Review role in context of employee preferences (1-2 hours). The current/anticipated role should be reviewed in the context of likes/dislikes. While it is unlikely that a person will like 100% of their job it is important that a person's role has a larger proportion of things that the employee likes than that which the employee doesn't like. This in turn results in a more motivated employee base. Some key things to look out for are if

- Employee dislikes are mission critical to the role.
- Employee likes match a key gap in another role.

In this section it is important to define any areas of importance and over time work with the employee to build solutions into their development plan and or discuss possible role changes.

Aligning employee preferences, competencies and development areas with the Corporation's objectives. This final, critical step is the employee meets with their Manager and Coach where the Coach hands off the employee analysis to the Manager. Engaging the manager fully, with the Coach and employee, readies the employee to engage in alignment discussions of the employee's PGP and the work groups and company's goals and strategies.

The Manager must be in clear control of the corporate strategy and how it impacts their function and work group. From this understanding the Manager can intelligently provide feedback to the employee and adjust their work assignments utilizing the above analysis. Triangulating the employee's preferences and competencies with the Corporation's objectives leads to great achievement and higher job satisfaction. The alignment process begins with the functional plan, derived and aligned with the corporate strategy, and further aligned with the work unit plan.

The work unit plan should be a culmination of projects aligned with key initiatives derived from the objectives in the Corporate and Functional plans. As an example: The Open Innovation Group in RD&E has a role in sourcing technologies from external parties to meet the innovation needs of the Corporation. Successful completion of this role requires a planning, searching and assessment activities and capabilities. In the example above this specific individual needs to develop planning capabilities in the context of sourcing external technologies. While planning is generic when applied to Open Innovation sourcing good planning capabilities now requires specific skills around intellectual property management, communication skills and timing.

Annual Performance Planning

The goal of performance planning is to help every employee contribute what they can to make the firm successful and not to find ways for the employee to fail by missing their objectives. Critical to this outcome is that ambiguity and uncertainty are recognized as part of any planning process and these need to be reconciled as new knowledge is acquired.

For example an employee's plan is case at the end of the previous year in which it'll be measured. Given the knowledge at that time certain objectives are defined with strategies for achieving them with appropriate metrics and a vision of what success looks like. Shortly into the planning cycle – the year the plan is valid for – information is received that indicates the objective cannot be achieved or shouldn't be achieved for a good business reason. As soon as this is known the plan needs to be revised so it remains current. If the planning method is too rigid then this revision may not be possible leading the employee and the firm to fail.

Another critical success factor in developing the annual plan is to be sure the metrics are truly measurable and reflective of achievement. Generally, the more definitive the objective the more *quantitative* the metrics can be and the more ambiguous the more *qualitative* the metrics. For example if the objective defines a certain number of tests will be performed, at a certain level of quality, over a period of time this is easily measured along with what defines above plan performance. However, if the objective involves a discovery that may or may not be possible, then the process of doing the research should be measured along with what was discovered. Further, in discovery research, unexpected events occur which are more valuable than the original objective and these need to be captured and not ignored because they aren't credited in the plan.

There are two basic performance-planning methods. The oldest is Management by Objectives, also known as the MBO process and a more recent method known by the abbreviation S.M.A.R.T. for Smart, Measurable, Assignable, Realistic and Time-bound.

Management by objectives (MBO), also known as management by results (MBR), is a process of defining objectives within an organization so that management and employees agree to the objectives and understand what they need to do in the organization in order to achieve them. The term "management by objectives" was first popularized by Peter Drucker in his 1954 book *The Practice of Management*.[37]

The essence of MBO is participative goal setting, choosing course of actions and decision-making. An important part of the MBO is the measurement and the comparison of the employee's actual performance with the standards set. Ideally, but not always, when employees themselves have been involved with the goal setting and choosing the course of action to be followed by them, they are more likely to fulfill their responsibilities.

According to George S. Odiorne, the system of management by objectives can be described as a process whereby the superior and subordinate jointly identify its common goals, define each individual's major areas of responsibility in terms of the results expected of him, and use these measures as guides for operating the unit and assessing the contribution of each of its members.[38]

MBO has its detractors and attention notably among them W. Edwards Deming, who argued that a lack of understanding of systems commonly results in the misapplication of objectives.[39] Additionally, Deming stated that setting production targets will encourage workers to meet those targets through whatever means necessary, which usually results in poor quality.[40] Point 7 of Deming's key principles encourages managers to abandon objectives in favor of leadership because he felt that a leader with an understanding of systems was more likely to guide workers to an appropriate solution than the incentive of an objective. Deming also pointed out that Drucker warned managers that a systemic view was required[41] and felt that Drucker's warning went largely unheeded by the practitioners of MBO.

---

[37] Drucker, Peter F., "The Practice of Management", in 1954. ISBN 0-06-011095-3

[38] Odiorne, George S., "Management by Objectives; a System of Managerial Leadership", New ISBN 0-06-011095-3 York: Pitman Pub., 1965.

[39] Deming, W. Edwards, "Out of the Crisis", The MIT Press, 1994, ISBN 0-262-54116-5

[40] Deming's 14 Points and Quality Project Leadership *J. Alex Sherrer, March 3, 2010*

[41] Drucker, Peter, "Management Tasks, Responsibilities, Practices", Harper & Row, 1973

An evolution of the MBO method is called S.M.A.R.T. for Specific, Measurable, Assignable, Realistic and Time-related. The S.M.A.R.T. method helps address Deming's objections by taking into account that at any given moment in time new knowledge can make the original performance "wrong" or ill conceived. Using the SMART method requires collaboration between the manager and employee so that a dialogue takes place and plans are updated on a periodic basis often quarterly.

The November 1981 issue of *Management Review* contained a paper by George T. Doran called *There's a S.M.A.R.T. way to write management's goals and objectives.*[42] It discussed the importance of objectives and the difficulty of setting them. Ideally speaking, each corporate, department, and section objective should be:

- *Specific* – target a specific area for improvement.
- *Measurable* – quantify or at least suggest an indicator of progress.
- *Assignable* – specify who will do it.
- *Realistic* – state what results can realistically be achieved, given available resources.
- *Time-related* – specify when the result(s) can be achieved.

Notice that these criteria don't say that all objectives must be quantified on all levels of management. In certain situations it is not realistic to attempt quantification, particularly in staff middle-management positions. Practicing managers and corporations can lose the benefit of a more abstract objective in order to gain quantification. It is the combination of the objective and its action plan that is really important. Therefore

Each letter in SMART[43] refers to a different criterion for judging objectives. Different sources use the letters to refer to different things. Typically accepted criteria are as follows. Choosing certain combinations of these labels can cause duplication, such as selecting 'attainable' and 'realistic', or can cause significant overlapping as in combining 'appropriate' and 'relevant' for example. The term 'agreed' is often used in management situations where buy-in from stakeholders is desirable (e.g. appraisal situations).

---

[42] Doran, G. T. (1981). "There's a S.M.A.R.T. way to write management's goals and objectives." *Management Review* (AMA FORUM) **70** (11): 35–36.

[43] Meyer, Paul J (2003). "What would you do if you knew you couldn't fail? Creating S.M.A.R.T. Goals". *Attitude Is Everything: If You Want to Succeed Above and Beyond.* Meyer Resource Group, Incorporated, The. ISBN 978-0-89811-304-4

Specific. The criterion stresses the need for a specific goal rather than a more general one. This means the goal is clear and unambiguous; without vagaries and platitudes. To make goals specific, they must tell a team exactly what's expected, why it's important, who's involved, where it's going to happen and which attributes are important. A specific goal will usually answer the five 'W' questions:

1. What: What do I want to accomplish?
2. Why: Specific reasons, purpose or benefits of accomplishing the goal.
3. Who: Who is involved?
4. Where: Identify a location.
5. Which: Identify requirements and constraints.

Measurable. The second criterion stresses the need for concrete criteria for measuring progress toward the attainment of the goal. The thought behind this is that if a goal is not measurable it is not possible to know whether a team is making progress toward successful completion. Measuring progress is supposed to help a team stay on track, reach its target dates and experience the exhilaration of achievement that spurs it on to continued effort required to reach the ultimate goal. A measurable goal will usually answer questions such as:

1. How much?
2. How many?
3. How will I know when it is accomplished?
4. Indicators should be quantifiable

Attainable. The third criterion stresses the importance of goals that are realistic and also attainable. Whilst an attainable goal may stretch a team in order to achieve it, the goal is not extreme. That is, the goals are neither out of reach nor below standard performance, since these may be considered meaningless. When you identify goals that are most important to you, you begin to figure out ways you can make them come true. You develop the attitudes, abilities, skills and financial capacity to reach them. The theory states that an attainable goal may cause goal-setters to identify previously overlooked opportunities to bring themselves closer to the achievement of their goals. An achievable goal will usually answer the question How?

- How can the goal be accomplished?
- How realistic is the goal based on other constraints?

Relevant. The fourth criterion stresses the importance of choosing goals that matter. A bank manager's goal to "Make 50 peanut butter and jelly sandwiches by 2pm" may be specific, measurable, attainable and time-bound but lacks relevance. Many times you will need support to accomplish a goal: resources, a champion voice, someone to knock down obstacles. Goals that are relevant to your boss, your team, your organization will receive that needed support. Relevant goals (when met) drive the team, department and organization forward. A goal that supports or is in alignment with other goals would be considered a relevant goal. A relevant goal can answer yes to these questions:

1. Does this seem worthwhile?
2. Is this the right time?
3. Does this match our other efforts/needs?
4. Are you the right person?
5. Is it applicable in the current socio- economic environment?

Time-bound. The fifth criterion stresses the importance of grounding goals within a time-frame, giving them a target date. A commitment to a deadline helps a team focus their efforts on completion of the goal on or before the due date. This part of the SMART goal criteria is intended to prevent goals from being overtaken by the day-to-day crises that invariably arise in an organization. A time-bound goal is intended to establish a sense of urgency. A time-bound goal will usually answer the question

1. When?
2. What can I do six months from now?
3. What can I do six weeks from now?
4. What can I do today?

Chapter 5 Summary

More and more people in the workforce, and most knowledge workers, will have to manage themselves. They will have to place themselves where they can make the greatest contribution; they will have to learn to develop themselves. They will have to learn how to stay young and mentally alive during a fifty-year working life. They will also have to learn how and when to change what they do, how they do it, and when they do it.

Knowledge workers are likely to outlive their employing organization. Even if knowledge workers postpone entry into the labor force as long as possible, such as staying in school into their late twenties to get a doctorate, they are likely to live into their eighties. And they are likely to have to keep working, even if only part-time, until they are at least seventy- five or older. The average working life, in other words, is likely to be fifty years, especially for knowledge workers. But the average life expectancy of a successful business is only thirty years, and even that is optimistic in today's turbulent times. Those that do survive will change their structure, the work they are doing, the knowledge they require, and the kind of people they employ.

Now, even people of modest abilities will have to learn to manage themselves. Knowledge workers facing drastically new demands must ask themselves questions such as the following:

1. What are my strengths?
2. How do I perform?
3. What are my values?
4. Where do I belong?
5. What is my contribution?
6. How do I take relationship responsibility?
7. How do I plan for the second half of my life?

Aligning business goals to talent of the employee base and with the company's strategic plan is critical to success. All successful businesses have a clear understanding of their strategy, which is then reflected in business goals that align with each employee's personal performance plan. This requires every level of management being committed and accountable for being sure that each employee's annual plan facilitates the execution of the strategy. These plans are living, breathing documents that are revised when and if the business circumstances change.

While technology will help facilitate the process the ultimate success factor is the conversation and understanding that exists between employees and their direct supervisors. With the advent of "Big Data" – databases so large and growing so fast they defy understanding – combined with the empowering nature of the internet drives decision making closest to the work hence favoring "flat" organizational designs.

Hierarchical designs were effective when data was limited and few leaders had the knowledge to interpret the data and act on it. Today's employees are "Knowledge Workers" and by virtue of being self-managed they are capable of acting on data and information impacting their roles.

The lubricant for the innovative culture is the combination of the proper alignment of strategy with personal performance objectives facilitated by an effective organizational design where information flows to where it is needed in a timely manner creating actionable knowledge leading to the best decisions possible.

Today, in the era of the knowledge worker, more responsibility will be offered lower in the organization. Instead of management making critical decisions they'll be made by the employee with the greatest knowledge and most likely closest to the customer. This new location of power requires that each employee have a well-defined and measurable annual plan. The best approach is to use the S.M.A.R.T. methodology combined with an open assessment of the ambiguity, or lack thereof, is establishing the objectives, strategies for achieving these objectives with metrics and a description of a successful outcome.

Chapter 5 Critical Questions

1. Does the employee's explicit and implicate objectives align with those of the business and how is this alignment described?
2. What evidence exists for knowing the planning process is effective?
3. How will the resulting performance plan will be measured and adjusted if required?
4. How will the Coach and employee's manager interact to be sure that role conflicts are avoided or managed if they occur?
5. How does the employee planning process facilitate the employee becoming more innovative as part of establishing an innovative culture?
6. How might the employee performance planning process inhibit the creation of an innovative culture?
7. How ambiguous are the objectives and how does this impact metrics?
8. Who is accountable for managing update reviews and how often will they occur?
9. What role do Human Resources have in the performance planning process?
10. How well does the plan align with the S.M.A.R.T method?

Chapter 6: Financial Planning Process

Planning is bringing the future into the present so that you can do something about it now.
~Alan Lakein ~

The Role of the Technologist: A Financial Perspective

New technologists start out with a limited understanding of finance, but they must develop an understanding of how investments in technology, especially their projects, create a return for the firm. This section explores some fundamental concepts of finance that are particularly useful to Technologists in relationship to decision-making. One caution: The Technologist must cultivate a strong partnership with the finance department and rely on its expertise in assessing potential risk and returns rather than pretending to be financial experts themselves. However, the Technologist must speak the language of finance in order to have this relationship. Importantly, financial results drive all firms – even those that are non-profits.

Finance is the study of the allocation of resources within the firm. It helps managers and companies of all sizes ask the right questions:

- How do they make investment decisions about the current use of resources for future gain?
- How should they manage the financing of investment decisions?
- What effect do these decisions have on shareholder value and other constituencies such as management, labor, suppliers, customers, government, and society over time?

Technology spending is in the short term (the current annual budget) is an expense, and over the longer term (five years) is an investment. In either case the resources must be used wisely. In both cases, financial considerations should drive decision-making and is the responsibility of anyone using the firm's resources. Technologists must consider resources entrusted to their use as a source of future value, and this value must be significantly better than other uses of these resources.

While there are many kinds of technical projects, this section will only consider two: Those that increase revenues at equal or greater profitability currently available and those that reduce costs. Projects increasing revenues are to grow the firm are often referred to as *"growing the top line,"* and those reducing costs as *"growing the bottom line."* Every technologist must realize that there are other potential uses of these resources, giving rise to a term called the *"discount rate"* or an alternative use of resources at equal risk and return. Technologists must always compete for resources, so it's their job to *"sell"* their idea as better than any alternative uses of resources.

Project Types – Revenue Growth vs. Cost Reduction

Revenue growth projects are often much higher risk and therefore the return needs to be higher, usually by a factor of 5-20 or more. Said another way, investments in R&D are uses of the firm's net income (e.g., cash after all expenses and taxes are paid).

For example, if a firm's net profit is 5%, then for every dollar of net income invested in R&D, $100 of revenue is required to break-even. The reason investments in technology make sense is that when successful, the revenues can exist for as long as the product is valuable to customers – the offering's product lifecycle. One complex concept, beyond the scope of this discussion, is the estimate of the net value of a new product if that product displaces (i.e., cannibalizes) an existing product. This estimate yields the true value of the innovation to the firm.

Projects reducing costs have a greater return than revenue growth projects because these are often calculated on a net income basis, so a 2-for-1 return is acceptable. For example, if a project reduces raw material costs by $1 a pound, then that $1 dollar becomes net profit. Such projects are often incremental in nature and, while important, are not sufficient as the entire portfolio. A proper balance of short-term cost savings projects with those that grow revenues at an acceptable profit margin yields a portfolio creating value over the longer term.

Like any management tool, finance cannot stand alone. Technologists need to harmonize the technical and financial considerations in their decisions. They must remember that their primary concern is creating value over time and that value comes from customers buying products and services in a competitive market. These offerings must consider all aspects of delivery and utilization to be successful. The technologist must use process tools like *Stage Gates* and *project management* to construct an offering that can be delivered in a finished form that is easy to use. An offering that is too difficult to make, deliver, or use will fall short of creating real value. All innovations must strive for leadership in their utility, be easily used, and repaired if need be. The technologist must consider all these constraints in developing their innovations.

Technologists are value creators, investing today in hopes of generating cash tomorrow. They must understand what cash flow will do; they must understand and manage risk; they must understand how value is determined. Technologists differentiate themselves by thinking through problems from the financial perspective.

Table 2. Key Relationships -- Technologists vs Accountants

Topic	Technologist as Financial Analyst	Financial Accounting	Comments
Cash	What is happening with the cash	How much cash is available	Views cash in present (current period) vs. future
Expenditures	Investment for future return	Expense against current earnings	Spending as an investment vs. cost
Economic Income	Focused on free cash flow[1]	Focused on total cash flow	Cash available for investment vs. current operations

[1]Free cash flows defined as net income plus depreciation, minus require investments in working capital, plant, and equipment. It takes into account both benefits and costs of investing.

In the following paragraphs, I identify certain concepts and tools of finance that are useful to technologists, followed by a description of how to create an R&D Budget that is aligned with specific outcomes described in objectives used to construct the annual plan. The annual plan is further described as a portfolio of projects and tasks which must be managed over the next planning period (usually 12 months). Conceptually, the technology annual plan and budget is a written along with a financial summary of the project portfolio and routine tasks by which the resources will be used over a given planning period (normally a year). Further, the annual technical plan and budget then links directly to every employee's annual plan. While very desirable, these absolute linkages are rarely achieved, but coherent planning is absolutely required of even the smallest firms.

Reading a Profit and Loss (P&L) Statement[44]

The profit and loss statement is the language of the business, and every technologist must learn to read a simple P&L statement. Doing so increases the technologist's credibility in the eyes of their commercial colleagues, and helps them understand how their work impacts the future of the firm.

---

[44] Understanding Finance: Expert Solutions to Everyday Challenges, Harvard Business School Press, 2007, ISBN-13:978-1-4221-1883-2

An excellent summary can be found in a brief publication titled *Understanding Finance* from Harvard Business School Press under their Pocket Mentor series. It is easy to understand and employ without being an accountant or finance expert. Attempting to be a financial *expert* will damage the credibility of the technologist, but knowing the language is key.

The Annual Plan and Budget

Aligning Resource Utilization with Outcomes

The Annual Plan and Budget (AP&B) is a document describing the use of resources against a series of high-level descriptors that will be embodied in projects and tasks in a given year. It is important that these two very different viewpoints are harmonized to communicate what each technologist is supposed to achieve and ultimately how they'll be measured. The AP&B should be a simple, easy-to-understand and measurable beginning with a recognizable format devoid of extraneous information.

Table 3. Planning Summary

Plan Element	Element Content
Plan Summary and Overview	Current situation, key issues and action plans
Vision, Mission and Objectives	What's our purpose, what will we achieve and how will we describe it?
Objective, Strategies and Action Plans	What will we work on, how will we be successful and what will we measure?
Financial and Resource Plan	Budget by unit and spending category including capital spending by project
Past Years Accomplishments	What resulted from recent investment
Appendix	Linkage to Strategic Plan 3 to 5 years forward.

Plan Summary and Overview

The plan summary and overview should very briefly summarize the plan in less than five pages and include a description of the organization's challenges and key issues. The intent of this section is to provide a concise description of what will be described in detail later in the planning document.

Vision, Mission and Objectives

The vision and mission statements should be internally consistent and concise in describing the purpose is for each function. For example, the vision and mission of an R&D function could be the following:

Vision: R&D provides the right technology and services, when and where needed, that assure the continued satisfaction of our customers and success of the corporation.

Mission: The R&D division provides valuable information, services, and technology critical to the development of offerings that meet or exceed our customers' expectations in a manner consistent with responsible care.

Objectives: The division supports corporate goals and objectives by:

- Creating valuable information through data oriented problem-solving.
- Enhancing our capability and maintaining the focus on core technologies that provide value-added products to our customers and assure a leadership position in our industry.
- Developing new technologies to provide future commercial impact.
- Providing the manufacturing capability for market development.
- Creating and protecting corporate intellectual property.
- Recruiting and developing capable, technical personnel.
- Reducing the time and cost required to create valuable information leading to products and services for customers.
- Leading the process of redefining the role of technology for the corporation to create maximum sustainable competitive advantage.
- Creating an environment where R&D staff achieve their full potential.
- Improving research and development processes for managing valuable information, ensuring acceptable ROI for these activities.

Strategies and Action Plans by Objective

This section of the plan links to the summary before it. It has each individual objective stated as it was in the summary with brief descriptions of the strategies to be employed and key issues to overcome with the action plans to be funded by the budget and implemented. It closes with a description of what success looks like. It identifies the leaders for each objective and those accountable for outcomes.

This summary treatment of the strategies is followed with more detailed descriptors of what is involved and the specific action plans required with milestones and a description of what success looks like. For example the strategies, objectives and action plans might look like the following.

Objective 1: Reduce the time and cost required for creating valuable information leading to products and services for our customers.
Team Members:
1.   Leader identified with team members to follow.
Primary Strategies:
   •   Continue identifying/implementing process improvement efforts.
Issues statement(s):
   (i)   Identifying the most attractive processes to improve given most processes don't stand alone.
   (ii)   Balance resources between improving the above processes and ongoing operations.
Action Plan(s):
1.   Promote the need to become more efficient within each department, encouraging employees to identify opportunities to be funded.
2.   Provide a source of funds to pay employees for their contributions beyond their normal compensation.

Vision of Success:
1.   Employees proactively identify opportunities for improvement.
2.   These opportunities are assessed and acted upon with funding or a reason for not funding the suggestion.
3.   Employees are recognized and reviewed with the R&D staff.
4.   Improved processes are monitored for expected results and reported on quarterly. Savings are reflected in future budgets.

Developing the Annual Operating Budget
   The descriptive portion of the plan is then represented in the divisional budget by department and spending category, such as…

1.   Direct against specific projects supported by the business units,
2.   Against corporate supported investments which impact multiple business units or reach beyond 3 years into the future,
3.   Market development manufacturing done within R&D for customer sampling.

   These corporate projects are funded in full view of all business units who can comment on their potential value but cannot stop the projects on their own. Administrative activities, depreciation and utilities are allocated against the project portfolio by a predetermined methodology. A simple methodology is to allocate indirect costs by size of the business unit. For example a business unit consuming 20% of the R&D budget would pay for 20% of the allocated costs. Another methodology is to allocate based on business unit revenues. The goal is to have as much of the budget directly assigned to specific projects captured via a project accounting system. Ideally, no more than 20% of the total budget should be allocated.

Since R&D is largely driven by personnel investments, the budget is slanted towards employee-related spending including salaries, benefits, and any long-term costs such as disability leave. The last element of the budget is capital expenditures on items such as equipment that are depreciated over a schedule dictated by the government rules. A typical budget might look like the following:

Operating Expenses	Year ($MM)
R&D Administration	2.1
Regulatory Compliance	1.7
IT Support	10.2
Overhead (depreciation, utilities)	1.8
Total Indirect Expenses	**15.8**
Direct Expenses to projects	**72.1**
Total Operating Expenses	**87.8**
Market Development Charges (Income)	1.0
Total R&D Budget	**86.8**
Staffing Plan	
Regular employees	638
Contract employees	90
Total staffing	**728**
Capital Expenditures	**21.2**

The operating budget would then be captured in a general ledger where expenses would be charged against very specific accounts such as salaries, benefits, utilities, specific supplies, etc. Each department budget would have expenses assigned similarly with people within each department charging against projects using a project number that aligned with either a business unit and market segment or a corporate account.

Corporate investments were intended to blunt any business unit from over-emphasizing the current year at the expense of the future since product development and product lifecycles we're so long. In businesses where this is not the case, the corporate investment could be eliminated or reduced since the business units should be able to reconcile their future and current-year investments.

Metrics: R&D Investments with Business Performance[4546]

There are many ways to assess the impact of R&D investments on the business. A common metric is the percent of revenues from products containing innovations developed within the last 3-5 years. This metric is often dependent on product lifecycles. Generally, the shorter the lifecycle the higher the percentage of innovations should be found in these products. If a smart phone has a lifecycle of 2 years, then the percentage of products containing innovations might approach 90% since a new product wouldn't be introduced if it wasn't more innovative (useful to customers) than the product it's replacing. Alternatively, if a product has a life cycle of 10 years and sales don't grow for an additional 2 years post-introduction, then a 5-year timeframe makes more sense, and a level of 50% of revenues from products released in the past 5 years would be significant.

Clearly, the metric must fit the business situation. Misapplication of the metric can lead to erroneous conclusions and ultimately bad decisions about the performance of R&D. The Industrial Research Institute (I.R.I.) has published many articles written by practitioners on how to measure the technology ROI. These methods are reported by actual practitioners and therefore are pertinent to any technologist learning how to measure their overall impact on their firms.

1994 IRI Survey and Analysis[4748]

In defining the value and effectiveness of innovation investments, most companies have reported on outcome-based metrics that include percent of revenues from innovation, trends in market share, customer satisfaction, and gross margins associated with innovation portfolios. These and other established metrics are used to demonstrate the degree of success of a company's investment in the design, production, marketing, and sales of products and services within an innovation portfolio. It is also well established that successful innovation requires the combined efforts of multiple operating functions. These functions include HR, marketing, regulatory, sales, legal, and value chain as well as R&D. The challenge of leadership within each of those functions is to define metrics that...

---

[45] Tipping, James W., Zeffren, Eugene and Fusfeld, Alan R. "Assessing the Value of Your Technology." *Research & Technology Management,* Sept-Oct. 1995, pp.22-39.

[46] Bean, Alden S., Russo, M. Jean and Whiteley, Roger L. "Benchmarking Your R&D: Results from IRI/CIMS Annual R&D Survey for FY'96." *Research & Technology Management,* Jan.-Feb. 1998, pp.21-30.

[47] RTEC (2007) Findings on the current state of RD&E measurement. Corporate Executive Board, Washington, DC

[48] Fusfeld et al. (2009) Measuring R&D Effectiveness: Metrics Surveys. Industrial Research Institute, Chicago, IL

1. Exist within their span of control.
2. Contribute to the overall enterprise value of innovation.
3. Include measurements of activities leading to successful innovation.

The purpose here is to define innovation metrics that R&D can measure, improve, and report as part of its role in innovation. Multiple functions in any given company drive successful innovation. Across all technology-driven industries, the following five managerial factors contain metrics that can be used to measure R&D's role in innovation:

1. Value Creation: Measurements of the value of innovation activities.
2. Portfolio Assessment: Measurements of the strength of the innovation portfolio relative to elements which include resource intensity, time-to-deliver and alignment to core competencies.
3. Business Integration: Measurements of not only the commitment of the company to R&D but the extent of teamwork and the ability to exploit both new and existing technology.
4. Asset Value of Technology: Measurements of both technical know-how and physical intellectual assets
5. Practice of R&D Processes to Support Innovation: Measurements of the efficiency and effectiveness of R&D processes including project management and other "best practices" in innovation management.

The above five factors originally outlined in 1995 have formed the foundation of metrics used by R&D organizations worldwide and are captured within the Technology Value Pyramid (TVP). More importantly, metrics R&D manages within the TVP categories must align to the operational and strategic needs of the firm. R&D must be founded on:

1. Having specific capabilities to discover, design, develop, and deliver, products and services supporting the business.
2. Being proactive in proposing solutions in support of the business strategy and objectives.
3. Understanding the product portfolio and the customer application of the products.
4. Having the capabilities to deliver product and application development supporting the global business's growth objectives.
5. Knowledge for optimizing customer processes (e.g. best practice sharing and performance monitoring).
6. Capabilities to drive cost out of our portfolio and ensure timely compliance with changes in the global regulatory landscape.
7. Delivering proprietary and disruptive technology platforms (either developed in-house or sourced externally).

The firm's R&D capabilities listed above of are consistent with the four factors: Processes, Asset Value of Technology, Business Integration, and Portfolio Assessment. Furthermore, each enable Value Creation as described in the TVP model. Examination of critical needs for improvement gets progressively closer to defining R&D metrics relevant to the firm. Key drivers for the R&D organization are (i) Strategic Technology Development, (ii) Product Lifecycle Management, including Portfolio & Project Management, and (iii) Customer Technical Service.

An overview of metrics from 1994, and associated end-states relevant to the firm, as described in the TVP are shown in the following tables, providing the firm's leadership a way of measuring the effectiveness of investments in innovation.

Table 4. 1994 R&D Innovation Metrics, Asset Value of Technology

Factor	The Firm's Need and End-State	Metric(s)
Asset Value of Technology Measurements of both technical know-how and physical intellectual assets	1. Quality of RD&E product development and service personnel for Innovation Management, Product Range Management and Product Services 2. Number and strength of patents 3. Sales protected by proprietary positions 4. Fraction of future sales and/or net income projected from projects in the RD&E pipeline	1. Rating scale from RD&E's internal customers (e.g., Marketing, Value Chain, Sales) and external customers (e.g., strategic accounts) 2. Percent of active patents which are known to be used to defend intellectual property of the firm 3. Percent of sales protected by patents owned by the firm and/or trade secrets or other exclusivity mechanisms 4. Forecasted sales and/or net income in project plan by year across innovation portfolio

Table 5. 1994 R&D Innovation Metrics, RD&E Processes

Factor	The Firm's Need and End-State	Metric(s)
RD&E Processes The efficiency and effectiveness of RD&E processes including project management and other "best practices" in innovation management	1. Fraction of projects in the total portfolio going through a defined project management system with defined milestones. 2. Percent across of projects of development milestones achieved 3. Global IT platform supporting all PPM and PLM activities 4. Platforms for the management of RD&E capacity and technical capabilities 5. Preservation (i.e., knowledge retention) of technical output 6. Cost efficiency of internal product development processes. 7. RD&E Employee Morale 8. Fraction of projects in the total portfolio going through a defined project management system with defined milestones. 9. Percent across of projects of development milestones achieved 10. Global IT platform supporting all PPM and PLM activities 11. Platforms for the management of RD&E capacity and technical capabilities 12. Preservation (i.e., knowledge retention) of technical output 13. Cost efficiency of internal product development processes.	1. Fraction of projects across total RD&E project portfolio 2. Percent of project milestones achieved within their targeted timeframe 3. Extent of geographic deployment (shared metric with IT and Marketing) 4. Extent of deployment of Time Tracking and Capability Inventory 5. Percent of technical reports authored and maintained on Agile 6. The cost and/or number of launched projects divided by the cost and/or number of launched projects 7. Survey-based ratings of key aspects of employee satisfaction 8. Fraction of projects across total RD&E project portfolio 9. Percent of project milestones achieved within their targeted timeframe (e.g., 3-months from initiation to reach field testing) 10. Extent of geographic deployment (shared metric with IT and Marketing) 11. Extent of deployment of Time Tracking and Capability Inventory 12. Percent of technical reports authored and maintained on Agile 13. The cost and/or number of launched projects divided by the cost and/or number of launched projects

Table 6. 1994 R&D Innovation Metrics, Business Integration

Factor	The Firm's Need and End-State	Metric(s)
Business Integration Measurements of not only the commitment of the company to RD&E but the extent of teamwork and the ability to exploit both new & existing technology	8. Current annual expenditures for RD&E staff and equipment benchmarked to competitors 9. Number of project definitions having Marketing approval 10. Alignment of RD&E to strategic marketing, with dedicated resources for ensuring on-the-ground technical product support, application expert service and consistent execution of engineering support functions 11. Fraction of RD&E project portfolio which is explicitly consistent with Diversey's AOP 12. Fraction of RD&E project portfolio which is responsive to emerging unmet requirements of Diversey customers 13. Fraction of projects in the RD&E with specific cross-functional teams assigned, subdivided by NPD project definitions and/or time requirements (short-term v. long-term)	4. RD&E budget relative to the firm's revenue and/or budget 5. Fraction of project portfolio 6. Extent of Deployment (rating scale) 7. Fraction of projects across total portfolio of projects 8. Fraction of projects across total portfolio of projects 9. Fraction of projects across total portfolio of projects

Table 7. 1994 R&D Innovation Metrics, Portfolio Assessment

Factor	The Firm's Need and End-State	Metric(s)
Portfolio Assessment Measurements of the strength of the innovation portfolio relative to elements which include resource intensity, time-to-deliver and alignment to core competencies	1. Fraction of projects discovered and initiated in-house versus use of externally source innovation resources 2. Cycle time from identification of customer need to availability of solution for commercialization 3. Distribution of technology investments by various dimensions, including • alignment to AOP, • risk vs. reward, • by technical platform • by resource intensity, • sustainability-driven, • regulatory-driven, • project type • Core Competency versus New competency • Global versus Regional 4. Extent of portfolio exploitation and/or search & re-apply 5. Extent and progress of RD&E's role in portfolio simplification	1. Fraction of projects across total portfolio of projects 2. Time from project approval to release into commercialization process 3. Fraction of projects, budget and FTEs across total portfolio of projects 4. Extent of Deployment (rating scale) 5. Progress by RD&E teams relative to established milestones

IRI Metrics 1994 Compared to 2009

The updated set of metrics to measure the effectiveness of R&D has been a major need for research managers for some time. In a 2009 survey of IRI participants, the need for metrics has ranked in the top three for several years. The enhanced importance of reliable metrics is being driven by several forces: The need to justify the investment in R&D to senior management, the desire to improve efficiency in the use of R&D resources, and the need for a means to estimate the value of the R&D investment for the future growth of the company.

The Technology Value Pyramid

One of the key challenges of implementing R&D metrics is matching metrics to the various levels and functions of the R&D organization, so that metrics are meaningful to the appropriate personnel. A bench scientist's metrics, for instance, should be related to his or her accomplishments, while the CEO or general manager should have more overarching metrics related to the performance of the organization under his or her responsibility. A metric for financial return makes sense for a CEO or CTO but has little direct meaning for a bench scientist.

Conversely, the number of patents issued may make sense as a measure of performance for the bench scientist but is not directly meaningful for the CEO. Categorizing metrics by their relevance to the particular components that make up the eventual value of the R&D investment addresses this by allowing metrics to be targeted to the most relevant levels of the organization. In this way, bench scientists can access relevant measures of their group's performance, while managers get the quantitative measures they need—not just to rate the return on the R&D investment but to answer the key question, "are we doing the right things?"

An earlier ROR group developed the TVP (Figure 7), a model that takes this approach to categorizing metrics. The TVP provides a hierarchy of metrics based on the fundamental elements of R&D value and the relationships of those elements to business results in the long and short term. Value creation metrics at the apex of the TVP investigate the financial returns arising from the investment in R&D. The returns are impacted by the Pyramid's next segments, portfolio assessment and integration with the business. Portfolio assessment metrics examine the distribution of the R&D investment in terms of risk, timing, and potential return. Metrics addressing integration with the business focus on the interaction of R&D and the business groups in terms of process, teamwork, and organization. The foundations of the TVP are the asset value of the technology and the practices of R&D. Asset value of technology metrics address the development of core competencies that are essential for growth and competitiveness. Metrics assessing the practices of R&D investigate the procedures, culture, and operations of the R&D organization and their ability to contribute to enhancing technology development.

For example, financial metrics fall in the outcome and strategy tier of the pyramid, while a measure of the number of technical reports produced falls in the foundations level. The group then surveyed 161 IRI members about the R&D metrics they used, asking participants to rank the 33 identified metrics in order of importance. Over the years, some companies have expressed a sense that the metrics available did not adequately quantify their own corporate needs. This resulted in the creation of newer metrics. Some of these new metrics were eventually added to the TVP dictionary, so that the list now incorporated into the TVP includes a total of 50 metrics.

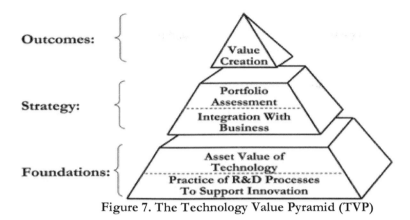

Figure 7. The Technology Value Pyramid (TVP)

Fifteen years after the publication of the original TVP survey in 1994, a new ROR subcommittee convened to revitalize the TVP, determine whether there has been a shift in the metrics used to measure R&D, and identify any new metrics that should be added to the TVP. The group also sought to determine whether the importance of particular metrics varies by industry or innovation strategy.

New surveys on R&D metrics

In an effort to answer these questions, the current group, measuring the effectiveness of R&D, administered two surveys. The first, survey A, was largely a repeat of the original 1994 survey; the intent of this instrument was to provide data to facilitate comparison in metrics usage between the original survey and this one and to measure changes in practice with regard to R&D metrics. Survey was administered at IRI's 2009 annual meeting; attendees were typically high-level R&D managers, vice presidents of R&D, and chief technical officers (CTOs). The survey listed the 33 metrics included in the original 1994 survey and asked respondents to rank them by order of importance in their organizations. We did not ask respondents to identify their organizations, but we did ask if they represented for-profit or not-for-profit corporations.

The second survey, Survey B, was a broader instrument that asked participants to rate the expanded list of 50 metrics on their importance to the respondents' organizations, using a scale of 1 (no importance) to 5 (top importance). Again, organizations were not identified, but we did ask respondents to identify the industry in which they worked. The group used this data to distinguish relationships between preferred metrics and industry, company type, and innovation game. Additionally, the survey solicited open-ended comments on the value and usage of metrics and methods used to collect data. Respondents were also asked to describe metrics that they felt were needed and list metrics that their corporation was using but that were not on the list. Survey B was administered to attendees at IRI 2008 member summit; again, this group comprised high-level R&D managers, vice presidents of R&D, and CTOs. One of the key challenges of implementing R&D metrics is matching metrics to the various levels and functions of the R&D organization.

Survey A was completed by 56 respondents from both corporate and not-for-profit organizations; the 1994 survey did not ask about for-profit versus not-for-profit status, but given that IRI's membership did not include not-for-profit organizations at that time, the original sample most likely included only for-profit corporations. Data from Survey A were compared to data from the 1994 administration of the same survey. The 2009 data are sorted by for-profit or not-for-profit to allow a better comparison of the data from 1994 to 2009.

Table 8. Top Ten Metrics in 1994 and 2009

1994	2009 For-Profit	2009 Not-For-Profit
Financial return	Financial return	Strategic Alignment
Strategic Alignment	Strategic Alignment	Accomplishments of project milestones
Projected value of R&D pipeline	Projected value of R&D pipeline	Quality of R&D personnel
Sales/gross profit from new products	Gross profit margin	Portfolio distribution of R&D projects
Portfolio distribution of R&D projects	Sales/gross profit from new products	Product quality and reliability
Market share	Accomplishments of project milestones	Rating of project benefits by customers
Customer satisfaction surveys	Achievements of R&D project objectives	External peer evaluation of R&D
Development cycle time	Quality of R&D personnel	Customer rating of technical capabilities
Gross profit margin	Level of business approval of projects	Number of technical reports
Product quality and reliability	Comparative manufacturing costs	Number of technical reports

Interestingly, the top three metrics from 1994 (financial return to the business, strategic alignment with the business, and projected value of the R&D pipeline) maintained their importance for for-profit corporations in the 2009 survey, but only the strategic alignment metric was judged of high value by the not-for-profit group.

A number of metrics ranked higher in 2009 rankings than they did in 1994, including achievement of R&D pipeline objectives, quality of R&D personnel, level of business approval of projects, comparative manufacturing costs, and effectiveness of transfer to manufacturing; none of these made the top 12 list in 1994, and all did in 2009. Other metrics lost ground, including portfolio distribution of R&D projects, market share, current spending level for technology, and customer satisfaction surveys; all were in the top 10 in 1994, and none were in 2009. Metrics ranked highly by for-profit respondents to the 2009 survey revealed a focus on financial returns, strategic business alignment, and quality, while not-for-profit respondents were focused on strategic alignment, accomplishment of milestones, quality of people, portfolio distribution, and clarity of project goals. The common thread in both groups was strategic alignment.

Survey B asked about companies' practices with regard to R&D metrics; the survey also asked participants to rate the metrics currently included in the TVP structure. There were 52 respondents.

Questions about company practices with regard to collecting and using metrics were revealing. While a minority of respondents indicated that their companies did not collect any metrics, most companies apparently feel compelled to measure the effectiveness of their R&D efforts. The most-reported uses for R&D metrics included:

- Providing data for project justification and decision-making processes.
- Enabling portfolio analysis, balancing, and tracking.
- Calculating ROI for R&D.
- Enhancing efficiency in product development.
- Driving performance and defining goals.
- Ensuring that R&D is aligned to the business strategy; and
- Benchmarking against intracompany units as well as outside companies.

About half of participants reported that their companies collect data for metrics on a quarterly basis; a quarter collect data either semiannually or annually. Most data must be collected by hand; only a small percentage of participants reported that their companies had automated data collection and metric generation processes. Return-on-Investment calculations, according to respondents, require some sort of project time tracking, in addition to other data collection.

Participants also rated the importance to their companies of each entry in the expanded list of TVP metrics (including those added after the original 1994 study), sorted by TVP level. As in survey a, financial return is a dominant theme, especially in the top two levels of the TVP. The top metrics for the value creation level are all financial, as are most of the top metrics at the strategy level. Other important strategy metrics include strategic alignment and probability of success.

Foundation metrics are associated with quantitative measures, such as number of patents, as well as more abstract metrics associated with people development and creativity.

Table 9. Top Five Metrics by TVP Level

Metric	Ranking
Outcome	
Financial Return	1
Gross Profit	2
Market Share	3
Project Value of Pipeline	4
IP Management	5
Strategy	
Financial Return	1
Project Value of Pipeline	2
Gross Profit	3
R&D Investment as percent of Sales	4
Strategic Alignment	5
Foundations	
IP Management	1
Number and Quality of Patents	2
People Development	3
Creativity	4
Cost vs. Budget	5

Respondents to survey B also identified a number of metrics that they felt should be added to the 50 currently included in the TVP; these fell into four broad groups:

- Open innovation metrics, including external vs. Internal R&D, percent of projects outsourced, and external innovation;
- Metrics to measure the effectiveness of R&D processes beyond financial, including, for instance, measures of efficiency in project management;
- Value creation metrics for technical service and support for existing products; and
- Not-for-profit metrics to measure the development of new capabilities, awards, professional activities, and bibliometrics.

Of particular interest were calls for additional metrics in R&D effectiveness and value creation. While the literature does describe some metrics in the area of R&D effectiveness beyond financial measures, most companies found these existing measures inadequate. Similarly, many participants reported a need for metrics to measure the effectiveness of technical service and support groups, which are often associated with R&D budgets, in order to show their value to the company. The closest metrics currently available in this area are related to cost savings, but these do not adequately address the issue.

Respondents also identified a number of issues with existing metrics, including the difficulty of collecting data and calculating and quantifying metrics, the lack of uniform standards for different business units or global sites, and inconsistency in the application of business-specific metrics across the company.

Respondents were sometimes skeptical of the value of metrics, attitudes reflected in comments that the easiest-to-measure metrics generally have the lowest value, that metrics are trailing measures that tend to focus on the short term, and that metrics tend to focus on inputs rather than outcomes. Respondents also worried that a reliance on metrics can lead to gaming the numbers to make a group look good. Respondents generally commented on the danger that metrics can influence behavior, for good or bad, and that poor choices of metrics can lead to bad business decisions. Finally, they commented on the difficulty of creating metrics that are meaningful to shareholders. And they lamented that, even with perfect metrics, doing all the right things does not guarantee success.

Shifts in ranking may reflect a number of changes in corporate culture and the context of innovation: the effects of the recession that began in 2008, which has driven a more inward and short-term focus and increased worries about finances, cash flow, and excess spending; the shift from Total Quality Management (TQM) with its emphasis on quality and the voice of the customer; the increased attention to corporate governance; and the rise of global competition. Recessionary anxieties are reflected in the increased importance of financial measures, such as the value of the R&D pipeline, manufacturing costs, and transfers to manufacturing, and in the decreased significance accorded to such metrics as portfolio distribution, market share, spending on technology, and customer satisfaction. The increased importance of business approvals and transfer to manufacturing may be a reflection of a closer focus on corporate governance. The shift away from TQM as a management paradigm may have driven down the importance of customer satisfaction as an R&D metric.

A third explanation for the emphasis on costs is global competition. In 1994, china was just beginning to replace some U.S. manufacturing. In today's worldwide marketplace, low price has become one of the most important criteria for product sales. This is reflected in the increased importance of manufacturing costs and transfers to manufacturing as R&D metrics.

There were also some differences noted in the metrics preferred depending on a company's innovation game and between corporations and not-for-profit organizations. For instance, consumer product companies tend to rely more heavily on quality metrics than other companies do, possibly because these industries lack the well-defined specifications and standards that generally guide companies working in the standalone or integrated systems areas. Companies in these areas are more likely to emphasize number of defects, efficiency, and system management and R&D metrics. Consumer products companies, on the other hand, must deal in a consumer market where a contaminated or poor quality product could generate major lawsuits, negative publicity, and bad will. Future events could influence following surveys; for instance, we might expect a higher emphasis on quality metrics in the petrochemical industry in the wake of the 2010 BP oil spill in the Gulf of Mexico.

There are also discernible differences in preferred metrics between for-profit and not-for-profit organizations. Not-for-profit companies are typically less concerned about financials and product sales; instead, they are focused on meeting goals and managing people and portfolios. The common thread linking corporations and not-for-profits is strategic alignment; both are concerned to make sure they're working on the right projects to support the core business. As the R&D model is changing to an open innovation perspective, metrics depicting these changes, and measuring their outcomes, are required.

As the R&D model is changing from exclusively internal development to an open innovation perspective, metrics depicting these changes, and measuring their outcomes, are required. Proposals for such metrics as percent of new intellectual property from licensing in or percent of new business created by licensed technology have been proposed. Fine-tuning these and integrating them into the TVP are important next steps; one part of that process will be determining in which levels of the hierarchy they belong. Since R&D will continue to evolve, identifying and integrating new metrics is a continuous process. The TVP should continue to develop as the repository of these metrics, along with their definitions, recommended uses, and references.

Conclusion

Concrete advice for selecting R&D metrics: First, it is important to recognize that some metrics are more important to specific industries and innovation strategies than others. *Choosing a metric, or benchmarking results, is best done within similar business types.* In a similar vein, before choosing a metric, it is important to understand what the company (and its stakeholders) will do with the results. To be effective, metrics must align with the business and technical strategies as well as with the immediate goals of measurement. The number of metrics that are collected should be limited to the minimum necessary to acquire a complete picture; at the same time, a few robust and clearly measurable metrics should be selected from each portion of the TVP. Even as measuring R&D performance becomes more important, metrics remain difficult and sometimes elusive.

References for Further Reading:

Andrew, J.P., Hannæs, K., Michael, D.C., Sirkin, H.L., Taylor, A. 2008. Measuring Innovation Survey 2008: Squandered Opportunities. Boston Consulting Group. Http://www.bcg.com/documents/file15302.pdf.

Cosner, R. R. 2010. The Industrial Research Institute's R&D Trends Forecast for 2010. Research-Technology Management 53(1): 14–22.

Donnelly, G., and Fink, R. 2000. A P&L for R&D. CFO Mag. Feb: 44–50.

European Industrial Research Management Association (EIRMA). 2004. Assessing R&D Effectiveness: WG62 Report. EIRMA Working Group Reports. Paris. Www.EIRMA.org/pubs/reports/wg62.pdf.

Germeraad, P. 2003. Measuring R&D in 2003. Research-Technology Management 46(6): 47–56.

Hauser, J. R. 1996. Metrics to value R&D: an annotated bibliography. Sloan Working Papers. Cambridge, MA: Sloan School of Management. Massachusetts Institute of Technology.

Mcgrath, M. E., and Romeri, M. N. 1994. The R&D Effectiveness Index: A Metric for Product Development Performance. Journal of Product Innovation Management 11(3): 213–220.

Miller, R., and Floricel, S. 2004. Value Creation and Games of Innovation. Research-Technology Management 47(6): 25–37.

Miller, R., and Olleros, X. 2008. To Manage Innovation, Learn The Architecture. Research-Technology Management 51(3): 17–27.

Roussel, P. A., Saad, K. N., and Erickson, T. J. 1991. Third Generation R&D: Managing The Link to Corporate Strategy. Boston, MA: Harvard Business Press.

Tipping, J., Zeffren, E., and Fusfeld, A. 1995. Assessing The Value of Your Technology. Research-Technology Management 38(5): 22–39.

Tirpak, T., Miller, R., Schwartz, L., and Kashdan, D. 2006. R&D Structure In a Changing World. Research-Technology Management 49(5): 19-26.

Financial Concepts for the Non-financial Technologist

Few, if any, technologists leaving school understand how to read a profit and loss (P&L) statement or are familiar with the key financial metrics of the firm. My goal is not to educate on financial terms but to share some concepts you'll need to understand while encouraging you to learn how to read the P&L. Within the P&L are messages about the health of the firm if you know what to look for. You need to understand the financial state of your firm to protect your own self-interests.

Of the many numbers to examine, the most important is *cash*. Cash is the life-blood of the firm and without it the firm goes bankrupt. Stock analysts are experts at dissecting income, cash flow, P&L statements, and balance sheets, so a first rule of thumb is to read several analysts' reports on your firm if it's publically traded. Carefully compare the observations and conclusions they make and assess them relative to consistency – is everyone is drawing the same conclusions or not? Then combine these analyses with your own assessment using the publically reported data and what you know internally. This will provide you a more educated and nuanced point of view. Private firms usually don't reveal this to anyone except the executive team, but talking with the commercial and financial departments helps.

Performance Evaluation and Incentive Compensation

The old adage holds: "Be careful what you measure because that's what you'll get." One basic tenet is individuals work to maximize their own wealth. Therefore, it's critical that the firm's incentive compensation system aligns increasing employee wealth creation with shareholder value. This demands that incentive schemes take into account both short and long term performance of the firm. Short-term metrics can involve net income, as expressed as earnings per share, free cash flow, and revenue growth. Longer term metrics including return on capital employed, return on assets, and revenue from new products sold over some timeframe help balance short and long term decision making. For example current earnings can be boosted in a given year by cutting costs at the expense of future earnings which suffer from delayed or avoided investments.

Incentive compensation often takes the form of stock options and grants combined with cash payments for meeting targets, with the logic being as shareholder price goes up so does employee wealth. However, many publically trade company's shares change with the market, and not just their own performance, so share-based incentive compensation needs to be balanced with metrics based on internal financial metrics. These can be free cash flow, new customer retention and acquisition, and productivity measures such a return on assets and capital employed.

Ultimately, the firm's valuation relies on the cash it generates, meaning "cash is king." All effective employee compensation schemes must align employee behavior to some cash metric.

Measuring Profitability

The manager's measure of profitability differs from the accountant's. Managers measure profitability on the basis of *net present value*, which is the difference between the present value of future cash flows and the initial investment, given the assessed riskiness of those flows. The accountant's measure of profitability (e.g., book return on equity) is often unrelated to the manager's measure. Book returns reflect the concept of matching income and expenses while ignoring expenditures necessary to produce the income. Moreover, book value is not the same as market value and is usually much lower.

Accounting Income versus Free Cash Flow

The technologist uses their project portfolio to increase free and total cash flows for the firm over some period of time such as 5 years. An accountant is concerned with income and total cash flows over the short term, be it a quarter or a year. A technologist much think like a financial analyst, instead of financial accountants, in that the *financial analyst must be able to describe what cash is doing to create future value for the firm whereas the accountant tries to match revenues and expenses over the near term accounting period.*

Accountants distinguish between *expenditures* and *expenses;* they define *net income* as the difference between revenue and expenses. Technologists define *economic income* as the difference between cash income and the sum of all cash outlays required to produce the cash income, whether called expenses or expenditures. That difference, called *free cash flow*, is the amount of cash income available for investment in new projects without hurting the cash flow stream required to operate the firm in the present.

Both roles are critical since the firm must perform well over the short term if there's to be a long term. Further, today's short term was yesterday's long term, meaning the short-term cash flows are a measure of how investments in past project portfolios are performing versus what was expected. Therefore, the technologist focuses on the difference between cash inflows and cash outflow over the period of the project portfolio and whether these flows are increasing and at an acceptable rate.

Ideally, the firm has sufficient free cash flow to make the required investments to grow shareholder value. An alternative source of cash for investments that could be attractive depending on interest rates and alternative uses of cash is to take on debt. Although important, debt is beyond the scope of this discussion.

Taxes and Cash

An important determinant of cash flow is taxation. Four kinds of decisions affect taxes: Legal (e.g., incorporation), investment, financing, and accounting. Managers must try to minimize the resources (corporate and personal) siphoned off to the government within the constraints of the law. To do otherwise would be to ignore one of the key responsibilities of management: Minimize costs in order to compete effectively. If one firm pays more taxes than an identical competitor, the first firm will fail. The ultimate losers will be the firm's constituencies.

Don't Run Out Of Cash

This is a fundamental role of finance (and the business generally). Just as blood sustains living organisms, cash sustains a business. Most competitive moves can be thought of as investments; even the decision to cut prices temporarily is an investment decision. In a competitive economy, the inevitable result of being unable to invest due to a cash constraint is atrophy and death. Not only is the company unable to seize profitable investment opportunities, but financial weaknesses might encourage the competition to attack. Forecasting and planning for future cash flow patterns, managers can avoid jeopardizing their firms' survival. Note that the definition of cash used is very broad. What one really has to have in mind is the potential to raise cash from inside and outside the firm. To obtain cash from external sources, however, there must be value within the firm that can be sold off.

Cash and Growth

Another important determinant of cash flow is the rate of sales growth. Growth in sales must be supported by growth in assets (working capital and fixed assets). In turn, growth in assets must be supported by increases in stockholder equity through retained earnings, stock sales, or increases in external liabilities. High growth rates may require successful firms to rely heavily on external funding.

It is essential that managers distinguish between real world and growth in prices from inflation. High inflation rates can have a much more damaging effect on the company's long-term financial health than high rates of real growth, especially in view of the historical cost basis for tax accounting used in the United States.

Pattern Recognition

A critical skill for managers is the ability to recognize and respond to patterns. Many patterns affect cash: Cyclical, seasonal, competitive, technological, regulatory, and tax. A hallmark of good managers is their ability to recognize an opportunity to create value *and* act on it. Becoming proficient at pattern recognition enables them to commit resources quickly to a perceived opportunity. By recognizing and responding to patterns of cash flow behavior, and using past and current information, successful managers seek to predict the future and to take action.

Pattern recognition helps managers make both defensive and offensive decisions. Consider the effects of a recession. Battening down the hatches, when the recession has been recognized, is an example of defensive action.

Deciding to accelerate an investment in capacity during a recession precisely because competition is battening down the hatches is an example of an offensive decision. Recognizing the event – a recession – and anticipating how the competition will react to it drives the company's decisions. Of course, managers cannot always identify the patterns that are affecting cash flows at a particular time. They may not know, for example, when a recession begins or ends; their reactions will therefore be delayed. If, however, they have studied the issues before they arise and have come up with a plan of action, they will do a better job than if they had not thought about the problem in the first place.

Scenario Planning

Scenario planning can be a useful way to analyze cash flows. The scenario is a numerical depiction of a logical consistent set of events that are likely to occur in the future. The scenario reflects past and potential management decisions. It also considers the probable moves of competitors and is a way of managing an uncertainty.

Scenario planning is not the same as worst-case, expected values, and best-case forecasting. Simplistic depictions of future events are not particularly useful. Consider the worst-case scenario. Rarely will all the elements of the worst-case scenario occur simultaneously. Moreover, these scenarios often fail to account for an explicit change in management decisions. They assume that management will keep making the same decisions it would have made had the expected outcomes occurred; in reality, managers may go so far as to abandon the project altogether. Best-case scenarios have the same pitfalls.

Nor is scenario planning the same thing as linear extrapolation. Few trends persist without interruption. Many planning errors are made because planners extrapolate from past data. During the 1970s, many banks lent to energy companies based on values that reflected the continuation of rapidly escalating oil and gas prices – rates above the expected rise in general prices. When oil and gas prices fell, both in absolute terms and relative to other places in the economy, the values on which loans had been made vanished. This example, which admittedly relies on hindsight, is nonetheless useful because the pattern has been and will be repeated time and time again.

An unwritten rule states that every forecast the manager makes will turn out (with hindsight) to be wrong. But by making internally consistent forecast that reflect reasoned management decisions and that are economically significant (i.e., not so unlikely as to be irrelevant), managers can manage in an uncertain world.

One final note: There is a crucial distinction between evaluating the effects of a particular event occurring and being able to predict the occurrence of the event with certainty. A good example is interest rates. No evidence indicates that any individual or group of individuals can predict interest rates with any precision. Nevertheless, managers must evaluate the consequences of interest rate changes.

One element of successful pattern recognition is the ability to recognize how current investment or financing decisions affect cash flows from the firm's existing assets or from future investment and financing decisions. Attributing these effects (whether positive or negative) to the decision under consideration is an important element of financial thinking.

Chapter 6 Summary

The first principle of all financial thinking is that cash is what is important. Because cash can be consumed – traded for other assets in the economy that have utility – all analysis of investment or financing decisions must focus on cash.

Finance is a way of thinking about cash, risk, and value. Managers must be able to view problems from the financial perspective as well as from other perspectives. But finance does not answer questions, nor does it make decisions. Finance can help identify the right questions to ask and narrow down the options. When viewed from the finance perspective, some decisions will turn out to be illogical or unfeasible. Deciding what should not or cannot be done is a valuable aid to managers.

Finance also teaches skepticism. The numbers of profitable investment opportunities thought to exist far exceed the actual number. The technologist shares, with management and the commercial teams, how a particular technical decision creates value, which often requires good judgment but not elaborate analysis. Financial analysis can occur, but its relevance needs to be defined. Often, numerical descriptions of events appear more relevant than they really are and need to be qualified by clear assumptions and expert judgment. Financial analysis, combined with expert judgment, helps R&D participate in charting the future course of the firm.

This chapter also dealt with the basics of technology budgeting and aligning these budgets with the annual operating expenses of the firm. A critical success factor is to keep indirect and allocated costs to less than 20% of the total budget while assigning the majority of the portfolio to projects directly sponsored by business units. Approximately 10% of the total project budget can be sponsored by the corporation to benefit multiple business units or to protect the overall business in the future. Often, business units will manage to the present year, and possibly 1 year beyond, but will not support work paying out for 5 years or more or involving basic understanding applied across multiple business units.

Supporting the R&D operating budget, which is assigned to specific projects or allocated across the portfolio, is a general ledger description of actual spending by specific accounts, be it salaries and benefits, supplies, continuing education, or staffing activities. This description of the budget allows the firm to recognize annual spending by conventional categories found in cost accounting processes. These expenses are generally direct, indirect, fixed, and variable, allowing the firm to correctly account for activities in the P&L statement. Often, R&D expenses are not broken out in detail but used internally as a management tool. This enables R&D management to analyze spending, making adjustments to ensure the correct resources are being deployed against the work requested over the period.

Measuring the impact of investments in technology is complex and very industry and firm dependent. This topic has been carefully studied over the years by the Industrial Research Institute, among other organizations, whose work should be consulted prior to selecting a set of metrics. A common metric is revenues from products and services enabled by an innovation within a certain time periods. The time frame selected must be consistent with the product and service life cycles. Longer lifecycles may yield low percentages of revenues from innovations vs. industries with very short product life cycles.

Finally, managers make better decisions combining financial analysis with expert judgment while avoiding over-analyzing the data, which can lead to paralysis and inaction.

Chapter 6 Critical Questions

Annual Planning
1. Where are you now?
2. What is your current situation?
3. How did you get to where you are today?
4. What were the factors and decisions that led to your current situation?
5. Is everything you are doing necessary to win and keep customers?
6. What savings could you generate by partnering with other companies to do work or carry overhead? (e.g., Open Innovation).
7. Could you share services to save time and money?
8. What activities would you outsource without reducing quality or service to your customers?

9. Where do you want to go from here?
10. What do you want to accomplish?
11. How much product from innovation would you be selling five years from now?
12. How do you get from where you are today to where you want to be in the future
13. What are the steps that you will have to take to create your ideal future R&D organization?
14. What obstacles will you have to overcome?
15. What problems will you have to solve?
16. Of all the problems or obstacles standing between you and your desired future outcomes, what are the biggest or most important?
17. What is holding you back?
18. What are the critical constraints or limiting factors for growth?
19. What additional knowledge, skills, or resources will you require to achieve your strategic objectives?
20. What additional competencies or capabilities will you need if you want to lead your field in the years ahead?
21. What is the one thing your organization was worst at this year? What single thing needs to happen to fix it?
22. What is the one thing your organization did best this year? What do you need to do to turn that success into a repeatable process?
23. Which individual or process was most responsible for standing in the way of your organization's success this year?
24. What are you going to do about it?
25. Which department, division, team or function was most responsible for standing in the way of your organization's success this year?
26. What are you going to do about it?
27. Which individual was most responsible for your organization's success this year?
28. How are you recognizing this achievement?
29. Which department, division, team or function was most responsible for your organization's success this year?
30. What are you going to do about it?
31. What is the single metric or measurement you least liked hearing about this year?
32. What will you do to prevent the same thing happening next year?
33. What is the single metric you will measure your success by (not how anyone else will measure your success-- how you will measure your own success).
34. What are you doing about it?
35. If you fired yourself today, and came back tomorrow as a new boss and could do anything, what would you do?

36. If a perfect competitor opened up across the street from you tomorrow, what would they be like?

R&D Metrics
1. Are you measuring the correct things? How do you know?
2. Which metrics align with your business and why?
3. How accurate are your measurements?
4. What does benchmarking tell you about your R&D group's performance?
5. Where does R&D rank among peer organizations? If not in the top quartile what needs to be done to get there?
6. How frequently does R&D measure itself?
7. Who audits R&D's metrics and what does the audit show?

R&D Financial Considerations
1. Do your R&D investments aligned with the financial goals of the firm?
2. Which financial metrics are most important and why?
3. How are these financial metrics used to manage R&D?
4. How do the incentive plans for R&D leadership align with creating shareholder value?
5. How does R&D leadership use scenario planning to make decisions?
6. How does R&D leadership use pattern recognition to guide decision making?
7. Who represents Finance on the R&D staff and what is their role?
8. Can all of R&D leadership read the firm's P&L and explain it relative to their decision making?
9. Does R&D leadership understand stock analyst reports?

Chapter 7: Critical Processes

To live means to finesse the processes to which one is subjugated
~ Bertolt Brecht ~

When processes become the end point, vs. the means to an end, you're finished
~ Unknown Author ~

When processes become ends in themselves, versus the means to an end, innovation begins to disappear. Sometimes the very quantitative metrics describing these processes make them end points in themselves, thereby killing innovation. Leadership must prevent this from occurring. It is risky using quantitative descriptions of data since doing so makes assumptions look like facts. This error will yield false confidence and significant errors that block innovation.

The intent of this section is to review the five primary tools leading to effective planning and execution of an innovation. Effective innovation requires that investments employ a portfolio management philosophy that links the investments to future financial return using an appropriate cost of money discount factor. Combining an investor's approach to deploying resources with a strategy for accessing ideas, technologies, and knowledge from external sources, which is often described under the heading of *open innovation*, manages the risk of processes becoming internally biased.

There are five processes employed to manage portfolio investments, beginning with roadmapping, describing where the strategy intends to take the enterprise, which leads to an investment scheme referred to as the *project portfolio*. Investments, described by the project portfolio, are assessed using the *Stage Gates* process. This process assesses the resources required to meet defined objectives for each project and the potential value being created. Projects are managed using *project management* tools at regular intervals. Finally, a *Product Life Cycle Management* tool is deployed which helps manage the product from "cradle to grave," allowing for the retirement of offerings which have lost value (e.g., profitability, growth, etc.). This chapter introduces these concepts along with several others as seen below:

Table 10. Critical Technology Processes

Process	Objectives	Metrics
Roadmapping	• Identifies market drivers • Recognizes critical to success industry nuances • Estimates financial potential	• Estimates timing • Defines problems • Describes solutions
Business Ethics	• Define the term • Review acceptable and unacceptable behaviors • Propose an enforcement methodology	• J&J Case studies • 12 Rules of Ethical Behavior • Violation reporting
Intellectual Property (IP)	• What is IP • How is it used as a business tool • Strategies for building a portfolio	• IP types and utility • Investment requirements • Curveball strategies
Project Portfolio Creation	• Defines investment options • Identifies financial returns • Evaluates investment dimensions (e.g., SWOT analysis)	• Identifies areas of risk • Aligns opportunities with internal competencies • Driver of the Open Innovation agenda
Open Innovation	• Mind set to look beyond the firm • Review effective methods • Highlight risks	• Describe process • Examples of successful programs • Review implementation process
Stage Gate Process	• Specifies investment decisions • Recognizes timing of outcomes • Manages and mitigates risk	• Defines value • Aligns with 3-5 Year business plan • Drive decisions about projects in portfolio
Project Management	• Describes the project (e.g., project brief, Work Break-Down, Structure, etc.) • Identifies resource deployment • Assigns individual accountability	• Assesses timing (e.g., GANTT charts) • Defines budget • Reports progress against plan
Product Life Cycle Management	• Definitions • Implementation • Strategic value in managing complexity	• Example process • Role of management
Dealing with "Big Data"	• Definition • Forecasting vs. predicting • Causation vs correlation	• "Foxes" vs. "Hedgehogs" • Bayesian statistics • Probabilistic thinking
Personal Annual Plan	• Drives personal performance plan • Frames areas of collaboration • Provides context for non-project work	• Identify strengths • Aligns skills with project portfolio • Drives recognition program
Annual Business Plan	• Revenue • Margin • Volume	• Geographic reach • Market penetration • Competitive responses

Roadmapping – Where to go

If you don't know where you're going any roadmap will get you there.
~Anonymous~

Roadmapping[49] [50] has emerged as a best practice for aligning business functions with corporate strategy and projecting with "precision" into the future. But what does roadmapping entail? The word "roadmap" generally evokes images of a two-dimensional map with lines representing roads drawn upon it. The roads are shown intersecting, circumnavigating, running in parallel and sometimes dead-ending. If one thinks about it, all of the roads are bi-directional, each affecting the course of the others that touch it.

The term "roadmapping" injects action into the map. Roads are actually being used to map a course of action, resulting in a roadmap that provides direction. Taking it one step further, "strategic roadmapping" involves manipulating the information contained in roadmaps to plan the best course of action for the future, aligning action with strategic objectives. Strategic roadmapping enables innovation leaders to gain a multidimensional view into the future and manipulate planning data to reveal the outcomes of their planning scenarios.

Creating roadmaps allows companies to project far into the future with the confidence that their strategic decisions are fueled by high-quality, up-to-date information and knowledge. Roadmapping is about more than just moving ahead in a common direction; it provides innovation leaders with the confidence that they are moving ahead in the right direction.

Further, roadmaps provide the framework for strategy creation, effectively turning strategy into action and tying strategic goals to tactical measures. This enables an organization to align day-to-day planning and projects to business priorities.

If applied as an enterprise framework, roadmapping has the potential to provide a bridge between all the tactical decision processes, different business functions, and organizations through the common element of time. Admittedly, this is an aspirational but nonetheless useful construct for creating innovative outcomes.

---

[49] Garcia, Marie L. Bray, Olin H. Fundamentals of Technology Roadmapping, Strategic Business Development Department, Sandia National Laboratories. E-mail: mgarci@sandia.gov ohbray@sandia.gov.
[50] Lee, Sungjoo, Park, Yongtae, Customization of technology roadmaps according to roadmapping, *Technological Forecasting & Social Change* 72 (2005) 567–583.

Roadmaps Provide Strategic Views of Enterprise Plans

Roadmaps are instrumental in increasing visibility, accountability, and collaboration at almost every level of planning, enabling stakeholders to see where they fit into the larger picture and what they are accountable for in the strategic process. In fact, thousands of leading companies around the world, including Motorola, Corning, Hewlett-Packard, and Lockheed Martin use roadmaps to improve planning processes.

Roadmaps clarify thinking among stakeholders and enable the rapid communication and sharing of ideas. They also reveal valuable linkages among functional areas of a business that are often disconnected from each other, much like the roads that link and disconnect across a map. Roadmaps should not just be viewed as the outputs of a process, but rather a snapshot of a "rolling" strategy at any moment in time; a strategy that must be kept current as conditions change.

Roadmapping as a Business Process

Roadmaps are valuable strategy tools because at their core they are all about making decisions. "What-if" scenarios, technology implications, product evolution, and supplier collaboration are often dedicated subjects of detailed roadmaps that support product portfolio decisions, merger and acquisition decisions, and even end-of-life or divestiture decisions. Time provides a common denominator on which any number of dimensions can be played out in advance, creating a canvas on which uncertainty and opportunity are managed into highly probable choices that create a company's future. Roadmapping software makes this process even easier.

Roadmapping is also a practice and a business process that involves capturing strategic information on a timeline. This data typically relates to business vision, objectives, strategies, market requirements, product or service plans, technologies, and capabilities. The collected data is then fed into various roadmaps, which include a theme, timeline, time-based elements, and links among these elements.

Strategic roadmaps are supported by tactical roadmaps describing markets, products, competitors, technologies, suppliers, regulatory and environmental elements as "landscapes," reflecting the planning horizon over multiple time periods. Time-based elements represent the availability of a technology, product, and market or decision point(s), and often the timing of an event may not be certain. Nevertheless, placing this information in the time domain is extremely important to consider its implications.

Corning, a leading diversified technology company, became focused on entering new markets, but strategic planning across the organization was not aligned with portfolio planning, R&D efforts, or market trends. The company used roadmapping across three divisions to align corporate strategy, R&D and portfolio planning. This helped to identify and select new market opportunities, enter markets early, and earn positive returns for the company within 24 months. The company also saw a decrease in development costs due to fewer last-minute changes that are hard to make further down the development chain.

Motorola, a global communications leader, used roadmapping software to track and organize tens of thousands of product roadmap documents distributed across the enterprise. The company reported saving more than $100 million in 12 months by consolidating strategic product planning projects across business units. By halting development on a chip that would become obsolete, it saved an additional $100 million. Today, thousands of users actively plan, collaborate, and view Motorola's innovation projects and new potential products using roadmapping software.

At Honeywell, the need for an improved roadmapping discipline grew out of a desire to prove the link between technology innovation, product development and customer needs. The company sought a business strategy tool that would help it evaluate conditions that impact the business, understand planned investments, and decide how to achieve business goals. In the first 12-18 months of deploying roadmapping software, the company improved visibility into upstream R&D efforts, ensuring that projects the company is investing in today are on target with what's important to the company's future. It now has the ability to leverage roadmaps across the entire enterprise, quickly adjust to ever changing conditions, and be confident that it is aligned with business objectives.

As these examples demonstrate, roadmapping provides companies with a multidimensional view of events and other significant milestones as they are anticipated to take place across time. Motorola was able to save money by consolidating project resources. Honeywell was able to ensure that projects they're working on today are in line with what's important for their company's future. Corning was able to bring products to market faster.

Companies that get the most out of their strategic roadmapping initiatives act decisively on the information revealed in their roadmaps. They take advantage of a roadmap's unique capability, creating alignment among business functions that move in and out of synch, unnoticed. And, although companies often use roadmaps to share plans, their purpose is often to stimulate thinking and improve a plan by managing the uncertainty contained therein. Roadmaps are effective because they help convert uncertainty into manageable risk. This is often one of the elusive facts of roadmapping that is not easily understood. Yet, every plan to address the future must take into account the level of confidence in each part of the plan, thereby identifying and reducing uncertainty, allowing risk to be more effectively managed while the plan is further developed.

Benefits of Roadmapping

Using roadmapping as a strategic planning process, companies benefit from the visibility achieved through increased access to information and the ability to model future scenarios. With roadmapping, executives no longer waste time gathering explicit data and tacit information to make decisions. They become informed innovation leaders who can view alternatives, perform "what-if" analysis and proceed with the best course of action.

Flexibility in roadmapping allows for quick modification of product offerings to meet market demands and enables the supply chain to adapt quickly to change. It also promotes in-depth collaboration among the company, its customers, and its suppliers. Roadmapping enables companies to monitor the progress of any number of product development programs in real-time and allows users to visualize where they fit into a larger network of collaborative projects. Other benefits of roadmapping are below:

- Sharpens strategic vision, resulting in better-informed decision-making.
- Produces greater alignment between R&D spending and product development initiatives.
- Manages data, product plans, and goals at a high level.
- Links markets, products, technologies, capabilities, and supplier intent.
- Enables discovery of technology re-use and synergy opportunities.
- Reveals gaps, challenges, and uncertainties in product, technology, and capability plans.
- Reveals long-term strategic weaknesses before they become critical.
- Communicates and provides visibility into strategic program direction across the organization.
- Enables growth of product portfolio in line with corporate and market demands.
- Provides direction to project teams and enables them to quickly see changes in strategic events or direction, increasing visibility into other functions to identify opportunities for reusing technology in other areas across the company.
- Because redundant work is minimized and technology re-use is expanded, companies experience improved time-to-market due to reduced product delays.
- Roadmapping is also an effective way to benchmark an organization's capabilities, identify new opportunities, and create forward- looking plans

A roadmap by its very name describes in a pictorial way a pathway to a future destination. Considering the adage that *a picture is worth 1000 words*, a roadmap will mean different things to different people. How a sales professional interprets a roadmap, will likely be different than a marketing professional, or someone from the R&D or manufacturing function. The best roadmaps are developed by multidisciplinary teams of these operating groups supported by other functions within the organization as needed, such as HR, IT, legal, finance, and so on.

A good roadmap provides direction, but it must be remembered that all roadmaps are estimates of future situations, and so all of the assumptions going into that description must be checked periodically for relevance.

Strategic roadmapping enables innovation leaders to gain a multidimensional view into the future by using sensitivity analysis to reveal the outcomes of their planning scenarios. Creating roadmaps allows companies to project far into the future with the confidence that their strategic decisions are reasonable as well as where they might be improved.

Roadmapping fueled by high-quality, up-to-date information and actionable knowledge provides a common direction for the organization to follow, with confidence that they are moving ahead in the right direction. Roadmapping effectively turns strategy into action; tying strategic goals to tactical measures. This enables an organization to tie day-to-day planning and projects to business priorities.

Business Ethics: Always Doing the Correct Things

Some years ago,[51] sociologist Raymond Baumhart asked business people, "What do ethics mean to you?" Among their replies were the following:

1.   "Ethics has to do with what my feelings tell me is right or wrong."
2.   "Ethics has to do with my religious beliefs."
3.   "Being ethical is doing what the law requires."
4.   "Ethics consists of the standards of behavior our society accepts."
5.   "I don't know what the word means."

These replies might be typical of our own. The meaning of "ethics" is hard to pin down, and the views many people have about ethics are shaky. Many people tend to equate ethics with their feelings. But being ethical is clearly not a matter of following one's feelings. A person following his or her feelings may recoil from doing what is right. In fact, feelings frequently deviate from what is ethical. Nor should one identify ethics with religion. Most religions, of course, advocate high ethical standards. Yet if ethics were confined to religion, then ethics would apply only to religious people. But ethics applies as much to the behavior of the atheist as to that of the devout

---

[51] This article appeared originally in *Issues in Ethics* IIE V1 N1 (Fall 1987).

religious person. Religion can set high ethical standards and can provide intense motivations for ethical behavior. Ethics, however, cannot be confined to religion nor is it the same as religion.

Being ethical is also not the same as following the law. The law often incorporates ethical standards to which most citizens subscribe. But laws, like feelings, can deviate from what is ethical. Our own pre-Civil War slavery laws and the old apartheid laws of present-day South Africa are grotesquely obvious examples of laws that deviate from what is ethical. Finally, being ethical is not the same as doing "whatever society accepts." In any society, most people accept standards that are, in fact, ethical. But standards of behavior in society can deviate from what is ethical. An entire society can become ethically corrupt. Nazi Germany is a good example of a morally corrupt society.

Moreover, if being ethical were doing "whatever society accepts," then to find out what is ethical, one would have to find out what society accepts. To decide what I should think about abortion, for example, I would have to take a survey of American society and then conforms to my beliefs to whatever society accepts.

But no one ever tries to decide an ethical issue by doing a survey. Further, the lack of social consensus on many issues makes it impossible to equate ethics with whatever society accepts. Some people accept abortion but many others do not. If being ethical was doing whatever society accepts, one would have to find an agreement on issues that does not, in fact, exist. What, then, is ethics?

Ethics is two things

First, ethics refers to well-founded standards of right and wrong that prescribe what humans ought to do, usually in terms of rights, obligations, and benefits to society, fairness, or specific virtues. Ethics, for example, refers to those standards that impose the reasonable obligations to refrain from rape, stealing, murder, assault, slander, and fraud. Ethical standards also include those that enjoin virtues of honesty, compassion, and loyalty. And, ethical standards include standards relating to rights, such as the right to life, the right to freedom from injury, and the right to privacy. Such standards are adequate standards of ethics because they are supported by consistent and well-founded reasons.

Secondly, ethics refers to the study and development of one's ethical standards. As mentioned above, feelings, laws, and social norms can deviate from what is ethical. So it is necessary to constantly examine one's standards to ensure that they are reasonable and well-founded. Ethics also means, then, the continuous effort of studying our own moral beliefs and our moral conduct, and striving to ensure that we, and the institutions we help to shape, live up to standards that are reasonable and solidly-based.

Critical for having an effective ethics policy is proper oversight where every employee is safe in reporting violations without fear.

This can take many forms, one of which is an "Ethics Hotline" where an employee can report their concerns anonymously to the Chief Ethics Officer for action at the highest level of the firm. The Chief Ethics Officer must be an executive of the firm, reporting on ethics issues directly to the Board of Directors and without informing their superiors. Often this role is played by the Human Resource executive, but another executive such as the Chief Legal Officer is another viable candidate. Finally the "Ethics Hotline" must also protect the firm from unethical behavior but the Chief Ethics Officer.

Doing it Right – A Case Study

The Legacy Of Johnson & Johnson and James Burke – An Extraordinary Leader

In 1982, the company most people knew for their Band-Aids and baby shampoo was headed by James Burke, a man who climbed to the CEO job based on his exceptional marketing skills, not his knowledge of medicine or pharmacology. Relatively few people knew that J&J owned the company that made the very popular pain reliever – Tylenol. In fact, it was Mr. Burke, who championed making Tylenol, popular consumer product having about 35% of the pain-reliever market when people who took the pills started dying.

On Sept. 29, 1982, two people living in Chicago died of cyanide poisoning. It was a huge case as one of them a 12-year-old girl and the common link between the deaths was that they both had taken Tylenol.

The Food and Drug Administration acted quickly as did Burke's Johnson & Johnson who owned McNeil Consumer Products, producers of the medicine. Burke ordered the immediate recall of 93,000 bottles of the pills that came from the lot implicated in the deaths.

From the outset, the response, personally directed by Mr. Burke demonstrated a level of accountability, transparency and candor that is still taught in business schools as a model of trust-building integrity. Within a few hours of the learning of the first deaths, J&J set up toll-free numbers manned by company employees. It also stopped all Tylenol advertising and sent 450,000 telex messages to doctors' offices, hospitals and trade groups.

Unfortunately, this was just the beginning of what would turn out to be a corporate crisis of historical significance. In the next four days, five more people died of cyanide poisoning. Hope that the problem was confined to the Chicago area evaporated when a bottle of Tylenol laced with a different poison, strychnine, was found in California. No one knew whether this was the work of the same person who poisoned the pills used in Chicago or a copycat poisoner.

Burke and his team met with both the FBI and FDA and suggested that all 31 million bottles of Tylenol capsules on American store shelves be removed. It would have been, by far, the largest recall in history and it's been http://www.jnj.com/connect/about-jnj/jnj-credo.

This decision cost the company $100 million dollars as it not only destroyed all 32 million bottles but it kept the drug off the shelves until it developed the first tamper-resistant bottles (setting a new standard for the industry).

Burke, with the sort of candor rare in top executives, later admitted that he didn't really know how much his decision would cost and that he was glad he didn't know because the huge price tag might have made it harder to do what he thought was right. He also said he didn't know whether Tylenol which had to re-enter a very competitive market would ever regain its market share,

In fact, the right thing turned out to be the smart thing as Tylenol did regain its market share within a year and Johnson & Johnson benefited from an unrivaled reputation. Even today, I doubt whether there is a business ethics class in America that does not discuss the Tylenol case as an exemplary model of corporate responsibility.

J&J's credo is literally carved in a huge block of stone in the company's New Jersey headquarters, and metaphorically in Jim Burke's reputation as one of the great business leaders of all time (in 2000 he was awarded the presidential Medal of Freedom and in 2003 Fortune Magazine named him one of history's 10 greatest CEOs).

12 Ethical Principles for Business Executives and All Employees

If recent history teaches us anything is that ethics and character count, especially in business. Huge organizations like Enron, Arthur Andersen and Health South have been destroyed and others were seriously damaged (AIG, Fannie Mae, Freddie Mac) by executives with massive ambition and intelligence but no moral compass. In today's ultra-competitive, high tech, interdependent business world, charisma without conscience and cleverness without character are a recipe for economic and personal failure of epic proportions. As President Theodore Roosevelt said, "To educate the mind without the morals is to educate a menace to society." Competitiveness, ambition and innovation will always be important to success but they must be regulated by core ethical principles like the ones described below.

Let's start with a basic definition: Ethical principles are universal standards of right and wrong prescribing the kind of behavior an ethical company or person should and should not engage in. These principles provide a guide to making decisions but they also establish the criteria by which your decisions will be judged by others.

In business, how people judge your character is critical to sustainable success because it is the basis of trust and credibility. Both of these essential assets can be destroyed by actions that are, or are perceived to be unethical. Thus, successful executives must be concerned with both their character and their reputation.

Your character is what you really are; your reputation is what people think of you.
~ Abraham Lincoln ~

Thus, your reputation is purely a function of perceptions (i.e., do people think your intentions and actions are honorable and ethical). While your character is determined and defined by your actions and whether your actions are honorable and ethical according to the 12 ethical principles:

1. Honesty. *Be honest in all communications and actions.* Ethical executives are, above all, worthy of trust and honesty is the cornerstone of trust. They are not only truthful, they are candid and forthright. Ethical executives do not deliberately mislead or deceive others by misrepresentations, overstatements, partial truths, selective omissions, or any other means and when trust requires it they supply relevant information and correct misapprehensions of fact.

2. Integrity. *Maintain personal integrity.* Ethical executives earn the trust of others through personal integrity. Integrity refers to a wholeness of character demonstrated by consistency between thoughts, words and actions. Maintaining integrity often requires moral courage, the inner strength to do the right thing even when it may cost more than they want to pay. They live by ethical principles despite great pressure to do otherwise. Ethical executives are principled, honorable, upright and scrupulous. They fight for their beliefs and do not sacrifice principle for expediency.

3. Promise-Keeping. *Keep promises and fulfill commitments.* Ethical executives can be trusted because they make every reasonable effort to fulfill the letter and spirit of their promises and commitments. They do not interpret agreements in an unreasonably technical or legalistic manner in order to rationalize non-compliance or create justifications for escaping their commitments.

4. Loyalty. *Be loyal within the framework of other ethical principles.* Ethical executives justify trust by being loyal to their organization and the people they work with. Ethical executives place a high value on protecting and advancing the lawful and legitimate interests of their companies and their colleagues. They do not, however, put their loyalty above other ethical principles or use loyalty to others as an excuse for unprincipled conduct. Ethical executives demonstrate loyalty by safeguarding their ability to make independent professional judgments. They avoid conflicts of interest and they do not use or disclose information learned in confidence for personal advantage. If they decide to accept other employment, ethical executives provide reasonable notice, respect the proprietary information of their former employer, and refuse to engage in any activities that take undue advantage of their previous positions.

5. Fairness. *Strive to be fair and just in all dealings.* Ethical executives are fundamentally committed to fairness. They do not exercise power arbitrarily nor do they use overreaching or indecent means to gain or maintain any advantage nor take undue advantage of another's mistakes or difficulties. Ethical executives manifest a commitment to justice, the equal treatment of individuals, tolerance for and acceptance of diversity. They are open-minded; willing to admit they are wrong and, where appropriate, they change their positions and beliefs.

6. Caring. *Demonstrate compassion and a genuine concern for the well-being of others.* Ethical executives are caring, compassionate, benevolent and kind. They understand the concept of stakeholders (those who have a stake in a decision because they are affected by it) and they always consider the business, financial and emotional consequences of their actions on all stakeholders. Ethical executives seek to accomplish their business objectives in a manner that causes the least harm and the greatest positive good.

7. Respect For Others. *Treat everyone with respect.* Ethical executives demonstrate respect for the human dignity, autonomy, privacy, rights, and interests of all those who have a stake in their decisions; they are courteous and treat all people with equal respect and dignity regardless of sex, race or national origin. Ethical executives adhere to the Golden Rule, striving to treat others the way they would like to be treated.

8. Law Abiding. *Obey the law.* Ethical executives abide by laws, rules and regulations relating to their business activities.

9. Commitment To Excellence. *Pursue excellence all the time in all things.* Ethical executives pursue excellence in performing their duties, are well-informed and prepared, and constantly endeavor to increase their proficiency in all areas of responsibility.

10. Leadership. *Exemplify honor and ethics.* Ethical executives are conscious of the responsibilities and opportunities of their position of leadership and seek to be positive ethical role models by their own conduct and by helping to create an environment in which principled reasoning and ethical decision-making are highly prized.

11. Reputation And Morale. *Build and protect and build the company's good reputation and the morale of its employees.* Ethical executives understand the importance of their own and their company's reputation as well as the importance of the pride and good morale of employees. Thus, they avoid words or actions that might undermine respect, and they take affirmative steps to correct or prevent inappropriate conduct of others.

12. Accountability. *Be accountable.* Ethical executives acknowledge and accept personal accountability for the ethical quality of their decisions and omissions to themselves, their colleagues, their companies, and their communities.

Intellectual Property: Protecting the Business

Intellectual property has the shelf life of a banana.
~ Bill Gates ~

Before you can protect your company's IP, you must identify it. Talk to your employees and take an inventory of any creative works (copyrights) your company owns, whether such works are used internally or sold to others. Determine how your company identifies and distinguishes its products and/or services from those offered by others in the marketplace (through use of trademarks). Figure out whether your company has any secrets that give it a competitive edge, and whether it has invented anything that may be eligible for patent protection. Don't forget to make sure that you have permission to use the names, images, or likenesses of all persons in your marketing collateral and on your company website, etc. Then, contact an intellectual property attorney to make sure that you did not miss anything and to help you through the registration process.

Methods for Protecting the Innovation – Intellectual Property

Every hour of every day each of us deals with one or more forms of intellectual property. We deal with it at home, at work, and during our free time. Every time we buy something we deal with brands (trademarks). Almost everything we read, listen to or watch is protected by copyright. Daily, we use inventions that are or were protected by patents. And every time we have a Coke or Pepsi, we are drinking something whose formula is a heavily guarded trade secret. Each one of us also has a right of publicity, which allows us each to determine how our name, image or likeness is used for profit. As a business owner, employee, or lawyer, the first step is learning how to identify your company or client's valuable intellectual property assets so you can then protect them.

There are 4 main areas of IP

- Copyrights are creative works of expression, such as artwork, photography, graphic design, music, text, source code, architectural works and boat hulls.
- Trademarks are what businesses use to identify and distinguish what they offer in the marketplace from that which is offered by others, and includes brands, logos, slogans, and taglines.
- Trade Secrets are business secrets that are not known, nor easily learned, by people outside the company.
- Patents are unique inventions, designs or processes.

IP rights are exclusive because they allow the owner to exclude others from using its IP.

Ownership of IP assets entitles the owner to certain rights. Most importantly, IP owners may prevent others from using their IP without permission and/or the payment of a fee (usually referred to a licensing fee or royalty rate). It is sometimes simpler to understand IP rights in terms of what the IP owner can prevent others from doing with its IP.

Copyrights owners have the sole and exclusive right to copy, transfer, and publicly perform or display (whichever is applicable) their works, as well as to create derivative works, which are works that are based upon the copyright owner's original creation. They may also prevent all others from exercising these rights without permission, which usually includes payment of a licensing and/or royalty fee.

Trademarks owners have the sole and exclusive right to use their mark on their goods and/or services and to prevent all others from using the same or a similar mark for the same or similar goods and services.

Trade Secrets owners have the sole and exclusive right to benefit from use of their secret(s) and to prevent their unauthorized use and disclosure.

Patent owners have the sole and exclusive right to create or utilize the invention/process covered by the patent and to prevent all others from creating/using an identical or equivalent invention or process.

IP owners may also transfer some or all of their rights permanently to one entity (by an assignment) or for a limited duration to one or more entities (through licensing). An assignment terminates the IP owner's rights and transfers those rights to a third party. Licensing enables an IP owner to continue to use its IP at the same time as one or more others are using it.

Beyond these forms of IP there are less obvious, but equally important, forms such as intimate relationships with members of the value chain including customers and suppliers, obtaining proprietary approvals for the company's offerings, regulatory actions that support the company's position among others intangible forms of IP like the company's reputation in the market, etc. These can be critically important when employed in the context of the business because they're asymmetrical, favoring the company over its competitors in ways that are hard to defeat, but tend to be situational and managed separately. One example is an exclusive supply arrangement between the company and a customer based on a personal relationship between the CEOs, which is very difficult to breach.

The duration of IP rights depends on the nature of the IP

No one else has or can legally use IP assets without your permission. Unauthorized use of IP is considered "infringement" and may be remedied by sending cease and desist letters or by filing a lawsuit.

Copyright duration depends upon who created the work and when. If the work was created and owned by an individual author after January 1, 1978, copyright protection lasts during the author's life, plus 70 years after the author's death. For works owned by a corporation ("works made for hire") that were created after January 1, 1978, the duration of copyright will be 95 years from first publication or 120 years from creation, whichever is shorter. For works created before 1978, one must determine who created the work and when, and then consult the Copyright Act to determine the duration of rights under the applicable version of the Act.

Trademark rights last as long as the mark is used properly. Proper use includes preventing infringing uses and avoiding naked licensing (licensing without quality control) of the mark. *Trade Secret* rights exist as long as the secret remains secret. Disclosure of the secret, even through unauthorized means, can eliminate the trade secret. *Patent* rights duration depend on the type of patent application filed and when it was filed. Design patents last for 14 years from the date granted. Utility patents filed before June 8, 1995 expire 17 years after issue or 20 years from filing, whichever is longer. Utility patents filed after June 8, 1995 expire 20 years after filing.

IP registration creates a formal government record of the asset. This record serves as proof of certain evidence in litigation, and is like a deed to the IP asset when a business is sold. *Copyright* registration is not required for rights to exits, but is required to sue someone for infringement. *Trademark* registration is not required for rights to exist, but provides numerous additional and important benefits that are only attainable through registration. *Trade Secrets* are not registered (as registration would reveal the secret, thereby destroying it). *Patents* are the only IP assets that must be registered for rights to exist.

The majority of our purchasing decisions are based on brand names; everything we read is subject to copyright protection; we use patented inventions every day and we frequently consume or otherwise use trade secrets. Here are some of the ways that the people in your company or client's company deal with IP:

Marketing
- trademarks (brands, taglines, slogans, logos).
- copyrights (logos, marketing collateral).

IT
- copyrights (source code).

Design
- trademarks (brands, taglines, slogans, logos.
- copyrights (logos, marketing collateral).

Management
- copyrights (company and product manuals, guidelines, plans and strategies).
- trade secrets.
- trademarks (promoting the company's brand(s).

Research and Development
- patents (inventions, processes).

Sales
- copyrights (sales brochures, pitches).
- trade secrets (your company's unique selling technique).

IP – Management Process Patent Strategy Objectives

To obtain a comprehensive patent estate that covers the products the enterprise plans to sell and processes it plans to use. The object will be (a) to obtain broad, valid and enforceable patents covering current and potential products and processes with no holes in the coverage, and (b) to avoid piecemeal filing.

Management Review of Invention Disclosures. Establish management review committees for each division or business segment to meet periodically (e.g., quarterly) to evaluate invention disclosures. Committee to have representatives from management with decision making authority, Research, Development and Engineering, Marketing and Sales and a dedicated Patent Attorney.

The Committee has four roles. The first and most critical is to rate inventions for value from multiple dimensions identifying those that are primary – requiring broad comprehensive patent protection. Next the Committee recognizes those inventions worth patenting but scope and cost are to be controlled within established limits. Finally the Committee decides on filings to be delayed pending further developments or not appropriate for filing patent application. This final role also involves recognizing intellectual property worth protecting in a different way such as trade secrets.

Employee Training. The Intellectual Property Department will hold periodic education sessions to insure new employees are knowledgeable in intellectual property protect and to educate new hires. These educational sessions will be held no less than twice annually. The basic program will cover the following:

- Patents - how to recognize patentable invention.
- Trade secret - how to protect trade secrets.
- Copyright - use of copyright notices.
- Trademark - proper trademark usage.

The program will also communicate appropriate recognition tools encouraging the recognition of company intellectual property while supporting collaboration critical to the innovation process and without creating competition among inventors. The incentive program is specifically design to encourage the filing of invention disclosures.

Record Keeping is critical given if litigation occurs all records can be obtained and often interpreted in ways unimagined by the inventor who wrote them. Hence being careful with record keeping is an imperative. Employee will receive notebooks for recording ideas, experiments, combined with an implementation system for numbering notebooks and controlling access to notebooks. Employees will be educated how to maintain proper invention records and will be tested periodically to assess continuing capability. Invention disclosure forms will develop and distributed to appropriate personnel for submitting ideas to management for consideration.

Protection of Confidential Technical and Business Information. The intellectual property team will develop, implement and monitor procedures for protecting confidential information at each business facility (i.e., offices, production plants, warehouses, research/ engineering centers) and share this accountability with the local management team. The program will be proactive and auditable using sign in/out requirement for all visitors including visitor identification tags, escorts complimented with limited access through monitored gates/reception areas. Confidentiality agreements to be signed by all employees with key employee signing more extensive confidentiality agreements that contain carefully drafted non-compete clauses. Confidentiality agreements with customers/suppliers will include forms that can be quickly prepared with minimal amount of information from the field. These will include but not be limited to the following:

1. one-way agreement with information going out from company.
2. one-way agreement with information coming into company.
3. two-way exchange of information.

In each case the company representative managing the relationship with the external party will be responsible for determining whether standard secrecy agreements are sufficient or whether a more sophisticated joint development agreement is needed. The Intellectual Property Law team will assist in this process as required. If other party makes improvements or inventions, based on company technology, joint development agreement required. Finally the Intellectual Property Law department will develop filing system (and possible database) for maintaining control of and access to confidentiality agreements.

Competitor Patents. It shall be the policy of the company not to infringe any valid patents of any competitor supported by taking the following steps:

4. Identify key competitors and/or technologies that are critical to the company.
5. Collect/review all patents that relate to such competitors and/or technologies.
6. Develop database for recording basic information concerning identified patents.
7. Periodically review patent literature for relevant patents and update database.
8. Competitor patents to be reviewed for impact on business plans and to access new technology of competitors from a technological perspective as well as a commercial perspective.

When adverse patents are identified, the appropriate invalidity/non-infringement opinions will be obtained, licenses sought, or design-arounds implemented with consultation from patent attorneys.

Monitoring of Infringing Products and Enforcement of Company Patents. A review committee for monitoring infringing products and enforcing the company's patents will allow salesmen/field personnel to be educated in identifying competitive products that may infringe the company's patents. Enforcement of the company's patents will include licensing and if need be litigation

Licensing of The Company's Technology. Identify technology/patents that the company's desires to maintain exclusively – these are not be licensed along with technology/patents that the company is willing to license. A team lead by the business unit's designate, supported by the Intellectual Property Department and R&D will determine if licensing is appropriate and the business unit we assign value. The business unit designate with help for Corporate Law will negotiate licensing agreements. In general licensing agreements will consider exclusive/non-exclusive arrangements, geographic and field of use limitations and royalty rates.

Trademarks. A survey will be conducted no less than annually identifying the inventory of all corporate trademarks for the purpose of identifying the trademarks considered to be most valuable to the company. This inventory will be used to obtain federal registrations to be obtained for all trademarks (including the corporate logo) deemed to be valuable. The most important trademarks are to be registered in foreign countries where business activity is significant or is expected to be significant for the products covered by such trademarks.

Guidelines regarding consistent use of trademarks to be established and distributed to label makers, advertisers, among others, will be monitored by the company for compliance and competitor trademark usage to be monitored for conflict with any the company's trademarks. Official Gazette of the U.S.P.T.O. to be monitored for trademarks that may be in conflict with the company's trademarks leading to oppositions to be filed in cases of serious conflict.

Copyrights. All literature published by the company, including advertisements, instruction manuals, packaging labels, and the like will contain proper copyright notice. The aforementioned IP protection process describes how patents, trade secrets, know-how, trademarks and copyrights will be managed.

The following framework only considers patent IP since these are commonly the most extensive forms of protection and require the greatest investment. A coherent IP strategy must be both multi-dimensional and customized supporting specific business outcomes. The intent is that one basic approach to managing patent IP can be applied across the business allowing for a separate approach needs to be employed for trade secrets, know-how, trademarks and other forms of IP.

A comprehensive patent IP management system must include the following elements:

Industry Characteristics
1. Relevance of IP in the industry.
2. Degree of competitiveness.
3. Innovation rate.
4. Product life cycles.
5. IP fit in firm.

Patent Estate Characteristics
6. Patent intent – defensive, offensive, revenue generating, providing negotiating leverage or supporting corporate image/brand.
7. Patent strategies – single or multi-application portfolio supported by a definitive filing approach – blanketing, fencing, surrounding, or networking.
8. Patent portfolio management – random, cost efficient, revenue maximizing, integrated with business operations, visionary by creating future opportunities and margin.
9. Patenting tactics – aggressive, active, selective, passive or reputational.

Patenting Approaches
10. Aggressive – very serious competitive tool. Primary business goal is extracting value from patents (e.g., IBM).
11. Active – driven by large degree of competition, need for legal protection and exclusion (e.g., specialty chemical industry).
12. Selective – used where innovation is high and product life cycles short (e.g., electronics).
13. Passive – protect core technology, slow rates of innovation, high capital costs and need freedom to operate (e.g., petrochemicals).
14. Reputation – driven company's image.

Patent Portfolio Characteristics
15. Size – the patent portfolio should be large enough and comprised of relevant patents to enable cross-licensing if desired.
16. Breadth – self-citations of strategic patents exceeds 20% indicates that the "patent fence" has become effective.
17. Velocity – time between granting of original strategic patents and patents for follow- on technology. With shorter time frames desired.

18. Momentum – refers to the growth trend of the patent portfolio in numbers of patents. Building portfolios growth on average by 10% annually.
19. Claim quality and scope – refer to enforceability of the claims and breadth of coverage per patent.
20. Geographic reach – describes reach and should defend where the business is located or anticipated.

Patent Intent – Definitions

Defensive intent – patent is used by a company to protect its own property against external competition in order to safeguard the developed technology and its commercialization. The patent is considered an effective weapon enabling the company to exclude competitors and secure as large a market share possible

Offensive intent – patent covers technology likely to be needed by, or is useful to, competitors where creating value comes from product sales, licensing and/or from strategic alliances formed to reach new markets

Increasing bargaining power intent – patent provides for a better negotiation positions for example in licensing agreements

Imagine intent – patent is considered an instrument aimed at bolstering a company's public image as a technologically strong enterprise

Promoting intent – patent protection is often viewed as the decisive tool to secure sufficient payback for R&D investments, especially in an environment of increased national and international technological competition. Patents can be used as a means of encouraging employee creativity and as a form of recognition

Patent Strategy – Elements

Single patent strategy – the company protects its technology asset with a single patent.

Multiple patents strategy – the company defends its technological asset with multiple patents. The strategies can be classified as followed:

- **Blanketing strategy** – the efforts are made to turn on area into a "minefield" of patents. This strategy is the less structured way of tracking out multiple patents. In this strategy a company patents not only the base technology but also peripheral and even unrelated technologies.

- **Fencing strategy** – is a more methodical approach of a "blanketing" strategy where different patents are developed blocking certain lines or directions of R&D (e.g. a range of variants of a chemical process).
- **Surrounding strategy** – a strategic patent is fenced in or surrounded by other patents. The surrounded patent(s) are generally less important than strategic patent, but collectively block the commercial use of patented technology even after the core patent has expired.
- **Networking strategy** – a technological area is protected with a close network of patents filings. This is a narrower form of a "fencing" strategy.

Patent Portfolio Management

A patent portfolio can be managed in different way according to the expectation that a company has about the contributions that his IP be making to the company's goal.

- **No criteria management** – the IP is considered a legal resource, an instrument to protect the company own technology but the management of these assets does not follow any criteria. Having a very high number of patents is the only guideline.
- **Cost cutting management** – a patent is still considered a legal instrument, but the management is focused on reducing IP costs. Patents are useful instruments to protect a company's core business, but the company to recognize that maintenance fees of patents are high and consequently refine and focus both IP creation and portfolio to control costs.
- **Revenue maximization management** – a patent is considered not only a legal instrument but a business tool, an instrument able to generate additional income. So the management of patent portfolios is driven by extracting revenue from licensing.
- **Integration management** – IP is embedded in the company's day-to-day operations and procedures. The focus is on IP not only as a legal and strategic asset but is also supportive of the decision making process.
- **Visionary management** – a patent is considered a tool to create opportunities for future margins. The company tries to foresee future trends and technologies and seeks actively to position itself as a leader in this field by acquiring or development IP that gives them this position.

Patent Portfolio Approaches

Aggressive. An aggressive approach to IP means patenting represents a significant investment and is viewed as a competitive tool and a critical part of the business strategy. IP management is oriented towards supporting the decision making process and is embedded in the company's day-to-day operations. The management of IP includes evaluating the progress of innovations toward commercialization, re-evaluating the strategic importance of each innovation, generating new patents identifying the technological area in which new or more patents are desired. Patents become an important value driver with the primary business goal being extracting value from the patent portfolio. This is a typical feature of high-tech (IT) firms. Patents are important tools because they:

- Grant a monopoly right that prohibits others from commercializing the patented technology without express permission from the patent holder.
- Are important because represent a source of income, helping the company finance measures to strengthen its competitive advantage.
- Reinforce the bargaining power of patent owner.

Having a wide and strong patent portfolio is a useful instrument in negotiations or cross-licensing agreements and the mere existence of a broad portfolio can intimidate negotiating with the company. This strategy requires holding of a large number of patents leading to a blanketing patent strategy where each patent has a large blocking power but comes with high costs.

Active. Specialty chemical is an industrial sector where an active strategy is commonly employed in protecting its core business. A specialty chemical firm applies for a patent to safeguard the developed technologies and their commercialization, and to protect the R&D investment from competition. For a specialty chemical firm the patent is a critical asset. The specialty chemical industry is characterized by high innovation rates and strong, determined competition. When competition is significant specialty chemical firms choose a defensible and focused network of patent filings where the firm protects its basic inventions from outflanking patents and also covers possible future applications.

In the specialty chemical industry patents can be considered an incentive system for research and development professionals. Patents are considered a critical means of driving revenues and creating profit.

Selective. Where industries are characterized by high innovation rates and short product life cycles, such as the electronics, the patent is considered as an instrument to spread know-how that will allow followers to copy the industry leader so trade secrets can be preferred forms of protection. Where patents are filed their purpose is to cover technological areas that are likely to be needed by, or are useful, to competitors. In this situation, the company files patents to block certain lines or direction of competitors' R&D rather than enable sales. The IP activities are strategically focused, looking outside the company and into the future. To be effective the company must be able to identify future trends of the marketplace and rival organizations and willing to use patents as bargaining instruments. A company, having a selective approach to IP, is broadly focused on technologies that can be developed and patented in anticipation of some future use.

Passive. A passive approach to IP uses patents to protect its core technology and enable freedom to operate. A passive approach is characterized by a small patent portfolio but one with a high technological capacity, large blocking power and substantial economic impact. This behavior is typical of a mature, slow growing industrial sector like petrochemicals. Its patent portfolio management is based on cost control and limiting coverage to well defined business areas. A review of selected patents will determine whether the company can terminate maintenance payments and still retain effective coverage.

Reputational. A reputation-based approach to IP management means considers patents as instruments to solely bolster a company's public image. The number of patent filed is considered as a proxy of firm's reputation consequently firms having this behavior adopt a blanketing patent strategy. But unlike aggressive approach, the patent can be the result of a modest investment. Companies with a reputation-based approach do not follow any criteria in IP management but hopes that by creating a large number of patents it can appear as a technologically strong enterprise. Having a very high number of patents is the only guideline of this IP management.

Patent Portfolio Characteristics

- **Size** – the patent portfolio should be large enough and comprised of relevant patents to enable cross-licensing if desired.
- **Breadth** – self-citations of strategic patents exceeds 20% indicates that the "patent fence" has become effective.
- **Velocity** – time between granting of original strategic patents and patents for follow-on technology. With shorter time frames desired.
- **Momentum** – refers to the growth trend of the patent portfolio in numbers of patents. Building portfolios growth on average by 10% annually.
- **Claim quality and scope** – refer to enforceability of the claims and breadth of coverage per patent.
- **Geographic reach** – describes reach and should defend where the business is located or anticipated.

Curveball Strategies: Additional Ways to Protect Your Technology[52]

Success in the marketplace is ultimately achieved by winning customers, not by defeating competitors. No matter how tough or clever you are, you have to deliver products or services, that customers value. After all, competitors eventually will catch on to the curves you're throwing and adjust their moves in response. Strategic hardball, playing rough and tough with competitors, employs smart strategies to defeat rivals. Strategic curveball, outfoxing competitors, can be just as effective in vanquishing the competition.

An Effective Curve Will Get Rivals to:

- **Do Something Dumb** that they otherwise wouldn't have that is, swing at a pitch that appears to be in the strike zone but in fact isn't, or
- **Not Do Something Smart** that they otherwise would have failed to swing at a pitch that appears not to be in the strike zone but in fact is.

Here's How to Throw Four Types of Curveballs

Draw your rival out of the profit zone. Lure competitors into disadvantageous areas, for example, by competing for, but intentionally failing to win, the business of less profitable customers. In a classic curveball move, Ecolab adopted a pricing strategy that helped Diversey win- to its detriment-these seemingly attractive customers: It priced its bids to small independents high enough to lose to Diversey but low enough to keep pressure on Diversey's margins.

Meanwhile, Ecolab focused on big chain accounts, which, although they commanded lower prices and were more difficult to acquire, were cheaper to serve. The high volumes they purchased generated economies of scale, and the number of outlets involved meant they were less likely to switch suppliers. Ecolab priced aggressively to win this business. The result was gross margins that, if the prices were matched by Diversey, would wreak havoc on its high-margin strategy.

Employ unfamiliar techniques. Knock rivals off balance by importing a technique used in another industry, for example, employing the retailer's hard sell in the stodgy world of retail financial services. The financial institutions mainly sought to keep costs down while preserving their market share and margins. Their one area of major investment was in customer relationship management techniques and technologies, designed to load up existing customers with ever more complicated products and product extensions in the hope of squeezing the last bit of profit from their wallets. Hornby used brash tactics to challenge the incumbents.

---

[52] "Curveball: Strategies to Fool the Competition", Stalk, Jr. George, HBR September, 2006.

Between 1999 and 2001, when the Halifax merged with the Bank of Scotland to become HBOS, the institution set for itself a goal of having the "best deal on the street" - an aim more reminiscent of Best Buy than Barclays Bank. It offered attractive deals including interest- bearing checking accounts and aggressively priced credit cards and loans that weren't tied to holding a mortgage with the bank. HBOS also ran its branches as retail sales outlets. They were remodeled to resemble High Street retailers, and the conversion of the branches went beyond cosmetics.

Managers exhorted the staff to close sales and rewarded them when they did. Incentive compensations, nearly unknown in the UK retail banking industry, further boosted lead generation and drove sales productivity to three times that of some rivals. In another parallel to the retail business, computer systems generated prompts for sales staff to use when interviewing prospective customers and provided back-office support from product IT systems Specialist and point of sale expertise allowed sales people to make immediate decisions on, say, a loan application and reduced the after- sales administrative burden of the sales team. Today, HBOS is the largest and one of the most profit- able retail banks in the UK, and it is growing at double-digit rates in overall revenue, revenue from new business, and profits.

Disguise your success. Veil your success by achieving an advantage through unlikely means- for example, generating product sales through your service operations. One way to throw competitors off balance is to mask high performance so rivals fail to see your success until it's too late. For example, you might drive sales through your service organization, making service technicians de facto sales representatives, effectively transforming a cost center into a profit center.

In the late 1990s, two companies, MedicTec and DiaDevice, not their real names, were in the business of designing, manufacturing, selling, and servicing a wide array of medical diagnostic equipment, ranging from $15,000 desktop devices to $6 million electronic behemoths that fill entire rooms. DiaDevice, the industry leader in a white coat was following them and, finding it hard to imagine that a doctor would be interested in this review, asked the engineering head about the interloper. The man turned out to be a service technician from DiaDevice, which had only a few pieces of equipment at the hospital. The real surprise, though: The technician was as- signed to the site full time.

This didn't make sense, Allan said to himself. MedicTec had significantly more equipment at the hospital but could *never* afford to dedicate a service technician to a customer of this size. Granted, providing a rapid and effective response to equipment problems was particularly important for DiaDevice as it strove to gain customers in North America.

But with service costs totaling between 15% and 20% of revenue at a company like MedicTec or DiaDevice, you didn't want to provide more service than was needed to keep a customer satisfied. Sophisticated algorithms for service scheduling, which took into account such things as the cost to customers of service interruptions, determined optimal service levels and guaranteed that "over-servicing" wouldn't occur. Standard industry algorithms would certainly not have justified a full-time service representative at this hospital.

How your company identifies & distinguishes its products & / or services in from those offered by others the marketplace (through use of trademarks). Figure out whether your company has any secrets that give it a competitive edge, and whether it has invented anything that may be eligible for patent protection. Don't forget to make sure that you have permission to use the names, But Allen was curious. Back at the office, he pulled together data on customers for whom many did offer a dedicated service engineer. Those customers were typically in major cities where service algorithms had indicated that a full-time service technician was cost-effective. Allan's review initially uncovered no surprises.

Although the sites with dedicated service technicians had lower equipment downtime rates and higher customer satisfaction scores, the differences weren't significant. The algorithm apparently was working, keeping service cost low with no serious decline in customer satisfaction.

Digging deeper, though, Allan saw that service contract renewal rates at these locations were roughly twice the national average for a medic tent customers, perhaps not Europe, was increasingly gaining market share in North America. MedicTec managers were convinced that DiaDevice was buying its way into the market with low- ball prices and that the only way to meet the challenge was to out-hustle the newcomer on the sales front.

MedicTec's service chief, Allan, decided to undertake his own evaluation of the problem. Breaking away from the demands of headquarters, he began a round of customer visits. At one site, the largest hospital in a midsize midwestern city, Allan toured the facility with the hospital's head of engineering, stopping at each piece of MedicTec equipment to discuss its operating strengths and weaknesses.

Perhaps not surprising given customers' satisfaction with the service they received. But that wasn't all: New equipment sales at sites with a dedicated service technician were *also* about twice the national average for MedicTec customers. Subsequent conversations with these customers revealed that MedicTec's on-site service engineers didn't only generate customer satisfaction and goodwill, many engineers pitched in to repair rival suppliers' products when they went down -they also tended to boost new equipment sales by influencing a hospital's request-for-proposals process.

Who better to provide input into the request for proposal (RFP), the hospital's purchasing team would reason, than an on-site technician who knew the strengths and weaknesses of all the equipment installed at the hospital, whichever the supplier, and who knew how best to fill gaps or extend the institution's capabilities to meet growing needs?

This clearly was what DiaDevice had set out to do-not in big hospitals where MedicTec already had dedicated service technicians but in the second-tier hospitals where MedicTec had determined that on-site service wasn't cost-effective. Here, DiaDevice was gaining share in both service-contract renewals and new equipment sales, virtually unopposed by MedicTec. It wasn't easy for Allan to convince his colleagues that MedicTec should place full-time technicians at the sites of customers ripe for poaching by DiaDevice. MedicTec's investment criteria were heavily driven by cost-oriented savings.

In the company's culture, it was better to place your bets on cost reduction, where you could control the game, than on growth or marketing, where the numbers were hypothetical and success depended on others. Only when Allan was able to predict accurately at which sites MedicTec would lose share in both service-contract renewals and new equipment sales did the company respond to DiaDevice's stealth moves.

Stealth sales can be exploited in industries where field service is an important element in customer satisfaction and is a large portion of a supplier's cost structure. Such industries include aircraft engines and components, mass storage devices, factory equipment, and process automation systems. The key is to determine the effect that more customer service will have on service contract renewals and follow- on sales, particularly of new products where successful ramp-ups are critical to achieving deep customer satisfaction.

Let rivals misinterpret your success. Allow rivals to act on a conventional but incomplete explanation for your success-for example, squeezing costs rather than aggressively utilizing assets. We look at a successful company and we understand why it's successful-or at least we think we do. Buzz about the firm's innovative strategy spreads through the industry. Business media pick up the story and retell it from every angle. Before long, competitors and non-competitors alike are trying to emulate the company's moves, which have taken on the mystique of media and business- school legends.

Often, the conventional assessment is wrong, or at least incomplete. A successful company can sit passively by his rivals overlook key source, or even the key source, of its outstanding performance and stumble in trying to replicate. Arrival smart enough to see all elements of the strategy, though, can realize similar success, nailing the curveball for a home run. Look at the recent history of low cost airlines. To meet the competitive challenge posed by startups such as Southwest, major carriers launch their own low-cost operations. Most of those initiatives Think how Continental light, Delta song, US Air's Metro, and United's TED have enjoyed less than stunning results. That's because most big carriers failed to appreciate and implement on of the key drivers of newcomers' outstanding performance.

Most of the elements of Southwest's strategy are available for public scrutiny: one aircraft model for the fleet, low landing fees at out-of-the-way airports, low training and labor costs, no pension obligations, and -most conspicuously, minimal in-flight amenities provided by fun, loving flight attendants dressed in Bermuda shorts. This view of Southwest's sources of success is accurate but incomplete.

The curveball Southwest threw its competitors and ultimately the industry is a strategy of extreme asset utilization. The company uses a production-oriented approach to scheduling, with the goal of keeping planes in the air as much of the time as possible.

Traditional carriers, on the other hand, typically have a customer-oriented approach to scheduling, one that will tolerate a plane remaining on the ground for, say, 20 extra minutes in order to pick up connecting passengers or accommodate business customers' preference for top-of-the-hour departures. Southwest structured its operations around being able to turn its planes at the gates within 20 minutes and get them flying again. This was a much faster turnaround time than legacy carriers' typical 60 to 90 minutes at the gate. By keeping its planes in the air 20% to 30% more hours, Southwest achieved higher asset utilization rates for aircraft *and* employees.

Southwest's point-to-point route network also enhanced asset utilization. In the hub- and-spoke network of most traditional carriers, a plane arriving late to a hub typically results in three planes being late leaving the gate, with at least six pilots and nine to 12 cabin attendants experiencing unplanned downtime. A late plane arrival in a point-to-point network affects the utilization of just one plane, two pilots, and three cabin attendants. The high asset utilization model is at least as important to Southwest's success as its reduced labor costs and bare- bones customer service. As asset turns increase, the prices required to maintain the return on assets can be reduced, which leads to lower fares, fuller planes, and, completing the virtuous circle, even greater asset utilization. As Southwest knockoffs appeared around the world, AirTran and JetBlue in the United States, Ryanair and Easy Jet in Europe, Virgin Blue in Australia -most legacy carriers failed to see the significance of asset utilization to the effectiveness of Southwest's strategy or were unable to escape the traditional approaches of their base businesses to emulate it.

Import successful business models. Competitive practices from another industry are most likely to succeed in slow-growing businesses with established supplier-customer relationships and stable market shares. In such cases, the industry participants are comfortable with their business models. Their cash flows are predictable and come from a core group of customers that they approach using sophisticated methods honed over time. In such a setting look around for strategies that have worked in other industries where this is the case and ask, "Why not try that here?"

Where Curveballs Come From

The opportunities to throw your competitor a curve are everywhere. We have described four in this article; there are many more. But how do you identify such opportunities? The best way is to look beyond the "averages". We manage our lives and our businesses using aver- ages. If we didn't, we'd be so overwhelmed with information that we couldn't manage at all. But this approach masks a gloriously rich world.

As soon as we choose an average on which to make decisions, we cut ourselves off from more detailed information that could lead to insight affecting our decisions and our results. The insights that led to the curveball strategies discussed here can be traced to looking beyond the averages: Making marginal customers seem attractive. Income statements and balance sheets are infested with averages. Dig beyond the aggregation of accounts and look for out- lying patterns in such areas as the cost to serve a customer or pricing by account size. When you do, you are likely to find new ways of looking at the business and its customers that were disguised by the aggregation of accounts. Chances are, if you have been misled by the aggregations your competitors have been, as well.

Importing best practices. The most egregious form of averaging is "industry practice!' When confronted with this standard way of doing things, look for an industry or industries where the practices are different. Don't let yourself be discouraged when people point out that there are good reasons why effective practices from one industry won't work in yours; that attitude makes companies more susceptible to a curveball.

Stealth sales. Ask an executive what his company's market share is and the answer will usually be an average. Drill deeper to determine the figure by account or by different service and sales force deployment models and you will see the data begin to scatter. In the scatter pattern between the best and the average results, it is very likely you will be able to identify new strategies others have missed.

Extreme asset utilization. The relevant, but ultimately unasked, question over the past decade or so has been: "How can low-cost airlines charge so much less than the savings from cutting costs suggest possible and still be so much more profitable and faster growing?" If the executives of legacy airlines looked more closely at their performance data they would see situations-when ground time for aircraft and crews is minimized, when airplanes and crews consistently make it back to home base at the end of the day -in which asset utilization is much higher than average. By dissecting asset utilization as a function of variables that drive that utilization, one can begin to see the outlines of a new way to run a business. Looking beyond the averages often yields new strategy and operational paradigms that help senior managers make better decisions and ensure they are acted upon on a day-to-day basis. By contrast, if competitors settle into managing the averages, they will not immediately, or even for an extended period, see the curveballs they are thrown.

Portfolio Creation – Why go there

Great portfolios come from making great decisions and knowing how to say no and meaning it.
~ Anonymous ~

The following scheme is for aligning strategy with critical market problems where the firm's core competencies align with market needs while meeting financial expectations. There are many specific schemes available for portfolio management.[53] [54] Regardless of which tools are employed, they must not become the end in themselves but serve the greater purpose of informing decisions.

A universal critical success factor is identifying problems which impact many customers in a given market segment so a successful solution can reach scale quickly. The problems and solutions must be defined in the context of the value proposition, satisfying the financial requirements of the firm and customer. From this analysis a detailed, written description of an offering is drafted, describing well-defined features and benefits as well as how the offering will satisfy the tenants of the value proposition. Concurrently, the offerings must be measurable against a defined set of metrics while having access to post- sale support resources.

The project leader is the primary owner of the outcomes, partnering with a marketing leader who owns the customer relationship and the product line management responsibilities. The project leader works closely with the resource managers to obtain access to support resources required to complete the project objectives. The basic schematic is shown below.

---

[53] Kodukula, Prasad, Project Portfolio Management: A Practitioner's Guide to Excellence, ISBN: 1-932159-42-8, Hardcover, October 2006.
[54] Blichfeldt bodil Stilling, Eskerod Pernille. Project Portfolio Management – There's More To It Than What Management Enacts, *International Journal Of Project Management* Volume 26, Issue 4, May 2008, pages 357– 365.

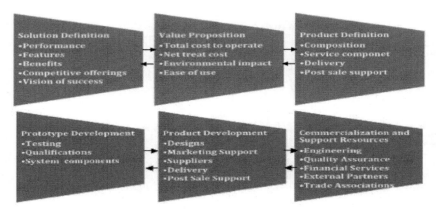

Figure 8. Portfolio Management Process

The primary project profile must be at the technology level aligning with the business strategy driven by selling out capacity. From the chemistry project descriptions will flow a view of application fits which helps define leverage for a given molecule and approach.

Project Analysis Criteria

Each project is subjected a series of basic measures including both project and financial descriptors. The non-financial measures are captured in the project brief, which becomes the primary source of data feeding the dashboard and project reports. Each project brief contains the following:

Date	Project is initiated
Project Platform	If appropriate
Project Title	Defined by commercial and technical leaders
Project Number	Numerical without descriptive data to preserve history and will be retired when the project is complete
Project Stage	Disc., Dev., or Commercialization
Technical Project Leaders	Resource manage and project manage
Commercial Project Leaders	Product and relationship manage
Purpose	Why is the investment being made?
Objective	What is to be accomplished?
Vision of Success	How will success be recognized?
Resources Requirements	How much will be invested (e.g., Operating budget, FTEs, Capital, etc.)
Action Plan	What will be done and when?
Timing	How long will it take?

Metrics	How will progress and success be measured (e.g., by project, product, etc.)?
Critical Path items	What's critical to success?
Results	What happened over a given period of time or money invested?
Reporting	When will information be communicated (e.g., monthly, quarterly, other)?

This brief, combined with the descriptors for discovery, development and commercialization projects will populate the profile log used to create reports from the data warehouse.

Universal project descriptors:

- Objectives – specific rational and purpose for doing the work.
- Vision of Success – written description of a successful technical outcome.
- Budget – people, external spending, capital etc.
- Schedule – timing to next milestone and completion.
- Metrics – how progress will be measured: budget, timing, technical achievements, application data, customer responses, etc.
- Readiness – IP, HS&E, supply capability, etc.

Universal financial and commercial descriptors:

- Revenue expectations – at maturity.
- Gross profit expectations – key assumptions.
- R&D Investment – internal and partners
- Competitive advantage – compared to currently offerings.
- Timing to first sale.

Collectively, these metrics drive decisions on prioritization. A narrative about assumptions must accompany each set of metrics. In estimating financial values and probabilities of commercial and technical success for discovery projects where uncertainty is high but risk is low, a description of *high*, *medium* or *low* should be used according to the table below:

Table 11. Example of Discovery Project Descriptors

Metric	High	Medium	Low	Comments
Revenues[1]	>$100MM	~$50MM	<$10MM	Global scope
Gross profit[1]	>30%	~20%	<15%	At scale
R&D investment[2]	>$1MM	~$0.5 MM	<$0.2five MM	Inclusive of partnerships
Competitive Advantage	New to the industry	Lower cost and better performance	Equal cost/performance	Based on customer feedback
Timing to sale	>3years	~1-3 years	<1 year	Based on customer feedback
IP Strength	Composition and applications	Applications only	FTO supported by trade secrets	As determined by legal counsel
HS&E	Requires Gov't registrations	Normal approvals (e.g., PMNs etc.)	Limited (e.g., MSDS etc.)	Supported by external analysis.
Probability of Success[3]	>75%	~50%	<25%	Risk based
Critical Technical Success Factors	Impact continuation of the project	Impact financial value of the investment	Resolution is defined	Must provide continuity between project updates

[1]At maturity, [2]Total program through development but not including launch. [3] "High probability" indicates no serious risks exist in accomplishing the objectives. "Medium probability" suggests 1-2 serious risks that could end the project but are well defined. "Low probability" indicates the risks are immeasurable and/or substantial concerns remain.

For probabilities of commercial and technical success, *high, medium* and *low* are defined as follows: As a project matures and moves towards application and product development, detailed financial projections are formulated by marketing defining specific revenues, gross profit and discount cash flows expectations built by customer, market segment, application and time frame. The key activity in managing the portfolio is a monthly review where decisions are made from the collective judgment of the technical and commercial leaders involved in the work. Portfolio owners would review those projects having significant channel along with a brief update on the overall portfolio's progress. For more advanced discovery projects moving into development and commercialization where investments and therefore risk increase dramatically, a more quantitative analysis is performed. It still relies on management judgment but is prompted by specific questions about value to the customer, technical feasibility, market attractiveness, and competitive advantage.

Information System Support

In order for the system to be relevant it must be current, accurate and easy to use by the project leaders and management. The IT system will be web-based with a "front end" built on a data warehouse driven by a relational database. This will eliminate the need for a structured data file and allow a flexible form of data capture (e.g., Word documents, Excel spread sheets, PowerPoint presentation, etc.) and retrieval. The front end will provide a dashboard of metrics supported by a series of programmed reports. Customized reports will be possible for "Power Users." All financial data will be audited by Finance on a periodic basis. Project identifiers will be numeric and not contain any descriptive information. Each project identifier will be used only once to preserve a projects history. All work associated with a given project, like spectral data, analysis, application tests results etc., will be recognized by the project identifier.

The database will collect data from various parts of the business process and in varying formats. A critical feature will be to collect data and information in forms it is normally collected for communication and used without modification. Ideally these documents will be dragged into the data warehouse where they can be searched and assembled at will or into standardized reports.

The reports will be customized according to the position the project holds in the Stage Gate process from discovery to launch. Exact terminology is to be determined but the concept is to add detail and confidence in the data as the project matures and to have the data content reflect this reality. Specifically, for early stage projects where certainty is low then high to low descriptors are to be used. As the project becomes better defined, quantitative measures will be used like revenues per unit time, gross profit, and investment requirements, all described in a common currency.

Open Innovation – Look Outside

Using someone else' innovation is the highest form of flattery
~ Anonymous ~

Open Innovation[55] [56] [57] – Vision and Strategy

The definition of Open Innovation (OI) is widely accepted to be what Henry Chesbrough called "a paradigm that assumes firms can, and should, use external ideas and internal and external paths to markets, as the firms look to advance their technology." The OI concept, first considered in the 1980s, emerged as a meaningful technology strategy in the middle 1990s and has been extensively viewed as a key to successes at companies like P&G, General Mills, IBM and others. OI is based on a firm joining forces with other world-class companies and organizations and sharing resources. Examples include:

- Pfizer and Warner-Lambert joining forces to market Lipitor.
- Clorox developing more than 75% of their innovations with external partners.
- IBM earning $1.2 billion per year out-licensing its technology.

This approach has also been dubbed by academics as "open-sourced innovation," or the more recent and wider "transformational growth." Innovative companies clearly recognize the critically important role open innovation plays in making their strategies successful. Ad-hoc processes in place, while effective, are neither efficient nor sustainable, and must be replaced with formal methodologies. The proposed methodologies must be owned, focused on current potential partners, initially suppliers, but rooted in benchmarked processes of leaders in Open Innovation techniques. Successful processes allow for unsolicited proposals from diverse places from entrepreneurs to major customers and must be as data-driven as possible. The initial framework should employ the WANT-FIND-GET-MANAGE system with a dedicated staff of professionals leading the effort.

[55] Huston, Larry, Sakkab, Nabil,. *Inside Proctor & Gamble's New Model for Innovation*, Harvard Business School Publishing, Boston, MA, March, 2006.
[56] Mortara, Letizia et al., *How to Implement Open Innovation: Lessons from Studying Large Multinational Companies,* University of Cambridge Institute for Manufacturing, 2006, ISBN:978-1-902546-75-09.
[57] Chesbrough, H. W. *Open Innovation: The New Imperative for Creating and Profiting from Technology*, Harvard Business School Publishing, Boston, MA, 2003

Situation Analysis

Common to each OI relationship are partner selection, partner motivation and reward structures, intellectual property management, internal project leadership and accountability, and ultimately, adequate leverage of internal investments as measured by the firm's financial results.

An illustrative example will focus on technology-related open innovation, although one could think of open innovation extending beyond technology and involving customer and marketing approaches. For example, the strategic alliance between Pepsi and Lipton not only involved a technologically co-developed innovation in mass-producing bottled tea from concentrate filled by Pepsi bottlers, but also allowed Lipton to reach consumers of ready-to- consume tea and Pepsi to spread out its plant and distribution overhead over more products.

Evaluating other companies, who have successfully employed OI, it is clear that formalizing the firms OI process will require a dedicated effort and must begin with a "supplier focused" strategy given this is where the quickest results will originate from while creating a model for the firm to employee with other entities such as universities, independent consultants and technology brokers, once the supplier-based system is established.

Supplier Focused OI

A Supplier Focused OI program will involve four specific elements:
- Efficiently identifying relevant external technologies.
- Deepening relationships with existing supplier-partners.
- Successfully managing intellectual property agreements.
- Effectively maintaining partnership relationships over time.

Critical success factors will be:

- A dedicated organizational team with skills to identify potential technologies for meeting the needs of projects aligned with strategy.
- Opportunities that are carefully selected to meet with business objectives over defined time frames.
- Partners uniquely positioned to supply technology-specific areas of technology.

The advantages of an effective supplier-focused OI program will be first access to technology in the firm's market applications, a relatively uncontested negotiating position with partners, and faster commercialization of the technologies accessed.

A variety of successful open innovation frameworks have been proposed and implemented. A key realization is that each successful program is assimilated with the company's culture and norms. Hence copying the "P&G" system likely won't work as well for any other firm. Beyond the supplier OI process, more advanced techniques can be used such as the following:

- Problem re-definition – General Mills
- Job design matrix – ExxonMobil
- Sustainable reuse ecosystem – Intel
- Peer group performance systems – BP
- Partnership-focused press release – P&G
- Technology broker management – Nine Sigma, Yet2.Com

These should only be employed once more rudimentary processes for suppliers are delivering results. While a comprehensive OI program has many dimensions, there are several common features requiring answers to the following questions:

- What external resources does the company need to fulfill its strategic intent?
- What mechanisms will the company employ to find these external resources?
- What processes will the company employ to access the resources?
- What tools and metrics will the company successfully use?

Roche has designated this framework the WANT-FIND-GET-MANAGE (WFGM) network and below is how Slowinski presents an elegant summary of the main elements of the WFGM network.[58]

The critical success factors of the WFGM process are:

1. Clear, long-term links with strategy.
2. Correct infrastructure (e.g. people, money, IT, etc.).
3. Clear tactical targets and accountability (e.g. road maps and support of senior leadership).
4. External contacts and relationships (e.g. networks, technology brokers).
5. Well designed and current financial models (e.g. develop business cases).
6. Aligned intellectual property strategy (e.g. clear options and negotiating capabilities).
7. Defined and institutionalized management process (e.g. assigned, documented and pro-actively managed).
8. Appropriate metrics and management team (e.g. measurable KPIs, experienced alliance management).

---

[58] Slowinski, G. *Reinventing Corporate Growth – Implementing the Transformational Growth Model,* Alliance Management Group Inc., Gladstone, NJ, 2005.

Alignment with Strategy

- **Gillette** maintains alignment with strategy by utilizing the model where the External Research Director (ERD) lives in the R&D world and has direct access to scientists, can find external technology in a timely fashion, and can make use of an effective reward system.
- Strategic WANTS are fairly stable for reasonable periods of time, while project level WANTS are more dynamic. As a project evolves and a scientist learns more about the technical challenge new WANTS emerge at random. The ERD keeps these aligned with strategy.

Business Unit Inclusion

At P&G the business units set three and five-year growth goals and develop a portfolio of initiatives to achieve these results. R&D then uses these portfolios of initiatives as the foundation for the innovation plan. There is an explicit inclusion of external resources in the innovation plan. There is a separate unit that executes the WANT and FIND. It's called the Connect and Develop Group (C&DG). The group comprises 50 technology entrepreneurs who understand the collaborative possibilities in the innovation portfolio and find the contact in the outside world. Typically multiple external opportunities are presented for each.

Importance of "Connectedness"

- **Internal connectivity:** Create virtual R&D networks to match problems with solutions (**DuPont's** problem-post chat rooms).
- **External connectedness:** the external OI network may vary in sophistication from **P&Gs** 50-strong global technology entrepreneur team, to one-scout per region. An additional option is to use the power of **NERAC** and use their search advisors as surrogate scouts.
- **Overall connectedness: Air Products** has had high success with a database linked to e-mail that ensures proper flow of information on OI opportunities to the relevant parties. Automated e-mails alert any scientist in the company on technical solutions and developments matching a set of keywords defined by them.
- A simple rating by the scientist helps the system improve the quality of the leads. Air Products claims that 78 percent of the information sent had not been previously seen by the technologists and that 92 percent of it is useful. Of these 30 percent are considered "worth the receivers time" and one in ten leads to a lab visit, CDA or sample exchange. Out of 20 of these, 1 or 2 result in products that return significant dollars.

The literature suggests firms follow a gradual path of adoption of OI principles. The first stage applies to the traditional centralized/internal R&D organization with not- invented-here biases and most R&D dollars invested in-house. Those WANTs are analyzed for strengths and weaknesses in an interactive process, which helps crystallize the project teams thinking on the final technological approach and further refine focus for the FIND team.

Since Henry Chesbrough's seminal work on Open Innovation in 2003 the literature has exploded with case studies. The following links provide a limited snapshot of what's available.

- Examples of how big companies can play well with others by Francine Gordon http://ad.vu/w77k.
- IBM and intrapreneurship - interview with Sharon Nunes, head of IBM Big Green Innovation: http://bit.ly/4Fd4ab.
- Children's Creativity Won't be Stopped by LEGO's Innovation by Hutch Carpenter: http://bit.ly/TA3p2.
- Intellectual Assets for (Open) Innovation - Braden Kelley interviews Jackie Hutter: http://bit.ly/10H1KP.
- How to effectively "kill" ideas and innovate faster by Zia Khan and Jon Katzenbach: http://bit.ly/2pMBmW.
- Five Key Characteristics of an Entrepreneur by Matt Heinz: http://bit.ly/DB3pB.
- Why LEGO's Open Innovation program works, why others don't and what are the lessons to be learned by Klaus Speidel http://wp.me/pwvbc-4F.

Table 12. Want-Find-Get-Manage (WFGM) Framework

WANT - External resources needed	Comments
• Build an effective infrastructure to identify internal needs • Use the strategic plan to identify technical resources the firm wants • Decide which resources will be generated internally and which will be sourced externally • Prioritize the external resource needs based on strategic intent, market potential and probability of success	Strategic level wants and Project level wants. Strategic Plan states business needs so they can be translated into a set of technical specifications or a technology roadmap supported by the following pieces of information: • Internal patents supporting business • External patents blocking us from executing our strategic intent • Internal patents blocking competitors • Which IP most likely will drive market share both today and in the future • Which IP must be acquired externally? • What is the total value of these assets (time and financial)?

FIND - What mechanisms will be used to find these resources
• Utilize internal and external sources to identify appropriate external resources
• Build linkages into internal product development process to include external resources
• Identify clear decision-making criteria for assessing the quality and quantity of external resources
• Select appropriate valuation models for assessing the impact of external resources on profitability
• Develop initial business case
	Comments
	• Unsolicited Proposals
	• The External Research Director
	• Internal connectedness
	• External connectedness
	• Other tools:
	  ○ Innocentive
	  ○ YourEncore
	  ○ NineSigma
	  ○ Yet2.com

GET - What processes will be used to plan, structure and negotiate an agreement to get the resource • Create a team to carry out the Get and Manage functions • Ensure team is represented by every corporate functional group with a stake in the potential relationship • Careful assessment of strategic and resource compatibility of potential partners • Determine guiding principles, deal structure and terms	Comments
MANAGE - Tools, metrics and management techniques to implement the relationship • Alliance management specialists • Fair and equitable to both parties conflict resolution strategies • Periodic alliance performance reviews • Capturing of learning(s) and transfer throughout organization	Comments

Stage Gates – Where to go First

I've made a decision and now I must face the consequences.
~ J. Michael Straczynski ~

Phased scope development and investment decision is a fundamental concept of chemical engineering and engineering economics, particularly since the 1940s as chemical complexity and scale of chemical processes grew. One source describes eight phases in the development of a chemical product starting with research, economic study, scale-up (pilot plant) and design leading to full funds authorization.[59]

In 1958, the American Association of Cost Engineers created four standard cost estimate type classifications to match these development and approval phases.[60] Other industries with complex products and projects picked up on the process. For example, NASA practiced the concept of phased development in the 1960s with its phased project planning or what is often called *phased review process.*

The phased review process was intended to break up the development of any project into a series of phases that could be individually reviewed in sequence. Review points at the end of each phase required that a number of criteria be met before the project could progress to the next phase. The phased review process consisted of five phases (Preliminary Analysis, Definition, Design, Development, Operations) with periodic development reviews between phases.[61] NASA's phased review process is considered a first generation process because it did not take into consideration the analysis of external markets in new product development.

Stage-Gate process was developed in the1980s as a "second-generation NPD process" and is different from phase-review because it is a business process (not just R&D or engineering), built in best practices uncovered from studying exemplary NPD projects, and incorporated tough go/kill gates. Dr. Robert Cooper and the Product Development Institute ultimately trademarked Stage-Gate in the United States.

A number of variants of Stage-Gate were developed by a range of consulting firms employing different names, such as "phase-gate" process or "gating" process.

---

[59] Chemical & Engineering News 29: 3246. 1951.
[60] AACE Bulletin". April 1958.
[61] Chao, L.P.; Tumer, I.; Ishii, K. (2005). "Design Process Error-Proofing: Benchmarking Gate and Phased Review Life-Cycle Models".*Proceedings of the ASME Design Engineering Technical Conference* (Long Beach, California).

Typical Stage-Gate

The need for product innovation has never been greater. Product lifecycles are shorter than ever, and pressure continues to mount for organic growth. Companies that fail to innovate face a grim future. The problem is that winning with new products is not so easy. Only one out of four development projects succeed commercially, and one-third of all new-product launches fail. What do the winners do differently? What are the critical drivers of success? What is a Stage-Gate process? In practice a Stage-Gate process can accelerate or retard innovation depending on how it's managed. Evidence of a failed Stage-Gate process includes the following:

- The data required by the process is unavailable, inaccurate or poorly understood yet it's employed to inform decisions.
- It becomes onerous demanding unavailable quantitative data be used in place of expert judgment.
- It is an end in itself – completing the Stage-Gate forms is more important than successfully innovating.
- Participants use the process to "Just Say No" based on their internal agendas.

Many more failure points in a Stage-Gate® Process can be identified but it's more constructive focusing on making the process effective in promoting innovation.

The Structure of the Stage-Gate® Process

Fashion these critical success factors into a Stage-Gate new product game plan – a conceptual and operational model for moving a new product project from idea to launch. This Stage-Gate system is a blueprint for managing the new product process to improve effectiveness and efficiency. The Stage-Gate system breaks the innovation process down into a predetermined set of stages, each stage consisting of a set of prescribed, cross-functional, and parallel activities. The entrance to each stage is a gate. These gates control the process and serve as the quality control and Go/Kill checkpoints

The Stages

The Stage-Gate system breaks the new product project into discrete and identifiable stages, typically four, five, or six in numbers. Each stage is designed to gather information needed to move the project forward to the next gate or decision point. Each stage is multi, or cross-functional since there are no "R&D stages" or "marketing stage." Rather, each stage consists of a set of parallel activities undertaken by people from different functional areas within the firm, but working together as a team led by a project team leader. In order to manage risk via a Stage-Gate scheme, the parallel activities within a stage must be designed to gather vital information (technical, market, financial, and so on) in order to drive down technical and business uncertainties.

Each stage costs more than the preceding one, so that the game plan is one of incremental commitment. As uncertainties decrease, expenditures are allowed to mount. Finally, flexibility is built in to promote acceleration of projects. In order to speed products to market, stages can overlap each other; long lead-time activities can be brought forward from one stage to an earlier one; projects can proceed into the next stage, even though the previous stage has not been totally completed; and stages can be collapsed and combined. The five key and overlapping stages are as follows:

Stage 1:   Preliminary Investigation: a quick investigation and scoping of the project. Typically, this stage is undertaken by a very small core team of technical and marketing people; it includes the first-cut homework, such as preliminary market assessment, preliminary technical assessment, and preliminary business assessment.

Stage 2: Detailed Investigation: the detailed homework leading to a business case. Includes market research (a user needs and wants study to identify requirements for the ideal product; competitive analysis; and a concept test to confirm purchase intent); detailed technical and manufacturing assessment; and a detailed financial and business analysis. This stage should be undertaken by a core team of marketing, technical, and manufacturing people – the beginnings of the ultimate project team in Stage 3. The deliverables from Stage 2 include a defined product (on paper: target market, product concept and benefits, and product requirements); a business justification (economic and business rationale); and a detailed plan of action for the next stages (including resource requirements and timing).

Stage 3 Development: the actual design and development of the new product. Here the development plan is implemented; a prototype or sample product is developed; and the product undergoes in-house testing along with limited customer testing (for example, rapid-prototype-and- tests with potential users). Additionally, the manufacturing process and requirements are mapped out; the marketing launch plan is developed; and the test plans for the next stage are defined. Stage 3 sees the project gain momentum, with a marked increase in resource commitment: Here the full cross-functional project team – marketing, technical, manufacturing, and perhaps quality assurance, purchasing, sales, and finance people – is in place.

Stage 4 Testing and Validation: the verification and validation of the proposed new product, its marketing, and its production. This stage witnesses extensive in-house product testing; customer field trials or trials in the marketplace; pilot or preproduction trials in the plant; and even test marketing or a trial sell. The deliverable is a fully tested product and production process, ready for commercialization. The project team and leader from Stage 3 remain accountable for actions and deliverables in 4.

Stage 5 Full Production and Market Launch: Full commercialization of the product. Stage 5 marks the beginning of full production and commercial selling. This stage sees the implementation of the marketing launch plan, the production plan, and the post launch activities, including monitoring and adjustment. While new members may be added to this "commercialization team," for example, from the sales force or from operations, the core project team from Stages 4 and 5 remains in place and accountable for commercialization, and beyond. There are no handoffs in this game! Note that there are two homework stages in this process: Stage 1, a quick homework phase, and Stage 2, which provides for a more detailed investigation. The result is superb up- front homework and sharp, early product definition (goal 4). Additionally, constant customer contact and a market orientation are evident throughout all five stages: The actions outlined in goal 3 are heavily featured in the process. These actions heighten the odds of delivering a superior product with real value to the customer (goal 6). Finally, a cross-functional team approach is mandatory in order to successfully execute each stage (goal 5).

Preceding each stage is an entry gate or a Go/Kill decision point, shown as diamonds in the diagram. Effective gates are central to the success of a fast-paced new product process:

- Gates serve as quality-control checkpoints, where quality of execution is the focus: Is this project being executed in a quality fashion?
- Gates also serve as *Go/Kill and prioritization decision points.* Gates provide for the funneling of projects, in which mediocre projects are culled out at each successive gate.
- Finally, gates are the points where the path forward for the next play or stage of the process is decided, along with resource commitments. Once again, quality of execution becomes a central issue.

Gate meetings are usually staffed by senior managers from different functions, who own the resources required by the project leader and team for the next stage. Gates have a common format:

- Inputs: These are the deliverables to a gate review – what the project leader and team deliver to the meeting are the results of the previous stage, based on a standard menu of deliverables for each gate.

- Criteria: these are questions or metrics on which the project is judged in order to make the Go/Kill and prioritization decision. They include both qualitative (for example, strategic fit; product superiority; market attractiveness) and quantitative criteria (financial return; risk via sensitivity analysis), and can include must-meet (mandatory) as well as should- meet (desirable) criteria.
- Outputs: These are the results of the gate review – a decision (Go/Kill/ Hold/Recycle); a prioritization level; resource commitments and action plan approved; and date and deliverables for next gate agreed on.

In the fastest Stage-Gate processes, gate decisions are made with incomplete information: This means that the project team is given a "Go" decision, conditional on positive results occurring early in the next stage. In this way, the project is not held up, awaiting the completion of one or two tasks from the previous stage.

Understanding the critical success factors – what separates high-performing business units and winning new products from the rest – is the first step toward improving one's own performance. Overhauling your new product process, and incorporating these success factors into this Stage-Gate process, is the way many companies are now winning at new products.

Critical Success Factors

Seek Differentiated, Superior Products. The highest success factor is the delivery of a differentiated product with unique customer benefits and superior value. But most new products miss the mark here.

The majority of products are tired "me too" products with little to distinguish them from the products of their competitors. A second, popular scenario, but one which also yields poor results, is the engineer building a monument to him – the technical solution in search of a market.

Often, "product superiority" is absent as a project selection criterion, while steps that with cycle-time reduction and the tendency to favor simple, inexpensive projects actually penalize the projects that will lead to product superiority.

Once you arrive at a viable product concept, test it constantly with the customer. This observation indicates why establishing the project portfolio with a balance of project types is critical. Incremental projects are more uncertain, and higher probability of success, reducing the risk for the project team but also reduces the value to the firm.

Up-Front Homework Pays Off. Too many new-product projects move from the idea stage right into development with little or no up-front homework. The results of this "ready, fire, aim" approach are usually disastrous. Solid pre-development homework drives up success rates significantly. Sadly, firms devote very little of a project's funding and person-days to these critical activities. More time and resources should be devoted to the activities that precede the design and development of the product. Up-front homework means undertaking thorough market and competitive analysis, research on the customers' needs and wants, concept testing, and technical and operations feasibility assessments. All of these activities in turn lead to the preparation of a full business case prior to beginning serious development work.

Build-In the Voice of the Customer. The people behind winning new-products have a strong dedication to the VOC. Those projects that feature high-quality marketing actions are blessed with more than double the success rates of projects with poor marketing actions. The VOC must be an integral part of the process. This begins with idea generation – focus groups, customer panels, and working with lead users. Use market research and customer reaction as input into the product's design, not just as a confirmation of it. Make the customer a part of the development process via constant rapid-prototype-and-test iterations. Finally, ensure that the launch is based on solid market information.

Demand Sharp, Stable and Early Product Definition. A failure to define the product before development begins is a major cause of both new –product failure and serious delays in time-to-market. In spite of the fact that early and stable product definition is consistently cited as a key to success, firms continue to perform poorly here. Terms such as "unstable product specs" and "project scope creep" describe far too many projects. Make it a rule: No project moves to the development stage without a sharp definition of the product, including target-market definition; the product concept and benefits to be delivered; the positioning strategy; and, finally, the product features, attributes, performance requirements, and high-level specs. This definition must be fact-based and signed off by the project team. Senior management should also commit itself to the definition.

Plan and Resource the Market Launch Early In the Game. Not surprisingly, a strong market launch underlies the success of any product. For example, winners devote more than twice as many person-days and dollars to the launch as do those that fail. Similarly, the quality of execution of the market launch is significantly higher for winners. The need for a quality launch – well planned, properly resourced, and well executed – should be obvious. But in some businesses, it's almost as though the launch is an afterthought – something to worry about after the product is fully developed.

Build tough Go/Kill decision points into your process – a funnel, not a tunnel. Many projects move too far into development without serious scrutiny. In fact, once a project begins, there is very little chance that it will ever be killed. The result is that many ill-conceived projects continue to move forward and scarce resources are allocated improperly. Having tough Go/Kill decision points or gates where managers decide whether to continue or not is strongly correlated to the profitability of new-product efforts. A project once "Killed" needs to go through the entire process from the start if it's to be "Resurrected". This institutes rigor and discipline protecting the integrity of the Stage-Gate process.

Organize Around True Cross-Functional Project Teams. Good organizational design is strongly linked to success. Projects that are organized with a cross-functional team, led by a strong project leader accountable for the entire project from beginning to end, dedicated and focused (as opposed to spread over many projects), stand a better chance of success. As previously discussed organizational design is a source of competitive advantage and must facilitate processes like Stage-Gate and not be inhibiting. Key is the design must make information flows timely and valuable.

Attack from a Position of Strength. This may be an old adage, but it certainly applies. The new product fares better when it leverages the business's core competencies. This means having a strong fit between the needs of the project and the resources, strengths and experience of the company in terms of marketing, distribution, selling, technology, and operations. These ingredients become checklist items in a scoring or rating model to help prioritize new-product projects. If your leverage score is low, then there must be other compelling reasons to proceed with the project. Leverage is not essential, but it certainly improves the odds of winning.

Given the Information Age we're operating in this leverage may come from an external partner than from within the firm. Successful Stage-Gate investment must consciously consider partnering as part of the criteria for a project to advance.

Build an International Orientation into Your New-Product Process. New products aimed at international markets and with international requirements built in from the outset fare better. By contrast, products that are developed for domestic markets and sold locally are not nearly as profitable. The strategy of "design for local needs and adjust for export later" usually does not work well. The goal is either a global product (one development effort and one product for the entire global market) or a "global" product (one development effort and one product, but with slight variants to satisfy each international market). An international orientation also means using cross-functional teams with members from different countries, and gathering information from multiple international markets.

The Role of Top Management Is Central To Success. Top management support is required for product innovation. But, many senior people get it wrong. Top management's main role is to set the stage for product innovation – to be a "behind-the-scenes" facilitator who is much less an actor, front and center. This stage-setting role is vital. Management must make the long-term commitment to innovation as a source of growth. It must develop a vision, objectives, and strategy supporting innovation. It must make available the necessary resources and ensure that they aren't diverted to more immediate needs in times of shortage. It must commit to a disciplined game plan to drive products to market. And, most importantly, senior management must empower project teams. Senior management's role is not to get involved in projects on a day-to-day basis, nor to constantly meddle and interfere in the project, nor to micromanage projects from afar, but to provide the needed leadership evident in the insights they bring to the process.

Project Management – Getting there

Discipline yourself, and others won't need to.
~ John Wooden ~

The purpose of this section is to gain an understanding of project management and to give a brief overview of the methodology that underpins most formally-run projects. Many organizations do not employ full time project managers, and it is common to pull together a project team to address a specific need.

While most people are not formally skilled in project methodology, taking a role in a project team can be an excellent learning opportunity and can enhance a person's career profile. However, professional project managers are very valuable resources given these skills are transferable across project types, meaning the project leader doesn't need to also be the technical or content leader at the same time.

A project is a temporary and one-time exercise that varies in duration. It is undertaken to address a specific need in an organization, which may be to create a product or service, or to change a business process. A project is initiated because of a perceived need in an organization. As a one-off undertaking, it will have a start and an end, constraints of budgets, time, and resources, and involves a purpose-built team. Projects are split into three phases *initiation*, *implementation*, and *closure*. Each phase has multiple checkpoints that must be met before the next phase begins.

All projects start with an idea for a product, service, new capability or other desired outcome. The idea is communicated to the project sponsors (the people who will fund the project) using what is called either a mandate or project charter. The mandate is a document structured in a way that lays out a clear method for proposing a project and should result in a business case for the project.

The implementation phase is about tracking and managing the project. The first thing that happens when the project begins is to use a Project Definition Report (PDR) to create a project plan that defines how to perform what is detailed on the PDR. The PDR is more of a summary of the project, so a detailed project plan must be created to fill in the fine detail of how the project will be run. The implementation phase is about tracking and managing the project. The first thing that happens when the project begins is to use the PDR to create a project plan that defines how to perform what is detailed on the PDR.

Progress Control is another responsibility of the Project Manager and is the monitoring of the project and the production of regular progress reports to communicate the progress of the project to all stakeholders of the project. All projects are designed for a specific period of time and the process of project closure is an important aspect of project management.

The purpose of a formal closedown to the project is to address all issues generated by the project, to release staff from the project and go through a 'lessons learnt' exercise.

Experienced Project Managers believe there are two key factors in determining the success of a project: 1. Recruitment and selection of suitably qualified project members to relevant project positions is essential. Recruiting of project team members should be handled with the same discipline and rigor as the recruitment of new employees to fulfill the ongoing positions in the business. 2. A well-documented methodology that is kept simple and easily adaptable to different sizes of projects is a critical foundation for ensuring project success.

What is a Project?

A project is a temporary and one-time exercise that varies in duration. It is undertaken to address a specific need in an organization, which may be to create a product or service or to change a business process. This is in direct contrast to how an organization generally works on a permanent basis to produce their goods or services. For example the work of an organization may be to manufacture trucks on a continual basis, therefore the work is considered functional as the organization creates the same products or services over-and- over again and people hold their roles on a semi-permanent basis.

A project is generally initiated by a perceived need in an organization. Being a one-off undertaking, it will have a start and an end, constraints of budgets, time and resources, and involves a purpose-built team. Project teams are made up of many different team members such as end users/customers (of a product or service), representatives from Information Technology (IT), a project leader, business analysts, trainers, the project sponsor, and other stakeholders.

What is Project Management?

Project management is the discipline of managing all the different resources and aspects of the project in such a way that the resources will deliver all the output that is required to complete the project within the defined scope, time, and cost constraints. These are agreed upon in the project initiation stage and by the time the project begins all stakeholders and team members will have a clear understanding and acceptance of the process, methodology and expected outcomes. A good project manager utilizes a formal process that can be audited and used as a blue print for the project, and this is achieved by employing a project management methodology.

Project Management Methodology

Generally, projects are split into three phases Initiation, Implementation and Closure. Each phase then has multiple checkpoints that must be met before the next phase begins. The degree to which a project is managed will depend on the size of the project. For a complex project in a large organization that involves a number of people, resources, time and money, a more structured approach is needed, and there will be more steps built into each stage of the project to ensure that the project delivers the anticipated end result. For a simple project in a small organization, agreed milestones, a few checklists and someone to co-ordinate the project may be all that is required.

Initiating a Project. All projects start with an idea for a product, service, new capability or other desired outcome. The idea is communicated to the project sponsors (the people who will fund the project) using what is called either a mandate or project charter. The mandate is a document structured in a way that lays out a clear method for proposing a project and should result in a business case for the project. Once the business case has been approved a more detailed document is prepared that explains the project and it is known as the 'The Project Definition Report' (PDR). The PDR is not only used to provide detailed information on the project, but is the report on which an assessment is made as to whether the project should proceed or not. Some of the key areas it covers are the scope of the project, results of any feasibility studies, and what it is intended to deliver. As well this document will identify the key people involved, resources required, costs and expected duration as well as benefits to the business. A project usually has a goal (the big picture) and this has to then be broken down into objectives you can use to measure whether you have achieved your aims.

From this list you must then identify what is known as *Key Success Criteria*, and these are the objectives that are critical to the success or failure of the project, even if other objectives are met. These obviously vary from project to project. Once the project has been given the go ahead, then a contract document is drawn up and the project sponsor uses this to give formal agreement to funding the project and for the project to begin. The initiation phase is then considered to be complete.

Implementing a Project. The implementation phase is about tracking and managing the project. The first thing that happens when the project begins is to use the PDR to create a project plan that defines how to perform what is detailed on the PDR.

The PDR is more of a summary of the project, so a detailed project plan must be created to fill in the fine detail of how the project will be run. The project plan is the central document that is used to manage the project for its duration so getting agreement and acceptance from all of the team on aspects such as the project milestones, phases and tasks, as well as who is responsible for each task, associated timelines and what deadlines are to be met.

Some of the stages in implementing a project are quality control, progress control, change control and risk management. The first aspect we will discuss is *risk management*, as once you have planned the project it is important to assess any factors that could have an impact upon it. 'Risk' in this case is considered to be anything that could negatively impact on the project meeting completion deadlines. For example losing team members due to illness or attrition, not having taken team members' annual leave into consideration, the possibility of having to retrain new team members, equipment not being delivered on time or contractors going out of business. A risk log is used to record and grade risks and carries an associated action plan to minimize the identified risk. Issues management is an associated area and refers to concerns related to the project raised by any stakeholder. This phase also involves the Project Manager in *quality control*, whereby regular reviews are made in formalized meetings to ensure the 'product' that is being produced by the project is reviewed against specific pre-defined standards.

Progress Control is another responsibility of the Project Manager and is the monitoring of the project and the production of regular progress reports to communicate the progress of the project to all stakeholders of the project. As most projects do not go exactly to plan, the process of progress control is to keep an eye on the direction of the project and monitor the degree to which the plan is followed and take appropriate action if stages are deviating from the plan by employing regular project tracking. This is achieved by having regular checkpoints during the course of the project that will have been established in the project definition. These meetings may be weekly and are used to monitor and control all that is going on with the project as well as capture statistics from each project team member on actual start and finish dates for their allocated tasks as well as estimates for the next round of tasks.

By the nature of most projects never going exactly to plan, changes will need to be made to the length, direction and type of tasks carried out by the team. This has to be fully documented by the Project Manager in the form of 'change control'. *Change control* involves the Project Manager in documenting requests for change, identifying the impact on the project if the change is to be implemented (e.g. will it affect the finish time of the project, will the project run over budget, are there enough resources) and then informing all stakeholders of the implications and alternatives that the request for change has identified. The implementation phase ends once the project has achieved its goals and objectives as detailed by the key success criteria in the PDR.

Closing a Project. All projects are designed for a specific period of time and the process of project closure is an important aspect of project management. The purpose of a formal closedown to the project is to address all issues generated by the project, to release staff from the project and go through a 'lessons learnt' exercise. At this stage a formal acceptance from the customer (the person for whom the process product has been created) is gained to indicate their sign- off on the project. This is generally done in the form of a customer acceptance form and is the formal acknowledgement from the customer that the project has ended. Once signed off, the project team is disbanded and no more work carried out. However the project team will come together for what is called a Project Review Meeting, to formally end the project and go over any outstanding issues such as ongoing maintenance, the closing of project files and conduct a team review of the project.

As a result a Project Closure Report is created to formalize how successfully the project has achieved its objectives, and how well the project has performed against its original business case, the scope, project plan, budget and allocated timeframes.

The Project Manager may also create a process improvement document that reviews the processes used by the project (e.g. what did we do well, what mistakes did we make) so that the organization can learn from this project and make further projects more successful. Because the project was run by a team of people who have spent a lot of time involved in the success of a particular piece of work, that has taken them out of their usual day-to-day activities it is important to hold some type of social closing event. This might be a dinner, drinks or some type of group activity where everyone can be recognized and rewarded for their efforts.

The project closure process is often the weakest link in project management because those tasked with closing the project are often pulled toward the next assignment. This costs the firm significant value by losing the descriptions of the lessons learned. Mitigate this by making the project manager's review dependent on having the closure process completed.

What does it take to be a Good Project Manager? Aside from understanding the methodology, there are other characteristics to keep in mind for successful project management. Given that any project is involved with a project team as well as the stakeholders, a good Project Manager needs to have not only excellent time management skills but also good people skills such as the following:

- Excellent communication skills
- Be a team player
- Superior interpersonal skills
- Skillful negotiator

References for Further Reading:

What is Project Management? Project Management Institute, Pmi.org.

Chatfield, Carl. "A short course in project management." Microsoft.

The Definitive Guide to Project Management. Nokes, Sebastian. 2nd Ed.n. London (Financial Times/Prentice Hall): 2007. ISBN 978-0-273-71097-4

Paul C. Dinsmore et al (2005) *The right projects done right!* John Wiley and Sons, 2005. p.35 and further. [42] Cattani, G., Ferriani, S., Frederiksen, L. and Florian, T. (2011) Project-Based Organizing and Strategic Management, Advances in Strategic Management, Vol 28, Emerald, ISBN 1780521936.

Lewis R. Ireland (2006) *Project Management.* McGraw-Hill Professional, 2006. ISBN 0-07-147160-X. p.110.

Joseph Phillips (2003). *PMP Project Management Professional Study Guide.* McGraw-Hill Professional, 2003. ISBN 0-07-223062-2 p.354.

PMI (2010). *A Guide to the Project Management Body of Knowledge* p.27-35.

Product Lifecycle Management (PLM)

Everything dies and must be buried before it begins to rot
~ Anonymous ~

What is PLM? *Product lifecycle management or PLM* is an all-encompassing approach for innovation, new product development and introduction (NPDI) and product information management from ideation to end of life. PLM enabling technology integrates people, data, processes, and business systems and provide a product information backbone for companies and their extended enterprise.

Business drivers. Innovation and new product development are essential for most companies to sustain future revenue growth. Customers demand more new products in shorter time intervals, often customized to their own needs. They want more attractive designs, better performance, better quality, lower prices, and instant availability. To meet these needs companies have to be able to collaborate closely within their own organization and with partners and suppliers located in various parts of the world. At the same time companies have to manage increasing product and manufacturing complexities due to a quickly growing number of environmental and regulatory rules and requirements.

The Problem. Accelerating innovation and increasing the number of successful new product introductions is a huge challenge for most organizations today because of their traditionally serial, fragmented, manual, and paper based processes. The result is that many companies suffer from NPDI practices that are slow, resource intensive, costly, inflexible, provide little visibility, and are difficult to manage and control.

The Solution – PLM. Through PLM the firm has the ability to integrate all product related data and processes and to eliminate boundaries in the value chain. PLM can significantly reduce non-value added activities and enable stakeholders to collaborate in real time using a consistent set of information throughout the entire product lifecycle.

As a result, *productivity improvements of over 60%* in NPDI-related activities have been achieved through PLM-enabled, enterprise-wide data and process optimization and integration that have allowed companies to do the following:

- Drive innovation.
- Accelerate Revenues.
- Increase Productivity.
- Reduce Costs.
- Improve Quality.
- Ensure Compliance.
- Shorten Time-to-Market.

In today's highly competitive, fast-paced and global business environment, well-designed and implemented PLM practices, processes and technologies that support an organization's strategies for innovation and growth can afford companies a real competitive advantage.

The inspiration for the burgeoning business process now known as PLM came from American Motors Corporation (AMC). The automaker was looking for a way to speed up its product development process to compete better against its larger competitors in 1985, according to François Castaing, Vice President for Product Engineering and Development. After introducing its compact Jeep Cherokee (XJ), the vehicle that launched the modern sport utility vehicle (SUV) market, AMC began development of a new model, that later came out as the Jeep Grand Cherokee. The first part in its quest for faster product development was computer-aided design (CAD) software system that makes engineers more productive. The second part in this effort was the new communication system that allowed conflicts to be resolved faster, as well as reducing costly engineering changes because all drawings and documents were in a central database. The product data management was so effective that after AMC was purchased by Chrysler, the system was expanded throughout the enterprise connecting everyone involved in designing and building products. While an early adopter of PLM technology, Chrysler was able to become the auto industry's lowest- cost producer, recording development costs that were half of the industry average by the mid-1990s.

Getting Started with PLM. Recommended steps to get off to a good start with PLM:

- Learn about PLM from unbiased sources
- PLM Books, Articles, Reports and Whitepapers;
- Websites dedicated to PLM, such as the *PLM Technology Guide*;
- Find and involve an experienced, independent PLM Consultant to help with the following steps;
- Define your immediate and long-term business needs and requirements based on your company's goals and objectives;
- Create a long-term PLM strategy and action plan;
- Identify potential areas of improvements in your organization based on industry best practices and latest available PLM technologies;
- Develop a PLM Business Case to be able to make an informed and financially sound decision regarding an investment in PLM;
- Analyze and compare the scope and functionality of different PLM Systems. Look for commercial-off-the-shelf (COTS) systems with available preconfigured industry solutions and a functional scope that can support your long-term PLM strategy;
- Conduct a methodical PLM Evaluation with 3 to 4 systems to find the best.

A Strategic Approach to PLM. PLM is a proven approach for managing the entire lifecycle of an offering from inception, through design and manufacture, to service and disposal[46]. A firm uses PLM for reducing the time and cost for introducing new innovations. PLM is data driven, IT enabled and highly collaborative between key operating groups such as RD&E, Marketing, Finance, Manufacturing, Supply Chain, and Regulatory Compliance and other functions.

PLM has strategic value by identifying offerings ready for retirement and freeing up resources for new innovations. In this capacity, PLM is the responsibility of the marketing organization in its role of guiding investments for creating future offerings. Constructed properly, marketing can use PLM to identify change drivers and inform investments in innovation projects. Specifically, PLM integrates people, data, processes and business systems providing a product information backbone for companies and their extended enterprise.[47] PLM is most useful when it is applied to project portfolios where the work is unambiguous. For example construction projects, where the blueprints and the designs are known, PLM techniques works very well because everything is well understood. In these portfolios time and cost are the primary risks to manage.

Conversely, in an R&D portfolio where ambiguity is high, PLM works best when applied to launch stage projects in a Stage Gate process. This high degree of ambiguity is often described as the "fuzzy front end," where applying PLM to the discovery phase of the R&D portfolio often leads to frustrated decision making because the required information is unavailable or worse poor decisions result because the lack of data.

PLM has many phases that can be readily researched with a simple Google search. It is important to recognize that projects don't run sequentially, or in isolation of other projects, especially in an R&D environment, so managing information flows between different people, organizations and systems is a critical success factor.

As previously discussed, the firm's organizational design structure is critical in managing information flows and therefore is a central part of a successful PLM program. Often, the organizational design is not factored into PLM activities, leading to disappointing outcomes. For example, a product being ready for retirement by one business entity may still have a useful life remaining for another business unit. An effective PLM process needs to reconcile these kinds of situations. Clearly, one of the greatest challenges a firm faces is "cutting the tail" of an aging product where low volume sales, while profitable on a percentage basis and desired by a few important customers, aren't generating sufficient money to support their hidden costs. These costs are often buried within an allocation system and difficult to measure. An effective PLM process utilizes methods to deal with this reality while fitting within the firm's norms of conducting business.

Successfully utilizing PLM depends on the co-ordination and management of product definition data, including managing changes and effectively communicating changes in a projects status. Using a "R.A.C.I." Model as a management technique provides clarity on who should be involved in PLM activities driven by their roles in the process by identifying who is Responsible, Accountable, Consulted and Informed.

PLM is highly dependent on well-integrated information technology systems reaching across the enterprise. The core PLM processes are effective portfolio management, project management, and financial accounting systems connected by an enterprise data management system

(EDM). The EDM connects all the other databases used in managing the portfolio from early stage discovery projects, as are common in R&D, all the way to measuring commercial offering's performance in the market place by generating financial results.

Linkage to other corporate systems such as Supply Chain Management (SCM), Customer Relationship Management (CRM), and Enterprise Resource Management (ERP) are common where firms employ best practices.

Finally, numerous collaborative product development tools[49] are available helping to manage the offerings lifecycle across the organization such as teleconferencing, data sharing, translation and warehouses where anyone involved with the PLM process can access and use data to fulfill their roles.

Strategic Value Assessment. The team then uses the findings to identify value drivers described in a Strategic Value Assessment (SVA). The SVA uses independent research benchmarks for PLM successfully employed by peer firms. The SVA will describe anticipated tangible and intangible costs and returns in terms of cash investments (e.g., IT infrastructure) and people's time (FTEs). Often intangible items can be estimated in cash terms using conversion factors. Often the cost of 1 FTE is estimated by dividing total budget by total FTEs. In sophisticated and low ambiguity situations opportunity costs – the cost of not doing something else – can be estimated.

Product Lifecycle Management (PLM) is a proven approach for reducing the time and cost for introducing a new innovation into the marketplace. PLM is data driven, IT enabled and highly collaborative between key operating groups such as RD&E, Marketing, Manufacturing, Supply Chain, Regulatory Compliance and Finance.

Many software solutions have developed to organize and integrate the different phases of a product's lifecycle. PLM should not be seen as a single software product but a collection of software tools and working methods integrated together to address either single stages of the lifecycle or connect different tasks or manage the whole process. Some software providers cover the whole PLM range while others single niche application. Some applications can span many fields of PLM with different modules within the same data model. It should be noted however that the simple classifications do not always fit exactly, many areas overlap and many software products cover more than one area or do not fit easily into one category. It should also not be forgotten that one of the main goals of PLM is to collect knowledge that can be reused for other projects and to coordinate simultaneous concurrent development of many products. This is where a user friendly Data Warehouse has unique value.

Although PLM can be thought of as an umbrella for activities such as product portfolio management (PPM), particularly with regards to new product development (NPD) and while there are several life-cycle models to consider, most are similar.

A PLM Framework

- Conducting a diagnostic of existing capabilities identifying redundant systems and capability gaps.
- Defining a system of record for data: Some of these capabilities and data elements could be managed in other applications.
- Qualify IT vendors for PLM system considering existing capabilities, time and cost for implementation and ease of use.
- Estimate integration costs for PLM is a component of the overall IT architecture.

Business Drivers

- Actionable insight to make informed product portfolio decisions;
- Replacement of low-margin product ranges by higher margin innovations;
- A defined method of managing product range and controlling offering proliferation;
- Improved business intelligence capability enabling business decisions on product range performance;
- Effectively managing the full lifecycle of products;
- Enable teams to work more effectively and efficiently with better collaboration and project management tools (time/resource management);
- Formalized stage gate processes, enabled with workflows, supporting global and regional initiatives;
- Consistent project management process with enabling tools and systems.
- One version of the truth for all product "DNA";
- Common, rationalized global definition and execution of master product data and standards;
- A single raw material and formulary management system;
- A common approach to Label and Artwork management if applicable;
- Easy access to data, skills and resources;
- Consistent approach to managing intellectual capital;
- Knowledge capture, storage and retrieval is transparent to the end-user;
- Ability to easily collaborate with suppliers, partners and customers;

- Enable the business to adapt and support new business models (Open Innovation, New Business Channels);
- Effective and efficient collaboration and data integration with suppliers, partners and customers;
- Reduce complexity and cost in supporting the IT application portfolio.
- Systems rationalization decreasing Total Cost of Operations and increasing ability to support;
- Don't proliferate spending on non-strategic/core applications (buy vs. build considerations).

Introducing PLM

Executive management requests a review of current systems and processes supporting innovation investments. The team identifies value drivers applicable to the firm's current offerings and future offerings as described by the project portfolio and validated by external benchmarks, which are then analyzed using the Strategic Value Assessment (SVA). The study yields a charter and recommendations on how to proceed with the introduction of a PLM process customized to the firm's business needs and supporting the business strategies. All relevant functions must be represented by, or on, the PLM team. These minimally include Marketing, Sales, Manufacturing and Supply Chain, R&D, IT, and Finance. If PLM is new to the company should consider the following 8 objectives as a starting point. Any PLM system should be modular, allowing cost-effective upgrading as the business requires.

Approach

- Conduct study to develop PLM purpose, vision and strategy with an execution plan for the company which:
  - o Considers current systems assessment and landscape,
  - o Uses SWOT analysis methodology to qualify the IT vendor
- Develop comprehensive systems requirements for PLM using advice from of Steering Committee and Power Users.
- Propose strategic alternatives showing soundness of fit.
- Conduct SVA showing implementation benefits, timing, ease of implementation and cost.
- Acquire executive alignment and business sponsorship on preferred solutions.
- Develop an execution plan recognizing the resource requirements and organizational impact.
  - o Identify critical changes in the firm's "norms of behavior",
- Identify supporting IT systems.

- Conduct Strategic Value Assessment showing benefits, timing, ease of implementation and cost of the proposal over time (often 1-3 years).
- Write a comprehensive implementation proposal.
- Frame the role of the executive team in communicating PLM to the organization,
- Recommend implementation participants using the R.A.C.I Model.

Table 13. IT Vendor SWOT Analysis

Strengths	Weaknesses
• Core capabilities for Project and Portfolio management • Strong workflow capabilities • User interface is easy to navigate • Software to Services ratio is approximately 1:1 • Single data model will allow for minimal integration and maximize consistency and reliability of product and project data • Recognized leader in PLM marketplace • High level customer satisfaction • Software license approach will allow the company to implement solution in modules and at our own pace • Commitment to the company and our industry vertical • Lowest risk option for entering into PLM	• Ideation functionality is weaker in comparison to other solutions • Analytical capabilities are not as robust as the other solutions • Vertical expertise in the company's industry
Opportunities	Threats
1. Received strong support from other functional business units that are stakeholders in the New Product Development and Commercialization process 2. Downstream potential for future PLM capabilities is very strong 3. Other modules show very strong promise 4. Vendor is showing great interest and commitment in the Consumer Packaged Goods vertical (where the company is classified) 5. Vendor has indicated future potential for recipe management functionality 6. Vendor has been very committed to winning the company's business and has demonstrated strong knowledge of our business and processes	1. PLM market is growing very rapidly and has potential for further consolidation. 2. Vendor's history is in the discrete high-technology vertical 3. Core database is architected around Oracle. Will need to secure skillsets for this 4. Introducing new technology/application into the company's application portfolio

Example of the PLM Team's Initial Goals and Objectives

- Define PLM for the company;
- Define PLM vision;
- Develop the implementation roadmap;
- Profile and evaluate PLM vendors and integration products (PLM/ERP);
- Benchmark company in current and future state vs. competitors and leading companies;
- Define Strategic Value of PLM;
- Confirm Executive/Leadership Team Alignment;
- Identify success factors and risk elements.

Example of External Benchmark Results from Instituting PLM

- Companies who use PLM for innovation and other product development processes have reported:
  o 30% reduction in project cycle-time
  o 50% increase in profitability per developed project
  o 30% increase in revenues derived from products introduced in last 3 years

Examples of Benchmark Companies

- **Large FMCG Company** – implemented Stage-Gate, Open Source and PLM program yielding innovation and 50% cycle-time reduction
- **Small FMCG Company** – implemented Stage-Gate process with technology. Increased up-front "kill rate" from 0 to 55%. Increased number of products introduced per year from 2 to 5 in 2005.
- **Equipment Company** – implemented Stage-Gate development process in conjunction with PLM as first phase of PLM project with executive dashboards for 200 projects across 3 divisions
- **Packaging Company** – linked suppliers directly to their open source innovation process yielding a 50% reduction in packaging project cycle time

Vendor Selection Criteria

- Recognized leader in the PLM software solution space;
- Has a proven track record for successful implementations and high customer satisfaction;
- Has the best understanding of the firm's needs having demonstrated the strongest commitment for successful introduction of a first generation PLM system;
- Capabilities and fit confirmed using independent market data;

- Proposal has cross-functional/regional business support;
- Software to services ratio is much better when compared to other options;
- Proposed PLM application suite has capabilities in PPM allowing leveraging of additional capabilities confirming fit and sun-setting of non-strategic applications;
- Architecture is based on a single database thus reducing integration costs and allowing company to build out future capabilities;
- Functionality in PPM exceeds the required capabilities that have been identified by the stakeholder group;
- Licensing structure allows for modular implementation of the solution.

References for Further Reading

The above material on PLM was adapted in part from the following sources:

- *About PLM*. CIMdata.
- *What is PLM?* PLM Technology Guide.
- Cunha, Luciano. Making PLM and ERP work together. onwindows.com.
- http://en.wikipedia.org/wiki/Collaborative_product_development

Big Data – Getting to Great Decisions

When human judgment and big data intersect there are some funny things that happen.
~ Nate Silver[62] ~

With the advent of the Internet circa 1995, data started becoming widely available to individuals on an unprecedented scale not seen since the introduction of the printing press in 1440. Books had existed prior to that but were not widely written nor read. They were luxury items for nobility, produced one copy at the time by scribes, which was a very expensive process, in turn making the accumulation of knowledge extremely difficult. Further, it required a heroic effort just to prevent the volume of recorded knowledge from actually *decreasing* since the books might decay faster than they could be reproduced. As was the case during the early days of the World Wide Web, however, the quality of information varied widely. The amount of information today is increasing much more rapidly than our understanding of what to do with it or our ability to differentiate the useful information from mistruths.

---

[62] Silver, Nate. *The Signal and the Noise*, The Penguin Press, 2012.

The impact of written communication on economic growth is unquestionable. GDP per capita in US dollars in the year 1080 was estimated to be about $200. With the advent of the printing press in 1440 and the steam engine in 1775, the GDP per capita grew to nearly $9,000, an impressive gain from the availability and application knowledge. It is important to recognize there are three forms of communication. There is raw *data*, which is often an expression of an observation. When that expression is assembled to communicate something, we call it *information*. When that information is understood it yields *knowledge* usable for making informed decisions. The transition from raw data to knowledge is critical for identifying insights enabling innovation to occur when people connect seemingly unrelated dots. Critical to effective decision-making, and therefore innovation, is the leader's ability to discern correct data from incorrect data. Often, decision-making is encumbered by the introduction of new data. An example of this is the "productivity paradox" of what was experienced in the United States in the 1970s. Computers were just being introduced, but the ability to use the information from these devices was limited, so productivity and economic efficacy actually declined as measured by R&D expenditures per patent application.

However, once decision makers could discern good from poor data and information, then the cost per patent in R&D expenditures began dropping. Clearly, numbers have no way of speaking for themselves. We speak for them and we imbue them with meaning that can be self-serving and detached from objective reality. So what does the future hold? Data is increasing exponentially at a rate of 2.5 quintrillion bytes of data per day, suggesting today's leaders are facing new challenges in their abilities to make good decisions.

Data-driven predictions can succeed, but they can also fail, especially when we deny our role in the process. Therefore, we must demand more of ourselves before we demand more of our data. The human brain is wired to recognize patterns, and when there is too much noise in the data people will create patterns that don't exist to fit their preconceived biases. The premise of this section is that leaders can apply something called Bayes's theorem, nominally a mathematical formula, which implies that innovators must think differently about their ideas and how to test them. Innovators must become more comfortable with probability and uncertainty and think more carefully about the assumptions and beliefs they bring to a problem.

Innovation leaders can be defined as persons who have differentiated insights about changes occurring around them compelling people to follow them even if this means subordinating their self-interest for the greater good. The innovation leader can obtain these differentiated insights by discerning signal, which is truth, from noise, which distracts us from the truth. That is what leads to making effective decisions.

Why predictions fail

It is first necessary to begin with definitions of two key terms: *prediction* and *forecast*. A *prediction* is a definitive and specific statement about when and where an event will occur. For example, a major earthquake will occur in Kyoto Japan on June 28, 2014. A *forecast* is a probabilistic statement usually over a longer time scale, such as there is a 60% chance of an earthquake in Southern California over the next 30 years.

The most dramatic failures of prediction usually have a lot in common. First, the focus is on those signals that describe the world as the observer would like it to be, not how it really is. Avoiding this confirmation bias error requires the observer to have an awareness and understanding of historical data and using this understanding to refine our assumptions, thereby creating a view of the world that is more aligned with the truth. A useful example of a failed prediction, driven by misreading noise as signal, was the housing bubble of 2008.

After adjusting for inflation, a $10,000 investment made in a home in 1896 would be worth just $10,600 in 1996. Although a home was not a profitable investment, it was considered a safe investment. The historical data on home ownership as an investment was clear. However, this historical data was ignored in favor of scenarios that supported much higher rates of appreciation and a misinterpretation of reality.

The situation worsened as prices became untethered from supply and demand as lenders, brokers, and rating agencies, all of who profited in one way or another from home sales, drove prices higher than the demand supported. Those involved were commonly referred to as "speculators." Historical data for investment returns from the housing market didn't support the conclusions being made from the data available from the 2000-2006 housing bubble, suggesting it was noise and anomalous. Dr. Robert Shiller, a Yale economist, recognized this but was dismissed.

Risk vs. Uncertainty: Critical to Decision Quality

Another cause of failed predictions is the confusion between assessing *risk* and *uncertainty*. *Risk* is something you can put a price on and you know the odds of it doing something predictable. *Uncertainty*, on the other hand, is risk that is hard to measure. When faced with an uncertain situation, it is likely that the leader's estimate might be off by a factor of 100 or by factor of 1,000, with no good way of knowing which it is. Risk generally greases the wheels of the free market economy by promoting investment, but uncertainty grinds that to a halt by slowing investment because it can't be easily estimated. When uncertainty is treated like well-defined risk, major errors in predictions become common. In complex systems, even slightly mismanaging risk can have large outcomes. This is the basis of *chaos theory*, which states that small changes to a complex system can have multiplied effects since so many elements of the system are connected to each other. It's a chain reaction. A good example of calculating risk is weather forecasting. Weather a very complex system and despite the tremendous increase in computing power, it's still difficult to forecast. However, weather forecasting today is much better than 50 years ago because we have the databases to analyze, yielding probabilities of events like rain or sunshine. A good example where forecasting remains very primitive is for earthquakes. The database is missing, and hence our ability to use history to forecast the future is limited.

Forecasting or predicting an earthquake has a high degree of uncertainty. The housing bubble was an example of leaders not managing risk by ignoring historical "signals" for current "noise" because the noise fit their aspirations of reality but not the truth. In the end those involved with the housing bubble fabricated uncertainty by denying history.

This error becomes much more serious for complex systems like the housing market. Again, chaos theory suggests that small changes in a highly integrated and complex system can cause surprisingly large effects. The housing market bubble was made worse by banks using leverage. The assets of the housing bubble, mortgages on real estate, became investment tools called mortgage-backed securities, providing the basis for banks to practice leverage against the housing industry. For example, Lehman Brothers in 2007 had a leverage ratio of 33 to 1, which means they had one dollar of capital for every thirty-three dollars of money at risk. This meant that if there were just a 3-4% decline in the value of its portfolio, Lehman Brothers would have a negative equity position and would potentially face bankruptcy. This is an example of chaos theory in the financial market.

In fact, 2007's total volume of trades in mortgage-backed securities was leveraged to about $80 trillion or about 6 times the size of the entire US economy! So what are the lessons to be learned by a leader when facing large amounts of data embedded in a highly complex, integrated system where small changes can have major consequences? Here are a few:

- Use historical data frame assumptions about future prediction.
- Carefully assess assumptions and avoid false confidence about the risk you're encountering.
- Recognize that in highly integrated complex systems small changes can have large outcomes.
- Insightful decisions require the leader to anticipate the impact of a failed decision on the organization.
- Leaders determine if the current context is relevant to the history. When these are not relevant, then the situation is termed an "out of sample" condition.

An "out of sample" example is where your experience of the past does not apply to the current case. A facetious example of this could be the argument for driving when you are intoxicated compared to the times you've driven while both sober and intoxicated. Assume you have taken 20,000 car trips and only experienced two minor accidents while having 19,998 uneventful trips. However, the 20,000 trips while sober don't tell you anything about the risk of driving while intoxicated because the context is different. Two lessons are as follows:

- We forget, or willfully ignore, that our models are simplifications of the world. We figure that if you make a mistake, it will happen at the margin. In complex systems, however, mistakes are not measured in degrees but in orders of magnitude. One of the pervasive risks that we face in the information age is that even if the amount of knowledge in the world is increasing, the gap between what we know and what we think we know may well be widening.

- The other lesson is to understand the difference between precision and accuracy. *Precision* measures the differences among a group of data, whereas *accuracy* measures the relationship of the data to the truth. Very precise predictions/forecasts can yield a false confidence that the prediction/forecast is also accurate. When a very precise forecast or prediction turns out to be wrong, it can be evidence of poor assumptions. Assumptions need to be tested before they're treated as facts or the truth. This is rarely done, especially when the assumption has a numerical description.

The Right Attitude for Making Better Predictions: "Foxes" vs. "Hedgehogs"

The foxes and hedgehogs are descriptors of different kinds of experts. *Foxes* are scrappy creatures that believe in a plethora of little ideas and taking a multitude of approaches towards a problem. They tend to be more tolerant of nuance, uncertainty, complexity, and dissenting opinions. *Hedgehogs* are type-A personalities who believe in big ideas, in governing principles about the world that behave as though they were physical laws and undergird everything in society. Hedgehogs are experts who know about one thing into which they try to fit everything. If hedgehogs are hunters always looking for the big kill, then foxes are gatherers. Should innovation leaders think like Foxes or Hedgehogs?

Hedgehogs tend to be more publicly visible than foxes. Consider the case of Dick Morris, former advisor to Bill Clinton, who now serves as a commentator for Fox News. Morris is a classic hedgehog, that when given the chance will make predictions as dramatic as possible. In 2005 Morris proclaimed G. W. Bush's handling of Hurricane Katrina would help Bush regain his standing with the public. On the eve of the 2008 elections he predicted that Barack Obama would win Tennessee and Arkansas. In 2010, Moore predicted that the Republicans could easily win 100 seats in the US House of Representatives. Finally, in 2011 he said that Donald Trump would run for the Republican nomination and win. The one thing all of these predictions had in common? They were all terribly wrong.

Foxes happen to make better predictions. They are quick to recognize how noisy the data can be, and they are less inclined to chase false signals. They know more about what they don't know. Foxes sometimes have trouble fitting into type-A cultures such as television, business, and politics. However, if you're looking for a doctor to predict the course of a medical condition or an investment advisor to maximize the return on your retirement savings, you may want to trust a fox.

If an innovator has a choice of being a fox or a hedgehog, they'd be better off choosing the fox's approach to decision-making. Foxes tend to make better decisions with experience, while the opposite is true of hedgehogs. Foxes may have empathetic convictions about the way the world ought to be, but they can usually separate that from their analysis of the way that the world actually is and how it is likely to be in the near future.

Hedgehogs, by contrast, have more trouble distinguishing fact from fiction in their observations. Instead, they create a blurring fusion between facts and values all lumped together. They take prejudicial views toward the evidence, seeing what they want to see and not really what's there. Too much information in the hands of the hedgehogs can be a bad thing. Hedgehogs having lots of information construct stories with protagonists and villains, winners and losers, climaxes and denouements — and, usually, happy ending for the home team. When innovators construct these stories, they can lose the ability to think critically. You can get lost in a narrative.

Principles for Dealing with Big Data: Think probabilistically

Instead of predicting one number, claiming to know exactly what will happen, it's better to articulate a range of possible outcomes. The most likely range of outcomes, enough to cover about half of all the possible options, are the most reasonable forecasts. The signature of a good forecast is that each of these probabilities turns out to be about right over time.

With practice, our estimates can get better. Hedgehogs are too stubborn to learn from their mistakes. Acknowledging the real world uncertainty in their forecasts would require them to acknowledge the imperfections of their theories about how the world is supposed to behave.

Table 14. The Difference Between Foxes and Hedgehogs

How Foxes Think	How Hedgehogs Think
Multidisciplinary: incorporate ideas from different disciplines and regardless of their origin on the political spectrum	**Specialized:** often have spent the bulk of their careers on one or two great problems may view the opinions of outsiders skeptically
Adaptable: find a new approach or pursue multiple approaches at the same time if they aren't sure the original one is working	**Stalwart:** stick to the same approach using new data to refine the original thought.
Self-critical: happy to acknowledge mistakes in their predictions accept the blame for itself them	**Stubborn:** mistakes are blamed on bad luck or an idiosyncratic circumstances such as a good model had a bad day
Tolerant of complexity: sees the universe as complicated, transfer point of many fundamental problems that are inherently unpredictable	**Order seeking:** expect that the world will be found to abide by relatively simple governing relationships once the signal was identified through the noise
Cautious: express their predictions in probabilistic terms and qualify their opinions	**Confident:** rarely hedge their predictions and are reluctant to change them
Empirical: rely more on observation than theory	**Ideological:** expect that solutions to many day to day problems are manifestations of some grander theory or struggle
Foxes are better forecasters	**Hedgehogs are weaker forecasters**

Today's forecast is the first forecast for the rest of your life

A serious misconception is that a good forecast shouldn't change. Certainly, if there are wild gyrations in your forecast from day-to-day, that may be a sign of either a badly designed model or that the phenomenon you are attempting to forecast isn't very consistent.

An example of this would be forecasting earthquakes where the data supporting the analysis is too weak to allow for good estimates. When the outcome is more certain, as a general election is in the late stages of the race, forecasting is more reliable. Ultimately, the right attitude is that innovators should make the best forecast possible today, regardless of what you said last week, last month, or last year. If you have reason to think that yesterday's forecast was wrong, there is no glory in sticking with it, although some people don't like this type of course-correcting analysis and mistake it for a sign of weakness. Making the most of limited information requires a willingness to update one's forecast as newer and better information becomes available. Failing to change your forecast for fear of embarrassment reveals a lack of courage.

Look for Consensus

The Hedgehogs fantasize that they will make a daring, audacious, outside-the-box prediction, one that differs radically from the consensus view on the subject. Every now and then, they might correctly make a forecast like this. However, the fantasy scenario is usually unlikely. Even though Foxes aren't really conformists by nature, they get worried any time their forecast differs radically from those produced by others, especially competitors. Foxes have developed the ability to emulate the consensus process in making their forecasts. Instead of asking questions of the whole group of experts, they are constantly asking questions of themselves. Often this implies that they will aggregate different types of information together, as a group of people with different ideas about the world naturally would, instead of treating any one piece of evidence as the Holy Grail.

Beware of Magic-Bullet Forecasts and Weighing Qualitative Information

Hedgehogs like models based on a few variables, since they are easily manipulated. Foxes, on the other hand, like combining economic data with polling data and other types of information, producing more reliable results. The lessons learned from political races indicate that too few variables in the model tend to cause major errors. The better approach is combining a variety of different sources of data and then creating a more correct model.

Most leaders have a stronger preference for more quantitative approaches in making forecasts. Hedgehogs can take any type of information and have it reinforce their biases, while Foxes, with practice and weighing different types of information, get benefits from accounting for qualitative along with quantitative factors.

The critical success factor for the innovator is to be as objective as possible in the face of ambiguous data and information. The way to become more objective is to recognize the influence that our assumptions play in our forecasts and to question ourselves about them. Innovators must learn how to express and quantify the uncertainty in their predictions.

They'll need to update their forecasts as facts and circumstances change. You need to recognize that there is wisdom in seeing the world from a different viewpoint. The more the innovator is willing to do these things, the more capable they'll be given a wide variety of information. You, as the innovation leader, will need to learn how to think like a Fox. The Fox recognizes limitations that human judgment imposes on predicting the world's course. Knowing these limits can help the innovator get a few more predictions or forecasts correct.

Balancing Data and Human Judgment

Critical to decision-making is balancing the use of data and human judgment. Often, the temptation is to analyze the available data and use it exclusively to frame our decisions. In reality, combining hard data analysis with human judgment leads to better outcomes than either alone. The challenge for the decision-making innovation leader is to recognize the nuances in using data and judgment yielding the most insightful decisions.

In general, statistical analysis of data is more effective in measuring performance than predicting or forecasting outcomes. A very useful data analysis methodology is often referred to as a "nearest neighbor analysis." This is a comparison of something new with something that is known and understood so you can apply that knowledge to the new element to render some understanding. A critical element of the successful nearest neighbor analysis is that the data sets analyzed must be closely related. As the new data and reference data diverge from a common background, the nearest neighbor analysis becomes less effective.

The nearest neighbor analysis is an excellent starting place to begin the decision-making process. One caution is that hard-to-categorize data is easily overlooked or misjudged. The innovation leader needs to carefully assess the data that they have collected for meaning. The critical mindset is understanding that there's a difference between *data, information,* and *knowledge.* Data is a representation of an event that can be assembled into information communicating something about the event that when understood can become knowledge that is useful in creating differentiated insights. Key for the innovation leader is that they generate differentiated insights, on a continuing basis, allowing their followers and organizations to create a sustainable competitive advantage.

In general, the best decisions occur when the innovation leader is able to look at the big picture and detailed data, information, and knowledge concurrently. This skill allows the innovation leader to see the situations they're facing from a 360° perspective. A nuance is that innovation leaders must learn is to look at situations and, rather than choosing among options, choose more than one option. This is been termed the "Tyranny of the Or," which means often when faced with choices, the best choice is choosing both options rather than one over the other.

Innovation leaders must integrate their experiences into insights that inform their choices. The more experiences the innovation leader has, the more likely they are to relate the current situation with some previous experience, providing a more relevant point of view for current decision. This can sometimes occur without conscious awareness. Using the subconscious part of the mind as a repository of past experiences can enhance judgment when making decisions like those already encountered. This is another example of a "nearest neighbor analysis," but one that occurs in the recesses of the mind. Using both the conscious and subconscious parts of the mind leads to the best decisions.

This is why "sleeping on it" sometimes results in insights not obvious when they were consciously assessed. The subconscious mind is also an integral part of our ability to complete hunches that are partially correct but insufficient alone in revealing an insightful path forward.

Dealing with Complexity

Many innovation leaders face complexity on a daily basis while recognizing the dimensions of complex systems is often under-appreciated in the decision-making process. When complex systems meet the criteria being of being both dynamic and nonlinear, then chaos theory applies. A dynamic system is one where behavior at one moment in time influences behavior in the future. Nonlinear systems mean that small changes can lead exponential, rather than additive, relationships. This last characteristic is particularly important when dealing with the quality of the data and information an innovation leader has at hand. Small errors in the data can lead to huge unexpected errors in the decisions that are made.

For the last 20 years computing power has increased dramatically. While allowing data to be analyzed in a more *efficient* manner, these analyses still need to be interpreted in order to be useful. An important technique that humans can use to analyze and interpret data is to depict the data in a visual form, such as graphs and charts that allow trends, outlying data, and other nuances critical to *effective* decision-making to be identified. This combination of *efficient* and *effective* use of data and information yielding knowledge enhances decision-making better than either one alone.

Given the complexity of most problems facing innovation leaders today, combined with the fact that many of these systems behave according to chaos theory, it is especially important that the innovation leader understand that sometimes the "exception is the rule." This means that rules of thumb and conventional wisdom may lead to disappointing results. Innovation leaders must be nuanced in the way they interpret their environment if they're going to generate differentiated insights.

Models, Signal, and Noise

Creating models is a reasonable approach when dealing with complexity and complex systems. Well-developed models can be an effective way of leveraging human judgment if the models are based on accurate, high-quality data and the users are aware of their biases. Models are used to *predict* or *forecast* a future event that the innovation leader can then use to make informed, insightful choices. A critical consideration of building models to make predictions and forecasts is how much our biases influence the outcomes obtained. We are all bound by our biases, and they often appear in the assumptions we make about situations we encounter. An assumption is a hypothetical expectation, in the form of a prediction or forecast, of a future outcome. Assumptions must be assessed using data leading to truth that can convert the assumption into a fact. All too often assumptions are considered to be facts, leading to grievous errors in decision-making. This is especially true when the assumption is described in a numerical form absent a range. In this case the human mind will associate the number to reality.

Effective use of assumptions requires the innovation leader to know how to ask questions uncovering the biases and flaws built into the assumptions. In many situations effective inquiry is absent since most modern education systems teach their student to provide answers and not raise meaningful questions. Many adults began their lives as highly curious children only to become adults, after eighteen years of education, who rarely question anything.

Next there is the data itself that we need to fashion into information and knowledge. Data arrives in two forms: *"signal"* and *"noise."* Signal is data that is meaningful and useful whereas noise is data that is wrong and therefore useless and even dangerous in decision-making. A common risk when facing large amounts of noise and little signal is that the observer begins fashioning the noise into a signal driven by their biases and desire for future outcomes. This erroneous outcome then appears in the form of assumptions that need to be assessed and even challenged before they are allowed to be used to drive decision-making.

Finally, it's important how data are used to create models in complex systems. The concept of *"over-fitting"* is when good signals are over-analyzed or mistaken for noise. Over-fitting errors can be where the data is too tight, leading to an overly-specific solution to a general problem, or too loose, leading to an overly-general solution. Over-fitting the model is most likely to occur when the data is limited and noisy, and when the understanding of the fundamental relationship is poor, which can be commonplace for complex systems.

Probabilistic Thinking: The Bayesian Approach

Given the challenges innovation leaders face with big data, what does one do that's useful? Fortunately, an obscure English statistician named Thomas Bayes left the world with the practice of learning about the unknown through approximation, getting closer and closer to the truth as evidence is gathered. The Bayesian method suggests that we need to make hypothetical but rational predictions about the future based on existing knowledge, then evaluate the outcome and make corrections.

This is also known as the *scientific method*. Bayes' theorem is concerned with *conditional probability*. This tells us the probability that a theory or hypothesis is true if some event has happened. In its most basic form, it is just an algebraic expression with three known variables and one unknown one. Suppose you come home and find a pair of strange underwear in your spouse's dresser drawer. You probably will ask yourself: What is the probability that your spouse is cheating on you?

The *condition* is that you found the underwear; the *hypothesis* you are interested in evaluating is the probability that you're being cheated on. The Bayesian method then gives you an answer to that sort of question, providing that you are willing to estimate three quantities: *First,* you need to estimate the probability of the underwear, as a condition of the hypothesis being true, that you are being cheated upon. Assume this is 50% probable. *Second,* you need to estimate the probability of the underwear's appearing on the condition the hypothesis is false. Assume this has a probability of 5%. *Third,* and most important, you need what in Bayesian method is a *prior probability*. Generally, 4% of the population is unfaithful to their spouse. Given this data set we can establish a *"posterior probability,"* which is the likelihood that we're being cheated on.

This relatively low probability of you being cheated on comes from the low prior probability of 4% based on historical data on your specific experience. This demonstrates the power of our prior knowledge (your spouse being faithful) in estimating future probabilities. Innovation leaders need to become comfortable in using the Bayesian Method.

Correlation vs. Causation

A once famous "leading indicator" of economic performance, for instance, was the winner of the Super Bowl. From Super Bowl I in 1967 through Super Bowl XXXI in 1997, the stock market gained an average of 14% the rest of the year when a team from the original National Football League (NFL) won the game. But it fell by almost 10% when the team from the original American Football League (AFL). Through June 1997 this indicator correctly "predicted" the stock market 28 out of 31 years.

A standard test of statistical significance, if taken literally, would have implied that there was only about a one chance in 4,700,000 possibilities that the relationship had emerged from chance alone. It was just a coincidence, of course. And eventually, the indicator began to perform badly. The important point here is that correlation can be merely coincidence, whereas causation is related to making the event occur.

Most have heard the maxim "correlation does not imply causation." Just because two variables have a statistical relationship with each other does not mean that one is responsible for the other. Figuring out what's truly causal and what's correlation is very difficult to do. The innovation leader has to be very careful to clearly identify noise versus signal. Noise is related to correlation whereas signal is related to causation. An innovation leader should almost never ignore data, especially when they are studying rare events, about which there isn't very much data to begin with. Ignoring data is often a tip-off that the innovation leaders overconfident, or is over-fitting the data to the model, and is only interested in showing a preconceived relationship rather than the relationship that actually exists. The other rationale for throwing out data is that there's been some fundamental shift in the problem that is being analyzed. Sometimes these arguments are valid to a certain extent. The problem is that you never know when the next paradigm shift will occur, and whether it will tend to make the data set more volatile or less so, stronger or weaker. However, anticipating these turning points is not easy.

It's important to recollect that in dynamic systems everything affects everything else in the system, putting a premium on the quality of your data set. Small errors in your data can result in large errors in your predictions or forecasts. This reality needs to be recognized by the innovation leader in the problem-solving process. Data quality counts, and data quality depends on the source of the data and in the biases of the interpreter of the data. The general rule is that bad data is worse than no data at all.

Managing the innovation leader's biases requires that they understand their assumptions by writing them down, using their assumptions to identify their biases, and consciously analyzing those biases relative to the problem they're trying to solve.

The Dangers of Extrapolation

Extrapolation is a very basic prediction or forecasting method simply involving the assumption that the current trend will continue indefinitely into the future. This is exceptionally risky in dynamic systems that behave according to chaos theory. An example of the dangers with extrapolation is how at the turn of the 20th century many city planners were concerned about the increasing use of horse-drawn carriages and horse manure.

"Knee-deep" in the issue in 1894, one writer in the Times of London predicted that by the 1940s, every street in London would be buried under 9 feet of manure. About 10 years later, fortunately, Henry Ford began producing his prototypes of the Model T and crisis was averted.

Extrapolation is specifically dangerous when the current data set is changing dramatically, making it even harder to predict or forecast relative to the past. Two examples of this are cases of AIDS and population growth. In 1980 the US had 99 cases of AIDS confirmed, and by 1984 there were 11,000 cases, and 560,000 cases by 1995. If the forecaster had used data suggesting linear growth of the cases from 1980, it would have been significantly *below* the actual number of cases diagnosed.

In 1682, William Petty projected that the population of the world would be 700 million people by 2012. The actual population of the world in 2011 was roughly 7,000,000,000, so Petty was off by a factor of 10 as a result of the industrial revolution allowing greater population growth.

Improving the Decision Making Process

It's clear that making effective decisions when faced with ambiguous big data sets governed by chaos theory is difficult. The following are some starting points that innovation leader can bear in mind as they face this kind of situation.

Always approach these kinds of decisions with the Bayesian mindset that the solutions are going to be *ranges of probabilities*. When we fail to think like "a Bayesian," false positives resulting from interpreting noise for signal become problems for all decision-making processes.

An important fact is that all models are inherently wrong, but some are useful. This means that you must interpret the outcomes of your models with the intent of making them better with each variation, and that no variation is final or complete. The goal is continuous incremental improvement of the model so it is more correct in the future.

Recognize that more data is not necessarily better. In the last 20 years, with the exponential growth in the availability of data and information, we can measure millions and millions of potentially interesting variables. The expectation is that we can use this data and information to make predictions and forecasts more accurate. Unfortunately, the quantity of the data, absent proper quality analysis of the data, makes predictions more prone to failure in the era of big data.

Use computers to do tactical and repetitive tasks and not strategic operations that require thought. With information processing power increasing at an exponential rate, it is important to look at a computer as a means to an end and not an end in itself.

Trial and error is a unique human process that can improve our understanding of big data, providing we come up with lots of ideas, examine them quickly, and then segregate the high quality results. Be careful to characterize the degree of uncertainty that is present in the data since the more uncertainty, the greater there is for error in the prediction. Innovation leaders often underestimate the uncertainty they're dealing with. When the data is very noisy, it is better to focus on the process used to analyze the data than on the results of the analysis.

Innovation leaders should ask whether they are applying the correct attitudes and aptitudes correlated with forecasting and predicting success over the long run, such as using effective Bayesian probabilistic analyses. Ideally, at least in the beginning, more information is better than less, but the innovation leader needs to make sure that its quality is controlled. Next, one needs to worry about being familiar with the tools that help you analyze the data set. While one doesn't need state-of-the-art computing technology, you do need to know how to use whatever technology you have. And finally, the innovation leader needs to worry about accuracy, about getting at the objective truth rather than about making the prediction that is most comforting to your biases.

The Power of Consensus

When two predictions or forecasts of the same data set differ those involved with making these need to either come to a consensus on what is most accurate or one needs to revise the forecast to match the others conclusions. The consensus seeking process takes advantage of the wisdom of crowds by which time most members of a group collect around a particular idea or alternative.

An extension of the idea of reaching consensus is aggregating different forecasts. There is strong empirical and theoretical evidence that there is a benefit from this activity suggesting that aggregated predictions and forecasts reduced error by as much as 15% to 20%. Three important rules of aggregating forecasts: The *first* is that aggregated forecasts or predictions, doesn't necessarily mean it will be good but that they're just likely to be better than those that are not aggregated. The *second* rule is the most robust wisdom of crowds will occur when the forecasts are made independently before being aggregated. Often, the aggregation process is simply averaging the data together. *Finally*, it's important to remember that the aggregate forecast or prediction, while better than the typical individual forecast or prediction, does not necessarily mean that it is better than the best individual forecast or prediction.

Searching for consensus has proven to be an effective way of reducing errors in forecasts or predictions innovation leader needs to be careful of "herding mentality." Herding occurs from deep psychological needs of most people, when making major decisions, to gather input from others, especially family, colleagues and friends, and even from competitors, if they're willing to give it to us. Often, the rallying cry is "follow the crowd," especially when you don't know any better. Whether this actually works to our advantage or not is speculative. A significant source of risk is when the innovation leader reaches out to an external party for advice and counsel. When that individual is very confident but not knowledgeable this confidence creates a false belief that the person has useful knowledge. When this person's confidence is not based on useful knowledge a bad decision is the outcome. Overconfidence, even among the knowledgeable individuals, is dangerous because it leads to "Hedgehog" behavior to fit reality to their biases, so their confidence is proven to be a source of truth.

Skepticism is healthy in finding signal in causality vs. noise and correlation there are three types of skepticism. The *first* flows from self-interest. This is obvious in that skeptic may present a doubting point of view to protect their self-interests from being attacked. The forecast or prediction may be accurate, but is threatening to the status quo and the self-interest of the skeptic. The *second* form of skepticism falls under the category of *the contrarian* where some people find it advantageous to align themselves with the crowd, while a smaller number will come to see themselves as persecuted outsiders or contrarians.

Contrarians are particularly powerful skeptics when the data is noisy and predictions/forecasts are hard to experience in a visceral way. The most important and **final** type of skeptic is the *scientific skeptic*. This kind of skepticism is very important, and some in the scientific community will have valid concerns about one aspect of the science or another, that need to be resolved in order to improve the prediction or the forecast.

Complexity, Uncertainty, and the Value of Consensus (or lack thereof)

Wrestling with complexity led to the development of chaos theory and the mindset that hard work, along with melding of computer power with human judgment, was the best way to deal with these issues. It is important to gather lots of feedback, allowing you to check your assumptions and incrementally improve your forecast or predictions, combined with a continuing deeper understanding of the system being assessed. An important caution is whenever you have a large number of variables applied to a rarely occurring phenomenon, there is the risk of overfeeding your model and mistaking noise in the past data for signal.

The goal of any model is to capture as much signal as possible and as little noise. Striking the right balance is not always so easy, and our ability to do so will be dictated by the strength of the theory and the quality and quantity of the data available.

It is important to recognize how much uncertainty there is in the data set and to estimate it properly. There are three distinct types of uncertainty that the innovation leader will encounter in complex big data situations.

The first is called *initial condition uncertainty*, these are the short-term factors that compete with the signal and impact the way we experience the data set. An example of initial condition uncertainty would be temperature swings over the short-term, when trying to forecast weather conditions. The second type of uncertainty is called *scenario uncertainty*, which increases with time. This concerns a variable that as it changes causes a greater impact on the prediction or forecast. An example from weather forecasting is the level of carbon dioxide and other greenhouse gases in the atmosphere. As these increase the impact on globe temperatures become more uncertain,

266

although one can predict general trends that the greater amount of these greenhouse gases in the atmosphere, the warmer the planet will become over the long-term. The final type of uncertainty is called *structural uncertainty*. This is the type of uncertainty that should worry the innovation leader the most because it is the most challenging to quantify. Structural uncertainty might increase slightly over time, and years can be self- reinforcing in the model is a dynamic system, like we will normally deal with complex data sets. Again, using a weather forecasting example, while it may be possible to estimate with reasonable certainty how much carbon dioxide it will be in the atmosphere, and its impact on climate, it is much more difficult to predict the impact of volcanoes or solar cycles on weather conditions.

Knowing What You Don't Know

Often knowing what you don't know is more valuable than knowing what to do know. While it's easy to recognize that knowing what you don't know is important it is very difficult to do in practice. In addition, a definition of signal is that it is an indication of the underlying truth behind a piece of data. The definition of noise is a random pattern that might easily be mistaken for signals. The absence of signal, and the presence of noise, can be almost as important as the presence of signal. . An example of this was the Japanese's radio silence that was observed before the attack on Pearl Harbor, 1941.

Previous to the attack, Japanese radio chatter was common and often unimportant. Just before the attack this "ideal chatter" disappeared, which might have been identified as a change and therefore a new risk.

The key for leaders in the era of big data is to use probabilistic thinking and good judgment driven by experience to make decisions that can be tested, leading to additional decisions. As the accuracy or meaning of the data becomes less trustworthy the decision-maker needs to think more like a "fox," taking the following approach:

1. **Multidisciplinary:** incorporate ideas from different disciplines and regardless of their origin on the political spectrum.
2. **Adaptable:** find a new approach or pursue multiple approaches at the same time if they aren't sure the original one is working.
3. **Self-critical:** happy to acknowledge mistakes in their predictions accept the blame for itself them.
4. **Tolerant of complexity:** sees the universe as complicated, transfer point of many fundamental problems that are inherently unpredictable Cautious: express their predictions in probabilistic terms and qualify their opinions Empirical: rely more on observation than theory.

Decision makers who think and act like "hedgehogs" will make poorer decisions overall some of which might be catastrophic. "Hedgehog Thinking" is…

1. **Specialized:** often have spent the bulk of their careers on one or two great problems may view the opinions of outsiders skeptically.
2. **Stalwart:** stick to the same approach using new data to refine the original thought.
3. **Stubborn:** mistakes are blamed on bad luck, or on idiosyncratic circumstances such as a good model had a bad day.
4. **Order seeking:** expect that the world will be found to abide by relatively simple governing relationships once the signal was identified through the noise.
5. **Confident:** rarely hedge their predictions and are reluctant to change them.

Finally applying Bayesian Statistics can help frame difficult decisions based on past knowledge and expected outcomes using numerical descriptions. A caution is that these numerical descriptions are still estimates and shouldn't be considered as more significant than the starting data set allows.

Chapter 7 Summary

The table below summarizes the key concepts covered in this chapter:

Process	Objectives	Metrics
Roadmapping	• Identifies market drivers • Recognizes critical to success industry nuances • Estimates financial potential	• Estimates timing • Defines problems • Describes solutions
Business Ethics	• Define the term • Review acceptable and unacceptable behaviors • Propose an enforcement methodology	• J&J Case studies • 12 Rules of Ethical Behavior • Violation reporting
Intellectual Property (IP)	• What is IP • How is it used as a business tool • Strategies for building a portfolio	• IP types and utility • Investment requirements • Curveball strategies
Project Portfolio Creation	• Defines investment options • Identifies financial returns • Evaluates investment dimensions (e.g., SWOT analysis)	• Identifies areas of risk • Aligns opportunities with internal competencies • Driver of the Open Innovation agenda
Open Innovation	• Mind set to look beyond the firm • Review effective methods • Highlight risks	• Describe process • Examples of successful programs • Review implementation process
Stage Gate Process	• Specifies investment decisions • Recognizes timing of outcomes • Manages and mitigates risk	• Defines value • Aligns with 3-5 Year business plan • Drive decisions about projects in portfolio
Project Management	• Describes the project (e.g., project brief, Work Break-Down, Structure, etc.) • Identifies resource deployment • Assigns individual accountability	• Assesses timing (e.g., GANTT charts) • Defines budget • Reports progress against plan
Product Life Cycle Management	• Definitions • Implementation • Strategic value in managing complexity	• Example process • Role of management
Dealing with "Big Data"	• Definition • Forecasting vs. predicting • Causation vs correlation	• "Foxes" vs. "Hedgehogs" • Bayesian statistics • Probabilistic thinking

Chapter 7 Critical Questions

General Questions about the Processes

1. Describe how your R&D processes are "means to an end and not an end in themselves"?
2. Processes that are an end vs. a means to an end are dangerous often corrupting the very work they were created to help.
3. Who owns each process, how is their role described and performance measured and is "processes ownership" managed over time?
4. Specifically process owners should rotate their ownership so not to become entrenched and blind to the weaknesses of the process or opportunities to improve it.
5. How do your processes compare to benchmarks in the marketplace?
6. Every process should be comparable to those used by others while be customized for the purpose at hand. This kind of analysis keeps the process anchored to methods proven to be effective. Benchmarking also enables the process owner to critically compare how their processes perform against those that are "best in breed".
7. How are the processes measured for effectiveness?
8. This is an internal measure of the process itself and not the outputs of the process. For example the number of projects being progressed through a Stage Gate® process is not an internal metric. The internal metric would be are the Gate reviews following the expected protocols and are variations of the protocol justified?
9. How are processes corrected should they lose impact because the firm's because the situation has changed, the process is being mismanaged or some combination of both?
10. What is done to keep processes current with changing business environments?
11. Who owns this assessment and how is senior management involved?
12. Who designed the "Dashboard" for management reporting from the processes and how are these "Dashboards" used by management?

Roadmapping

1. Which changes can be expected to drive the Roadmap (trends, scenarios)?
2. Which opportunities and challenges will these changes produce?
3. Which future is desirable?
4. Which disruptive events could occur?
5. Which successful future strategies can be derived from this?
6. How does the Roadmap align with strategy, objectives and resource deployment?
7. How do Roadmaps represent markets, customers and change forces?

8. How can the Roadmap be made simpler, easy to understand, and more insightful?
9. How will the Roadmap be customized for various audiences to insure clear communication is achieved? What do Roadmaps communicate to Executive Leadership, Marketing, Sales, Human Resources, Manufacturing and other key stakeholders?
10. What support exists for projects found in the Roadmap? What are the critical assumptions? How are they validated?
11. How will Roadmaps be used to create corporate, divisional, department and personal annual performance plans?
12. How will the Roadmaps be updated?

Business Ethics
1. Have you defined the problem accurately?
2. How would you define the problem if you stood on the other side of the fence?
3. How did this situation occur in the first place?
4. To whom and to what do you give your loyalty as a person and as a member of the organization?
5. What is your intention in making this decision?
6. How does this intention compare with the probable results?
7. Whom could your decision or action injure?
8. Can you discuss the problem with the affected parties before you make your decision?
9. Are you confident that your position will be as valid over a long period of time as it seems now?
10. Could you disclose without qualm your decision or action to your boss, your CEO, the board of directors, your family, society as a whole?
11. What is the symbolic potential of your action if understood? If misunderstood?
12. Under what conditions would you allow exceptions to your stand?
13. Explain the conditions under which whistleblowing might be justified. Six conditions:
    - A product or policy of an organization needs to possess the potential to do harm to some members of society.
    - The concerned employee should first of all report the facts, as far as they are known, to their immediate superior.
    - If the immediate superior fails to act effectively, the concerned employee should take the matter to more senior managers, exhausting all available internal channels in the process.
    - The prospective whistleblower should hold documentary evidence that can be presented to external audiences.

- The prospective whistleblower must believe that the necessary changes will be implemented as a result of their whistleblowing act.
- The sixth condition is a general one and it is that the whistleblower must be acting in good faith, without malice.

Intellectual Property (IP)
1. What kinds of IP are important to your firm and why?
2. Who is involved with generating IP and how is it managed?
3. What role does the IP attorney play in the managing the firm's IP?
4. What are the formal guidelines for managing the firm's IP?
5. How is IP employed by the firm? Right to use? Exclusion of competition? Demonstrate market leadership? Etc.
6. What role do individuals play in enforcing the firm's IP position?
7. How are patent claims reviewed and by whom?
8. What guidance is offered on how to capture IP in writing?
9. How does the firm capture new IP?
10. How is IP aligned with the firm's business strategies?

Portfolio Creation
1. How is the portfolio a reflection of the roadmap?
2. What skills are required to take advantage of the opportunities represented by the portfolio?
3. How does the portfolio satisfy the needs of the business and firm itself?
4. How is the portfolio managed? Monthly, quarterly, annually etc.?
5. How will the portfolio impact the firm's key financial metrics over the next year? Next 5 years?
6. What should be removed from the portfolio? Why?
7. Who is accountable for the portfolio and how are resources deployed against it?
8. How are the projects sponsored by the firm reflective of the portfolio?
9. Is this project aligned with core competencies? (Yes or No - qualitative)
10. What is the project's NPV? (value - quantitative)
11. How well does a project support strategic initiatives? (very well; well; average; not so well; poorly - a 5-point scale).
12. What are our resource objectives?
13. What are our critical resource limitations?
14. What do we think is most important?
15. Which ideas and needs are worth developing into business cases?
16. What strategic initiatives does this project support?
17. Does the value equation, fully consider all uncertainty and risk?
18. What are the inter-project dependencies?
19. Why we doing this project?
20. Which current and proposed projects should be in the portfolio?

21. Will a project cause excessive multi-tasking, or delay other work?
22. What are the key risk areas for each portfolio?
23. What areas of uncertainty endanger the realization of benefits?

Open Innovation

1. To what level of satisfaction are your technology needs met by your internal R&D? Explain.
2. Does your company make a practice of looking to bring in outside IP and technology? Is this done opportunistically or do you have a formal, systematic to doing so?
3. Is looking outside for technology that can be leveraged everyone's job– or is there a distinct group dedicated to doing this? What types of people fulfill this role?
4. What specific goals or objectives do you have regarding bringing in technology? What incentives are tied to these goals?
5. Where do you typically look for outside ideas and technology: e.g.: universities, start-ups, competitors, conferences, or companies in peripheral industries?
6. How would you characterize your efforts to bring in technology:
7. Would you say that typically when you bring-in or jointly develop an outside technology, it is to address an incremental product improvement or a breakthrough product?
8. Do you typically work with 'proven' technologies used in other applications, or are you trying to develop something entirely new?
9. Do you typically bring in technology that leverages core R&D capabilities, or does it feel more like outsourcing non-core needs?
10. How has bringing in outside technology helped your company?
11. Has the impact been significant?
12. What has the impact been?
13. How would you characterize your efforts to take out technology?
14. When something is developed internally that doesn't fit with your business model, do you have a practice of taking the IP or technology assets out to the marketplace?
15. When something that was initially developed internally is deemed "dead," are efforts made to find companies or partners that might be interested in it? Is this done opportunistically or is there a formal mechanism to do this?
16. Are there specific goals around when a technology asset can be taken out to the marketplace?
17. Who or what group has responsibility for doing this? How are they incented?
18. What impact has taking IP or technologies you have chosen not to commercialize out to the market, had on the company?

Stage Gates
1. How does your Stage Gate® process (the process) secure the Voice of the Customer (VOC)?
2. What evidence is available that senior management is committed to the Stage Gate® process?
3. How does the organizational structure and processes that support the Stage Gates® process? Inhibit it?
4. Where did the process originate? Was it done by stakeholders who will use it or by third parties (e.g., external consultants)?
5. How relevant and accurate is the data used to support decision making at each stage of the process? It the data verified or audited?
6. How does IT support the process and is data available broadly to stakeholders in real time?
7. Do communities of interest provide insights facilitating decision-making?
8. How many attractive new product concepts are becoming available for development because of the process? What are they worth to the firm?
9. How does the process help project team secure resources for introduction?
10. Does the process "kill" projects? What's the ratio of projects that advance into development to these that are killed?
11. How does the process help project leaders focus on reducing uncertainties as early as possible?

Project Management
1. What are the business goals the project is aiming to achieve?
2. What business benefits will these goals deliver if achieved?
3. What will be the consequences to the business (financial, reputation etc.) if the project does not go ahead or fails to deliver the objectives?
4. Are there any easy-to-implement alternatives to this project? Sometimes other solutions are available that do not require the cost implications of a full-blown project.
5. Are there any disadvantages to implementing this project? Staff redundancies might be an obvious one, but there might be some that are less obvious.
6. Who is the main stakeholder, with ultimate responsibility for driving the project forward? It is important that someone senior takes ownership of a project – that person should never be the project manager.
7. Who is responsible for ensuring appropriate resources (time, people and money) are allocated to the project? This should be someone with the authority to allocate whatever resources are required.

8. Who will be responsible for deciding whether the project goes ahead or not after the initial investigations? This will often be a group of people, sometimes with conflicting aims.
9. Is the new project dependent on the successful delivery of a current project? If so, a full report on the status of the project already underway should be obtained before committing to the new project.
10. What are the success criteria that will indicate the objectives have been met and the benefits delivered?
11. Will new equipment/products be required to facilitate project delivery for example is new software needed?
12. Will there be any necessary staff changes (redundancies or new hires)?
13. Will existing staff require re-training, for example, to learn new business processes?
14. Which individuals, teams or departments will be involved in the project?
15. Who will be responsible for documenting the business requirements in detail?
16. Who will determine interim and final deadlines? Projects where the marketing department, for example, decide on a deadline for an IT project have a far less chance of success than when informed estimates are made about the resources required.
17. How much contingency will be available in the budget?
18. Who will be responsible for making the decisions to include or exclude requested changes once the project is underway?
19. Will the project deliverables need to be tested and, if so, by whom?
20. Who will provide the final approval of the project deliverable?

Product Life-Cycle Management (PLM)
1. How can PLM be sued to increase collaboration increasing innovation?
2. How will PLM reduced time and cost to market?
3. How does PLM help reach financial targets?
4. How will PLM improved product quality and reliability?
5. How will PLM reduce prototyping costs?
6. How does PLM increase efficiency by reusing data from other projects?
7. How PLM help with product optimization?
8. How will PLM reduced waste in development and manufacturing?
9. How does PLM create savings through the complete integration of development task?
10. How will PLM help meet compliance requirements?
11. How does PLM provide contract manufacturers with access to a centralized product record reducing cost to serve?
12. How does PLM improve forecasting to reduce material costs and help estimate financial results?

13. How does PLM facilitate communication between parts of the firm especially R&D, Marketing and Manufacturing/Supply Chain?
14. Who owns the PLM process?
15. What IT platform is used supporting the PLM database?
16. How visible is the PLM database to critical users? How user friendly is the PLM system?
17. What metrics are employed to assess PLM's effectiveness in reducing the firms cost from complexity such as retiring aging products before their profitability wanes?
18. How are the product record histories preserved?

Big Data
1. What is the role of intuition in the era of big data?
2. Have machines and data supplanted the human mind?
3. A key piece of big data is its reliance on "unstructured" and "semi-structured" data.
4. Can you explain what's going on here?
5. Want to launch a successful big data initiative? Get practical. Read more[63]
6. Data visualization is becoming more popular than ever. Will dataviz be a requirement for people to be able to understand the insights that big data can deliver?
7. Data science, some say, is actually a mix of art and science -- the art of knowing what to look at amidst a profusion of information.
8. Can you explain a bit about this? How people can develop those skills?
9. We seem to be entering an era of exponential growth of data.
10. Is there a point at which many enterprise systems will cease to operate?
11. How will big data impact small businesses?
12. Will we see an era where every business (even barbershops or corner stores) will somehow be leveraging big data?
13. Can you talk about how big data will trickle down and impact individuals?
14. Are there direct ways this will impact our day-to-day lives in the coming years?
15. Are "big data skills" something that everyone will need to learn moving forward?
16. What skills do workers need to sharpen to prepare for the era of big data?

---

[63] Big Data Innovation: Time to Focus. http://www.informationweek.com/big-data/commentary/big-data-analytics/big-data-innovation-time-to-focus/240161285?itc=edit_in_body_cross

Chapter 8: Critical Internal Interfaces

R&D can be an investment or a cost depending on how well the R&D function creates shareholder value. The more shareholder value created, the more this spending appears to be a good investment. When R&D fails to create shareholder value, investments in R&D become costs that must be minimized. Measuring returns from R&D investments is often difficult, as described below, so the value created by R&D becomes very subjective. Since perception is reality, R&D needs to generate confidence in the critical parts of the organization for investments in R&D being well-placed.

The simplest measure of value creation from an R&D investment is whether or not it returned the cost of capital to the firm. The cost of capital considers alternate uses of cash such as investing in a vehicle that has very low risk with a known return. A reasonable benchmark would be 10% return on that investment, although in today's market it could be significantly less. Investing in R&D becomes attractive when the returns are substantially greater than the cost of capital, such as a 10/1 to 20/1 return. Measuring the return on R&D investments is complicated and often ambiguous. For example, introducing a new product could involve cannibalizing existing products with well-established rates of return.

Further, the money invested in R&D is after-taxes, making it very costly. If a company's profit margin is 5%, then every dollar invested in R&D requires $20 of revenue to break even. This is where the 10/1 to 20/1 expected returns comes from. The overall return from a new product is further complicated by difficulty in measuring the actual costs associated with its development. Direct costs are easy to measure whereas indirect and allocated costs are not.

Revenue growth can occur over years, making total returns subject to estimating the opportunity costs associated with other uses of funds. This is where project portfolio management is critical. Were the right products developed? Valuation of new products needs to be discounted by the products it "cannibalizes."

Future costs for servicing the new product can reduce the actual returns obtained. These are difficult to estimate prior to actual market experience. Finally, many new products fail outright to generate any return, which means these investments are lost and need to be recouped by other new products.

Normally, revenues from new products, as a percent of total revenues, over a specific timeframe (usually five years) define the returns from R&D investments. While a blunt metric, benchmarking data suggests that the most effective R&D investments, from a portfolio of products introduced over time, will generate between 35% and 45% of the total revenue stream at the five-year point post-introduction. Said another way, how much of a given year's revenues came from new products in the past 5 years?

One additional complexity is that the research and development function often spends money on activities that are not related to new product development. For example, many R&D functions spend resources on doing some level of basic research generating knowledge, servicing existing products, or as administrative and overhead costs, neither of which generate any revenues. These activities are essential in maintaining the existing business, but further pressure the R&D investment from achieving the required returns.

Perceptions of R&D

Each of these interactions is described below, along with how R&D can make them fruitful. The intent of this section is to offer advice on how the R&D leadership team and then individual contributors need to perform. However, R&D's role varies depending on the function involved in the interaction. R&D interacts with almost every part of an organization, but the 6 below are most important:

R&D-Partner Role Matrix

Function	R&D Role
Marketing and Sales	Vendor of services
Human Resources	Equal partners
Finance	Customer
Manufacturing	Vendor of services
Corporate Administration	Subordinate Partner

General Interactions

R&D functions are very specialized and therefore opaque to other parts of the company. For this reason, it is incumbent upon R&D to learn and demonstrate the norms of behavior expected by their partners in the organization. An example is how R&D personnel must adjust the way they communicate, appear, and collaborate to be effective. It is easier for R&D personnel to learn how their partner functions operate than it is for their partner functions to learn how R&D operates. Simplistically, R&D must speak the language of their partners versus expecting their partners to learn the R&D language. Take the following for example:

Attire worn by R&D professionals should be compatible with that worn by their partner organizations. In a meeting with marketing, the R&D participant should dress like their marketing colleagues. Often this means that the R&D professional should not look like they plan to be working in the laboratory instead of meeting with someone with a commercial point of view. This may mean leaving their "lab coats" back in the lab. During interaction with marketing, R&D personnel need to avoid using jargon that while clear within R&D is mysterious to someone with a commercial back ground. Most importantly, R&D personnel should *never* discount the value of their commercial colleagues just because they don't have an advanced technical degree.

Marketing and Sales – Vendor of Services

The role of *marketing and sales* is to represent the customer to the internal functions of the firm. In performing this role, marketing and sales often take the side of the customer when discussing the customer's needs and wants. Marketing and sales supporting the customer's needs is not negative. The role of the technical function is to manage expectations appropriately so that they don't over-commit and under-deliver on the products and services the customer wants. Take the following for example:

The technical community should never promise to deliver an invention by a certain moment in time or date. Inventions are inherently unpredictable, some of which may never be accomplished, so by setting a date for delivery, you're almost certain to miss that commitment.

Marketing and sales must clearly define what they want, when they want it, and how much are they willing to spend or invest to obtain what the customer wants. A critical component of an interaction between marketing and sales and technical staff is a clear specification of what success looks like.

The best approach is for the technical community and marketing and sales is to use "probabilistic thinking" as described in the section of Chapter 7 on *big data*. R&D delivers estimates, informing decisions about the value of a given investment, relative to what the customer is willing to pay for.

Human Resources (HR) – Equal Partner

Technology development is clearly a "people game," and so the relationship between the technical functions and HR needs to be symbiotic. Specifically, the two parties must plan and engage in hiring, motivating, and retaining technical professionals. HR, being a part of the R&D planning team where annual and strategic plans are developed, provides internal consulting on HR issues they encounter in the routine managing of their functions. Take the following for example:

1. R&D is responsible for identifying the universities where they wish to recruit from with HR then establishing the relationship with the school.
2. R&D and HR share accountability for the recruiting program using a set of joint metrics.
3. HR leads the effort of managing performance by establishing guidelines for performance and compensation. R&D then works within these guidelines in leading their teams.
4. HR and R&D leadership work together in dealing with performance issues, especially if a termination is a possible outcome.

Finance – Customer

Finance supplies services to R&D leadership, helping them in developing operating budgets, strategic plans, and investments in capital projects. In this role, finance also serves as expert consultants helping measure R&D effectiveness (see Chapter 6's section on metrics), estimating the potential returns on R&D projects, and managing overall risk involved in R&D activities. R&D needs to educate finance professionals on the risk factors inherent in innovation so that appropriate discount factors are applied. Take the following for example:

Developing budgets can be straight forward, but with finance involved the R&D leadership team has a partner to explain and defend the numbers. Further, budgets for large organizations can become complex, involving direct and indirect expenses, fixed and variable costs, depreciation, and most importantly, returns on the R&D investment. A trap to avoid is treating R&D as a cost versus an investment. Finance should work with the R&D leadership team to express the investment in terms of potential returns from either new products or servicing existing customers. Finance partners with R&D to maintain its infrastructure, keeping it current and anticipating future needs of the business. Allowing infrastructure to age or become irrelevant is a strategic mistake.

Manufacturing – Customer

R&D and Manufacturing often have a deep relationship in many businesses since new products will move from R&D into some kind of pilot production and then eventually full-scale production. In these cases, manufacturing relies on R&D to provide a robust process by which to manufacture and then act as an expert consultant as things change over time. For R&D, "birthing" a new product is only the beginning, and as "parents" of these products R&D must engage with manufacturing when support these offerings is required. Consider the following:

Manufacturing's role is to deliver high quality offerings to customers with a consistent quality supporting the brands established by marketing and sales. Manufacturing being more variable than R&D requires R&D to understand this variation so it can be managed. Manufacturing will experience unforeseen events with raw materials, processing conditions, and contamination where R&D's expertise is required to manage through these situations. R&D should proactively, via their engineering capabilities, offer manufacturing options for reducing costs and/or increasing quality in existing offerings. Most cost reductions in manufacturing end up as expanded margin, which helps marketing and sales reach their goals.

Corporate Administration – Equal Partners

R&D leadership, especially at the Division Head or Vice President level, must have a meaningful and effective partnership with their peers in other functions as well as the CEO, COO, and Board of Directors. Corporate administration functions include the CEO and COO, legal, investor relations, corporate secretary, ethics (if separate from HR or Legal), and so on. These relationships become critical success factors when developing the firm's overall vision and tactical plans for making that vision a reality. Relationships based on trust and genuine caring, for the good of each other and the firm, resonate throughout the entire organization. Internal conflict at the top of the organization is devastating to the firm's overall capability of succeeding. Consider the following:

The head of R&D needs to know, respect, and perhaps even like their peers in corporate administration, especially legal and investor relations. These leaders should meet one-on-one on a regular basis (no less than monthly) and discuss how they can support and proactively help each other avoid risks wherever possible. For example, legal leadership needs to know as early as possible of issues impacting intellectual property. This must occur before they're so problematic they result in harm to the firm. Finally, and most importantly, R&D leadership needs to inform the CEO and COO of the unexpected, be it good or (especially) bad.

Chapter 8 Summary

R&D can be an investment or a cost depending on how well the R&D function creates shareholder value. The more shareholder value created, the more this spending appears to be a good investment. When R&D fails to create shareholder value, investments in R&D become costs that must be minimized. Measuring returns from R&D investments is often difficult as the value created by R&D is very perceptional. Since perception is reality, R&D needs to generate confidence in the critical parts of the organization that investments in R&D are well placed. Investing in R&D becomes attractive when the returns are substantially greater than the cost of capital such as a 10/1 to 20/1 return. However, measuring the return on R&D investments is complicated and often ambiguous. The overall return from a new product is further complicated by the following:

1. Difficulty in measuring the actual costs associated with its development.
2. Revenue growth can occur over years, making total returns subject to estimating the opportunity costs associated with other uses of funds.
3. Valuation of new products needs to be discounted by products it "cannibalizes."
4. Future costs for servicing the new product can reduce the actual returns obtained.
5. Finally, many new products fail outright to generate any return, which means these investments are lost and need to be recouped by other new products.

While a blunt metric, if 35%-45% of revenues come from new products as a percent of total revenues over five years, this suggests that the R&D is a reasonable investment. However, the R&D function often spends money on activities that are not related to some level of basic research generating knowledge, servicing existing products, or as administrative and overhead costs, neither of which generate any revenues. These activities are essential in maintaining the existing business but further pressure the R&D investment from achieving the required returns.

How R&D interacts with internal partners and stakeholders will define perceptions, which become reality. R&D must impress these stakeholders or risk being considered a cost or worse, an impediment. R&D interacts with almost every part of an organization but the 6 shown in the R&D–Partner Matrix are most important:

R&D-Partner Role Matrix

Function	R&D Role
Marketing and Sales	Vendor of services
Human Resources	Equal partners
Finance	Customer
Manufacturing	Vendor of services
Corporate Administration	Subordinate Partner

Finally, R&D functions are very specialized and therefore opaque to other parts of the company. For this reason, it is incumbent upon R&D to learn and demonstrate the norms of behavior expected by their partners in the organization. An example, R&D personnel must adjust the way they communicate, appear, and collaborate to be effective. Most importantly, R&D personnel should *never* discount the value of their commercial colleagues because they lack an advanced technical degree. Finally, R&D personnel must create confidence in the eyes of the external customer so they want access to the firm's R&D resources.

Chapter 8 Critical Questions

General
1. How often does R&D leadership meet with their partners and what is discussed?
2. What role do the R&D partners play in developing the annual and strategic plans?
3. How do the R&D partners represent R&D to their functions?
4. How active are the business unit partners in working with R&D? Do they provide guidance?
5. How can these partnerships be improved and why?
6. How long do the same partner representatives stay with R&D?

Human Resources as Equal Partners
1. How does HR guide R&D leadership in critical personnel decisions from recruiting, hiring, development, motivation and retention?
2. What is the relationship between the senior leader in R&D and their counterpart in HR? Is the HR partner a confidant? Is it collaborative, adversarial, remote etc.?
3. How often and where do meetings occur between HR and R&D leadership? How many meetings are formal with agendas, minutes and action plans vs. informal?
4. How does HR help resolve conflicts among the R&D leadership team?

5. How does the HR leadership advocate on behalf of R&D when confronted with issues beyond the R&D remit?

Marketing and Sales with R&D as a Vendor of Services

1. How often does R&D leadership meet with Marketing and Sales? What is the context for regular meetings? Conflict? Information exchanges? Facilitating alignment etc.?
2. What other channels of communication exist between R&D and Marketing and Sales? How do they work? How is e-mail used vs. in-person discussions?
3. How are conflicts resolved between the R&D plan needing to serve the entire firm and the needs of the individual business units represented by Marketing and Sales?
4. Are conflicts resolved "locally" or elevated to the CEO/COO? Under what conditions are conflicts elevated? What role does HR play in conflict resolution?
5. What are the "Norms of Behaviors" agreed to between R&D and Marketing and Sales? Are these upheld and if not what happens?

Finance as a R&D Customer

1. What does R&D leadership need from Finance in developing and monitoring the annual and strategic plans?
2. How does R&D ask for and use advice from Finance?
3. How does Finance balance their responsibilities to the firm and R&D?
4. What role does Finance play in developing metrics and measuring R&D performance?
5. What role does Finance play in estimating the ROI from R&D investments?

Manufacturing with R&D as a Vendor of Services

1. Is the relationship collaborative or contractual? Under what circumstances?
2. How does R&D communicate with manufacturing? Who owns the relationship within R&D?
3. What services does R&D provide to Manufacturing? Process development, trouble shooting, product qualifications etc.
4. How often does senior leadership from R&D meet with their counterparts in Manufacturing? Where do they meet? For how long? Is it formal or informal?
5. Are conflicts resolved "locally" or elevated to the CEO/COO? Under what conditions are conflicts elevated? What role does HR play in conflict resolution?

6.   What are the "Norms of Behaviors" agreed to between R&D and Manufacturing? Are these upheld and if not what happens?

Corporate Administration as a Service Provider to R&D

1.   Does the senior most leader of R&D meet regularly (e.g., monthly) with their supervisor – the CEO or COO? What is discussed? How are the meetings shared?
2.   Does the next level of R&D leadership meet with the CEO/COO at least quarterly sharing departmental progress against plan? What kind of feedback is obtained and how is it acted upon?
3.   How does R&D and Legal share accountability for the firm's intellectual property? Is this a team effort or remote? How is intellectual property developed and protected?
4.   When, and in what context, does R&D help influence investor appreciation of the firm as a good investment?
5.   How do the Corporate Secretary and R&D leadership help the CEO/COO position the R&D investment with the Board of Directors so they understand the risks involved and returns being appreciated from investments in R&D?

ABOUT THE AUTHOR

Dr. Di Biase is the president of Premier Insights, LLC, an innovation practices consultancy, a member of Cornerstone Angels, a Chicago-based angel investor group, served as the Chief Executive Officer of Laser Application Technologies, a high technology company delivering technology to the food service industry, as a Vistage Chair, currently mentors CEOs of technology-based start-ups, and is an adjunct professor at Benedictine University.

Previously, Dr. Di Biase served as the Chief Scientific Officer of Elevance Renewable Sciences a high technology specialty chemicals company and as the Senior Vice President and Chief Scientific Officer for the Research Development and Engineering Department at Diversey Inc. In these roles he was responsible for technology innovation, research, development efforts, and technical resource management. Dr. Di Biase also served as interim Senior Vice President of Human Resources.

Before joining JohnsonDiversey, Dr. Di Biase spent 26 years with the Lubrizol Corporation, where he held a variety of leadership positions, including general management roles and Vice President – Research, Development and Engineering and Vice President – Emulsified Products.

He is a 1974 graduate of St. John Fisher College with a Bachelor of Science degree in chemistry and earning a doctorate degree in chemistry from Pennsylvania State University in 1978.

Dr. Di Biase is also a past member of the Board of Trustees for the Mt. Union College and the Industrial Research Institute and sits on the Science Advisory Board for The Pennsylvania State University. He has served as chairman of The Lubrizol Foundation Scholarship Committee, Chairman of the Northeastern Ohio Section of the American Chemical Society, Board member of the Cleveland Area Research Directors (CARD) and in The Boy Scouts of America where he served in a variety of posts. Dr. Di Biase has been honored by The Pennsylvania State University College of Science with its 2007 Distinguished Alumni Award. He is also an adjunct professor at Benedictine University and guest lecturer on entrepreneurship and innovation at the Kellogg School of Business at Northwestern University.

INDEX

Made in the USA
Middletown, DE
17 May 2015